RETHINKING HOUSEHOLDS

The study of living arrangements has been undertaken by various disciplines in the social sciences, such as family history, anthropology, demography and household economics. This resulted in independent formulations, often disparate and contradictory, some of which assume that household formation depends on a natural desire of individuals or married couples to live together (collectivism), others presuppose the contrary (atomism), and most unwittingly mingle both points of view simultaneously.

From a multidisciplinary perspective, Michel Verdon proves in this study the absurdity of 'collectivistic sets of suppositions', building a powerful case for a radically new atomistic perspective on living arrangements. Recognizing residence as a separate and crucial dimension of reality, he submits that contradictions in the European cultural code yield on the part of families and of adults not constituting parts of couples a spontaneous preference to reside independently of others. The reasons why they do not do so in some places and at some moments in time are contingent on various economic and political constraints.

The author has thoroughly surveyed the theoretical literature in the various disciplines dealing with living arrangements and found it possible to unify them all under this new 'atomistic set of suppositions'. Straddling the fields of anthropology and family history while borrowing key insights from household economics and demography, this book aims at dispelling a host of false assumptions in much of the literature on living arrangements while introducing a new framework for multidisciplinary communication and analysis.

Born in Montreal **Michel Verdon** studied anthropology at the Université de Montréal and at Cambridge University where he obtained his PhD in social anthropology in 1975. He taught social anthropology at Cambridge from 1979 to 1984 and is now Professor of Anthropology at the Université de Montréal. He is the author of *Keynes and the Classics*, also published by Routledge.

ROUTLEDGE RESEARCH IN GENDER AND
SOCIETY

RETHINKING HOUSEHOLDS

An atomistic perspective on European living arrangements

Michel Verdon

ROUTLEDGE

London and New York

First published 1998
by Routledge
11 New Fetter Lane, London EC4P 4EE

Simultaneously published in the USA and Canada
by Routledge
29 West 35th Street, New York, NY 10001

© 1998 Michel Verdon

Typeset in Garamond by Routledge
Printed and bound in Great Britain by TJ International, Padstow, Cornwall

British Library Cataloguing in Publication Data
A catalogue record for this book is available from the British Library

Library of Congress Cataloguing in Publication Data
Verdon, Michel.
Rethinking Households: an atomistic perspective on European living
arrangements / Michel Verdon.
p. cm. – (Routledge research in gender and society; 3)
Includes bibliographical references and index.
1. Households–Europe. 2. Households–Canada. 3. Family–Europe.
Households–Economic aspects–Cross-cultural studies.
I. Series.
HB3581.A3V47   1998
306.85–dc21   98–15336
CIP

ISBN 0–415–18195–X

FOR MY CHILDREN, PATRICK, JULIE
AND ELOÏSE,
WHO TAUGHT ME SO MUCH ABOUT
CORESIDENCE

CONTENTS

CONTENTS

ILLUSTRATIONS

Figure

Tables

ACKNOWLEDGEMENTS

This book grew out of a seminar which Francis Zimmermann, Directeur d'Etudes at the Ecole des Hautes Etudes en Sciences Sociales (EHESS), invited me to give at the Laboratoire d'anthropologie of the Collège de France in May 1994. I had by then written various publications on the stem family, and decided to look at the Pyrenean case again. What I thought would be a simple rehash of old ideas ended up turning my earlier theses upside down.

Richard Wall, of the Cambridge Group for the History of Population and Social Structure, provided the second main impetus, luring me into publishing a refined version of this seminar in *Continuity and Change*. He and Lloyd Bonfield, co-editor of *Continuity and Change*, fed many critical ideas and comments into this initial statement.

On the advice of Richard Grew, editor of *Comparative Studies in Society and History*, I decided to expand the theoretical aspect of the article, too condensed and esoteric when it appeared in article form, and to apply this theoretical framework to cases other than the Pyrenees. The rest of the story takes place at the Cambridge Group itself, where I opted to spend a sabbatical year in 1997–8. During this time, Richard Smith, Director of the Group, helped enormously with the chapter on medieval England. Peter Laslett and Richard Wall, in particular, gave the manuscript a close look, as did Pier Paolo Viazzo of the Department of Anthropology of the University of Turin, and helped greatly in giving it its final shape. To all of these people, but also to other members of the Cambridge Group who helped in other ways, either by their comments at my seminar or through purely material help (and here, I have particularly in mind Ann Thompson), I offer my most sincere and heartfelt thanks.

Finally, I also wish to address very special thanks to the Association of Commonwealth Universities, the financial support of which made my stay in England possible. I wish to thank most particularly the Commonwealth Awards Division and Mr Terry Illsley, its Director, as well as Mrs Anderson, who so kindly helped me with all the administrative aspects.

Last, but not least, my wife Heather not only co-authored Chapter 8 of this book, but helped me articulate the whole volume more than anyone else, through the endless discussions which surrounded every chapter. Her help has simply been invaluable.

Part I

TOWARDS AN ATOMISTIC
SET OF AXIOMS

INTRODUCTION

When he published *The World We Have Lost* in 1965, Peter Laslett dropped a bomb on the historical community. Historians had hitherto believed that preindustrial people (and especially women) married young, that preindustrial families were large and their households complex. According to this traditional historical perspective, the great demographic transition to older age at first marriage, to smaller families and to less complex households followed the Industrial Revolution. Using data from English villages, Laslett undermined this traditional view: English households appeared to have been small and mostly nuclear for many centuries before the Industrial Revolution, and women had married relatively late over the same period. With the collaboration of the pioneer of historical demography, Louis Henry and his student Antoinette Fauve-Chamoux on the one hand, and Laslett and his collaborators on the other, this led to a momentous colloquium which resulted in another landmark in the so-called history of the family, namely *Household and Family in Past Time* (Laslett and Wall 1972). With a few qualifications, the results confirmed what Laslett had perceived in the early 1960s, a theme which he later refined (Laslett 1977, 1983) and which Hajnal repeated in 1983. Over the same years (1969), Laslett and Wrigley had created a now famous research unit, the Cambridge Group for the History of Population and Social Structure (referred to simply as the Cambridge Group in the rest of this book). The various researchers of the Cambridge Group followed their respective paths, but it is no exaggeration to say that Laslett influenced their work by creating a brand of family history revolving mostly around a specific definition of 'household' (Laslett 1972; Hammel and Laslett 1974) and a corresponding typology founded on household composition. This aspect of family history, I shall call 'household history'.

Almost from the beginning, historical studies in household composition came under heavy fire. Many anthropologists, who had been studying 'domestic groups' for decades, did not take very kindly to this kind of approach (for the anthropological critique, see below, Chapter 2), and many family and social historians followed suit. Most of these critiques bore on the two key pillars of the type of household history carried out by the Cambridge Group, namely the very concept of household, and the typology based on it. I shall dedicate Chapter 2 to reviewing those critiques.

Recently, another social historian, D.S. Smith, criticized the very same studies from a different angle (Smith 1993), one which, from my point of view, reaches to more fundamental issues. He first challenged Laslett's claim that historians prior to him believed preindustrial households to be large and complex. Accusing Laslett of historical short-sightedness, Smith bluntly indicts him of having invented the myth he claims to have refuted. Second, he accuses family historians of theoretical blindness, of neglecting what he calls 'underlying philosophical assumptions' because of their obsession with facts. To illustrate his case, he singles out the discovery of quasi-ubiquitous nuclear households in England and Northern Europe. Instead of getting embroiled in factual concerns with statistics and representativity, he questions the assumptions that underlie current debates, pointing out that only two fundamental stances can be taken about such a phenomenon: either 'a strong, neoindividualist conception', or a cultural view, itself weak or strong. Convinced that only a neoindividualist viewpoint will stir the debate in the right direction, he lashes against the cultural interpretation:

> The weak, cultural [view] is less important for social science than the strong neoindividualist conception. Instead of locating the elemental motivation for human action at the level of the individual actor, it merely comments on the 'peculiarities of the English'. . . . In this weak variant, all cultures are weird, with the English or, by extension, the northwestern European being only the most peculiar of the lot. In the strong version of the theory, the rest of the world outside England and northwestern Europe is peculiar, burdened with coercive institutions and practices.
>
> (Smith 1993: 345)

In his opinion, Macfarlane and Todd epitomize the most extreme examples of this weak, cultural variant (Smith 1993: 347; Macfarlane 1978; Todd 1985). In contrast, the strong, neoindividualist approach puts the individual (and individualist) actor back at the centre of the stage, and would inspire new and more fruitful questions:

> If people have a real choice, the strong version of the [neoindividualist] theory predicts that they will live in households no more complex than those of the simple family. Complex households consequently are the result of coercive institutions or norms. Nuclear households are close to being natural, biologically based units.
>
> (Smith 1993: 347)

According to Smith, this 'strong' neoindividualist version finds its ultimate justification in sociobiology (the 'natural' proclivity of parents to invest in their children) and, if it had been taken seriously, it 'would have created a far more productive and interesting controversy: between the individual and the social as units of analysis, and between the biological and the cultural as the main determinants of behavior' (348).

Smith thus reaches out to anthropology, but to a brand of anthropology (sociobiology) that most of its 'self-respecting' (that is, politically correct . . .) practitioners would hastily repudiate. Despite what some might regard as a questionable assumption, I cannot help feeling that in some respects Smith is asking the right questions.

In the debate on the comparative study of households, anthropologists may have added important riders to premature conclusions on the part of historians, warning them that the concept of household is not a self-evident category, and that they might have lumped disparate entities together. It is unclear to me, however, whether anthropologists themselves have taken things much further or not, for a case could be made that they threw the baby out with the bath water. Indeed, many of their objections have led them to abandon altogether anthropology's original programme, namely comparative analysis. Ironically enough, it is now mostly historians, and especially household historians, who have taken up the flag.

As an anthropologist, I have worked on living arrangements somewhat in the manner of the Cambridge Group (Verdon 1979a, 1979b, 1980a, 1980b, 1987, 1991, 1996a) and, though aware of the difficulties marring this type of research, I nonetheless still believe it possible to give back credibility both to the historical and the comparative studies of households. In this endeavour also I consider that D.S. Smith must be taken very seriously, for he is the first to shift the emphasis from discussions on the household to what he mistakenly calls 'underlying philosophical assumptions' (the term 'philosophical' is somewhat misleading in this context; one may speak of authors' 'underlying assumptions' about the nature of the phenomena they study, of their underlying presuppositions, postulates or set of axioms, but the link to philosophy is on the whole too indirect to be of any great heuristic value in the type of analysis he advocates). Smith's questions will thus take us directly to the key conceptual issues plaguing household history.

However, Smith seems unaware that his strong, neoindividualist set of axioms also lives in the works of some family economists interested in household formation (Ermisch and Overton 1985, for instance), economists whose conceptual grid now supports new developments in family demography (Burch and Matthews 1987; Juby 1993). In brief, demographers studying contemporary European families and households, anthropologists interested in European kinship, as well as family historians, not to mention household economists, are trying to account for household composition and, willy-nilly, will ultimately have to share a common set of axioms. In other words, we are no longer talking about a renewed dialogue between family historians and anthropologists but about a 'conference' between many more interlocutors.

Hence the present venture: I wish to take things where Smith has left them and strive to elaborate a new conceptual and theoretical framework which could sort out, clarify and unify diverse attempts to study household composition in Europe. As we shall see, this new set of axioms will superficially look like Smith's neoindividualism, but superficially only.

As a result, this book will be divided in two parts. In the first part I will seek to develop an atomistic set of presuppositions from considerations stemming from anthropology and family demography; in the second, I shall endeavour to demonstrate its heuristic validity by applying it first to two European areas with types of households which have overwhelmingly been described as extremely collectivistic, namely pre-emancipation Russian multiple family households and Western Pyrenean stem families. A chapter on the question of English neolocality and contemporary household 'atomization' in Canada (1971–86) will follow, and I will end by contrasting the set of postulates I developed for Europe to the one which would have to be elaborated in a radically different cultural setting, namely among the Abutia Ewe of southeastern Ghana. Needless to say, I do not see my contribution as an empirical one, since I have selected empirical cases for their paradigmatic value, and will rely on secondary sources when discussing them. What this book strives to achieve is to clarify some issues that have tended to get more and more clouded as years went by; as such, it remains an essentially programmatic statement.

I have subtitled this book 'An atomistic perspective on *European* living arrangements'. In reality, I would have preferred to write 'Western living arrangements', but 'The West' is one of those realities which makes sense only to those who do not feel they belong to it. As it is, I have therefore chosen Europe, and implicitly North America of European extraction, and I have written of Europe as if it formed a unified cultural area. I am aware of the raging debates surrounding the notion of 'cultural area', and of the futility of trying to define them in general. Furthermore, I am equally aware that, within Europe, some areas display sufficient homogeneity to warrant sub-demarcations. But over time and space, so many factors have shaped diversely the European social and cultural landscape that it would be most naive to present it either as a well-delineated, uniform social space, or as neatly subdivided into easily categorized areas. Beneath the variations, however, some convergent themes do make it useful to evoke such a fuzzy concept as Europe. I therefore deny it any cultural boundaries, and confess to using it loosely for its immediate presentational convenience. The same themes that pervade the literature on European residence might be found much further afield, but my concern is not to delineate cultural areas; it is to identify some common elements which warrant the framework I elaborate.

Finally, I have limited myself to European populations and North American populations of European extraction, partly because this is the literature I know and about which I have written over the years, but mostly because moving further afield would have involved me in different cultural contexts and would possibly have called for vastly dissimilar sets of axioms, as the contrast with Abutia suggests. And, within this general geographical category, I have chosen paradigmatic examples which were presented either as extremely collectivistic or extremely individualistic, to demonstrate how misleading such categorizations are and how, underneath all, the same axioms can be seen to run. I have therefore wilfully neglected such important areas as India, China, Japan, not to mention the Arab world, because each one of them might have called for a different book.

1

THE UBIQUITY OF
COLLECTIVISTIC
ASSUMPTIONS

In the Introduction, we saw D.S. Smith claiming that Laslett more or less invented the theses he proceeded to demolish, and advocating that we pry into 'underlying philosophical assumptions', especially into what he calls the neoindividualist and the cultural assumptions in the study of households. In this chapter, I shall argue that the sets of axioms underlying debates on household composition do not set neoindividualism against culturalism, but 'atomism' against collectivism. I shall show that collectivistic sets of axioms (which Laslett allegedly invented to make his claims 'revolutionary', according to Smith) do pervade the whole literature, anthropological as well as historical, on areas characterized by complex household types. Ultimately, however, I shall converge with Smith by showing that collectivistic assumptions seem inevitably to lead to culturalism. From there, I shall conclude that only 'atomistic' assumptions can rescue household history.

Understanding axioms and their implications

Before tackling the question of underlying assumptions, I feel it necessary to spell out what underlying assumptions, or more appositely a 'set of axioms' really implies, that our choice of assumptions (or axioms) dictates what we will deem problematical (what we define as a problem). To understand better the relationship between the two, I shall evoke a classical paradigmatic case, namely one from the history of dynamics (that part of physics dealing with the study of movement).

Every physical (and social) theory must posit some things about the outside world. Let us start with Aristotelian dynamics. Aristotle posited that the natural tendency of matter was not to move once in its 'natural place' (for the purpose of this demonstration, we shall conveniently forget his theory of natural places), axiomatically declaring rest, or absence of motion (immobility), to be matter's natural proclivity. From this set of axioms it followed logically and necessarily that if matter resists movement and movement is found to exist, it must therefore be problematical and a phenomenon to be explained. Aristotle's set of axioms thus led him to the central set of problems that haunted the Schoolmen: why do things move, if they resist movement by their very nature?

Galileo completely inverted the terms of this representation. He posited axiomatically that matter is intrinsically mobile and that it would move indefinitely at a constant velocity unless acted upon (this is physics' principle of 'inertial motion'). In other words, matter moving at a constant velocity will by nature conserve this velocity and *resist* changes to it. These new assumptions about movement wholly transformed the traditional questions. Logically, Galileo could no longer ask why things move since he declared matter to be intrinsically mobile, and he therefore had to explain why matter undergoes *changes* in velocity (in other words, why one witnesses acceleration and deceleration in the real world). This radically new understanding of what is problematical about movement launched dynamics on its scientific course, freeing it from the circular arguments emanating from the Aristotelian set of axioms. Why, then, does matter speed up or slow down, if by nature it should move at a constant velocity? Galileo found the answer in the existence of hindrances to movement or in the action of forces: matter's constant velocity will decrease if hampered by the medium through which it travels (hindrances), or increase if attracted by a force.

There is an important corollary to this relationship between what we understand to be problematical, and the underlying set of assumptions which make us see things in that way. Inertial motion belonged to Galileo's set of axioms, but that does not imply that he could escape asking the question, why does matter sometimes retain its constant velocity? However, if both constant velocity (or inertial motion) and its opposite (namely acceleration or deceleration) called for answers, these answers stood in symmetrical but inverted positions. To account for acceleration or deceleration he had to invoke factors which overcame matter's resistance to changes in velocity; these were, as we have seen, either hindrances or forces. To explain constant velocity (inertial motion), on the other hand, he had to argue in the opposite fashion. Because inertial motion formed part of his basic presuppositions, it could be explained only by assuming the *absence* of hindrances and forces.

From physics let us move closer to home, namely to agricultural history. In the agricultural history of French-speaking Quebec, a formidable (and strongly ideological) debate arose around the fact that nineteenth-century French-speaking Québecois supposedly did not commercialize while their English-speaking neighbours did. In this polemic, some historians turned to neoclassical economics for an answer (following an anthropological usage, I shall call those historians 'formalist') and, among agricultural historians of Quebec they, more than most, clearly understood the manner in which a set of axioms dictates the manner in which we define what is problematical. Someone unaware of this distinction would indeed claim that both commercialization and its absence are problematical, that both call for explanations. 'Yes', the formalists would reply, 'but in radically different ways'.

For a number of theoretical reasons (having to do with the maximization of utility), the formalists hold that if a market exists and conditions of access are good, farmers will 'naturally' commercialize. In brief, given market conditions approaching perfection, they take commercialization as a natural proclivity of economic agents. This constitutes their underlying assumptions. Supposing that economic agents are rational (we will deal with the question of irrationality in Chapter 5), their reluctance to commercialize needs to be explained (is problematical) and should stem from market imperfections (hindrances); this would account for the Franco-Québecois' alleged economic backwardness. Remove those hindrances (that is, create easier access to credit and markets) and they will 'naturally' commercialize; this would account for the Anglo-Québecois and English-Canadian response. Clearly, both commercialization and its absence have to be made intelligible, but the two call for inverted factors. Lack of commercialization derives from the *presence* of hindrances, whereas commercialization flows from their *absence*.

Endless examples could be adduced from anthropology, sociology and the like, but I hope the distinction to be clear enough to go ahead with our present topic, household composition. I have cited those cases to show that the study of residence, like that of any social phenomenon, does not escape this necessary relationship between our set of axioms and what we deem problematical. Unfortunately, the issues in the study of households have never been stated in those terms. To my knowledge, D.S. Smith is the first to have made a step in this direction and, in my opinion, he failed to infer all the logical consequences. When we explicitly set apart axioms from the manner in which they channel what we regard as problems, we can reformulate his question in a simpler and clearer fashion. In short, students of European residence must decide what is to be explained (is problematical), and what is to be posited (taken as axiomatic); *furthermore, in all scientific practice (and in philosophy of science) one choice excludes the other* (with some important exceptions, such as the contemporary theory of light, which prove the proverbial rule). Either one assumes on the part of Europeans a tendency to live in complex households and has to explain the emergence of less complex and, ultimately, nuclear households, invoking for that purpose external factors either inhibiting their formation (normally demographic ones) or undermining them (the rise of individualism in its many guises) – I will call this a 'collectivistic' set of axioms; or one may on the contrary suppose that European households will spontaneously tend to nuclearize, if unhindered; complex ones must then be made intelligible in terms of hindrances, coercion, or both. This, in my terminology and for reasons explained below, makes up what I will call an 'atomistic' set of axioms. If this last set of presuppositions seems to repeat Smith's, it does so only apparently, as we shall see in Chapter 4. With these clarifications out of the way, we may now return to the study of residence.

Collectivism in the study of complex households

Let us first assess Smith's main grievance against Laslett, namely that the latter invented the myth he sought to supplant. In his accusation, Smith's argument revolves almost entirely around the relationship between industrialization and the nuclearization of the household. According to Smith, Laslett assumes that previous historians connected the two causally and, against this whole tradition, the author of *The World We Have Lost* would profess to have discovered that English nuclear households preceded industrialization by three hundred years or so.

If Smith wishes to uncover family history's underlying set of axioms, his essay must belong partly to epistemology and, from an epistemological point of view, it makes little difference whether historians placed large and complex households before the Industrial Revolution or in the early Middle Ages. What matters is the view of an evolution from large and complex households to small and nuclear ones. Second, he claims not to find any evidence that historians held such views, save a few Americans who were 'influential for roughly the two decades between the mid-1930s and the mid-1950s' (Smith 1993: 326, elaborated on 338ff.). In his search for sources of this alleged myth he comes across nineteenth-century evolutionists whose views seemed to prove Laslett's thesis right, but he swiftly dismisses them by arguing that their vision of history was but a simple dichotomy of ideal types:

> However, the purpose of these polar concepts [so characteristic of evolutionists, such as the evolution from status to contract, from *Gemeinschaft* to *Gesellschaft*, and the like] is not to periodize the past. Dichotomized in this manner, time is a moral rather than a historical concept.
>
> (Smith 1993: 336)

About the evolutionists, Smith is more than partial. Engels's and Durkheim's (and all the evolutionists') polar types were linked by a continuum which did represent the unfolding of time. Furthermore, Smith omits one universal belief of this evolutionary thinking, namely the assumption that 'primitives' were not individuated, that they were 'group-creatures', so to speak, and that only groups enjoyed full ontological status; that is, only groups were true phenomena in their own right, individuals were only epiphenomenal, deprived of any individuality. As a result of this fusion of the individual with the group the evolutionists declared the so-called primitives collectivistic and contrasted them to individualistic 'civilized' societies.

It is true that the evolutionists did not write about household composition, and this because they confused household and family, as many still do, including Smith in this critique of Laslett. Had they been acutely aware of household composition, however, it is more than plausible that they would also have depicted it in terms of an evolution from collectivistic to individualist forms, that is, from complex to nuclear households. What obtained for the general movement from the primitive to the civilized would have equally extended to the general movement from 'primitive' (i.e. medieval) to contemporary Europe (see Netting *et al.* 1984a).

Finally, if Smith had consulted a different set of authors he would have easily noticed that this nineteenth-century evolutionary heritage did permeate the literature. In fact, as I shall argue, historians and anthropologists alike have transplanted to the very history of Europe this evolutionary sketch from collectivistic 'primitives' to individualistic 'civilized people'. This, for instance, can be seen in the works of many authors in search of grand syntheses, such as Ariès (1973), Flandrin (1976), Shorter (1977) and others, all of whom describe the evolution of European society as a movement from collectivism to individualism. But it lives in a host of other works and, in this first chapter, I plan to ferret these collectivistic presuppositions out of their burrows, and to assess what collectivistic presuppositions actually lead to.

The first and obvious place to look in a search for collectivistic presuppositions is the history and ethnography of complex households. Indeed, I believe that collectivism thrives most happily in the literature dealing with those areas typified by a large proportion of complex households. By this, I do not claim that all authors writing about these areas espouse collectivistic sets of axioms. Far from it: some argue from a purely atomistic point of view, albeit most often implicitly, others from a collectivistic viewpoint, whereas others still unwittingly mix atomistic and collectivistic perspectives in the same texts. Where authors mix their set of axioms, I shall write of 'axiomatic dualism'. Now, let us turn to some of the most famous areas of complex households, and of collectivistic anthropology or family history.

Collectivism and the stem family: Quebec and the Western Pyrenees

Collectivistic axioms about the stem family reach back to the very first writings on the subject, to the works of Le Play and of his followers. Ultraconservative, appalled by the French Revolution and what he considered the growth of individualism and the disintegration of the very fabric of French society, Le Play discovered in the Western Pyrenean stem family the coveted model to reinject traditional family values while preparing individuals for a changing world. He saw in the stem family a felicitous compromise between the 'patriarchal family' (which he also called *famille communautaire*, or 'communal family') and the 'unstable family' (the 'nuclear family'), but he also thought that the stem family was threatened by the growing individualism of contemporary society and the inability of fathers, under the Napoleonic code, to make wills and transmit most of their property to a single heir (Le Play 1907).

Demolins, one of Le Play's most famous disciples, realized that Le Play had confused two different types of stem families. In some areas patriarchal families retained their conservative and communal values but bequeathed their possessions to one son only because of land scarcity and demographic pressures. Demolins dubbed this type of family 'quasi-patriarchal' or 'quasi-communal'. In other areas, however, the patriarchal family had been transformed by new circumstances which thrust individuals towards new types of productive activities, stimulating their spirit of initiative and enterprise, and leading young people to create new households upon their marriage. The father, forsaken and afraid to see his farm abandoned after his death, lured one son to stay with him by appointing him his only heir. According to Demolins, only this type would deserve the appellation 'stem family', and he christened it the 'particularist family'. In Demolins's scheme the 'particularist family' included Le Play's *famille instable* in its most extreme form in the Anglo-Saxon world, and was historically the most recent development in family types (Demolins 1893).

Immensely successful in France and even translated into English, Demolins's publications thus explicitly contrasted communal or quasi-communal families with particularist ones. Patriarchal families mercilessly subordinated individual interests to collective ones, whereas particularist families saw collective interests overpowered by individual ones; at marriage every child moved out of the parental house and followed his whims, regardless of the needs of the parental household (which, for instance, might have needed his manpower). Thus the evolutionist picture of a movement from collectivism to individualism, as old as evolutionism itself, resurfaced in family history.

The debate on the stem family in France died down at the turn of the century but, interestingly enough, Le Play's work had its most immediate and important impact on Quebec ethnography and sociology from the late 1890s onward. In Quebec, stem families were not isolated on inaccessible mountain tops as they are in much of France; on the contrary, they dominated the rural landscape. Furthermore, Léon Gérin, Quebec's first and perhaps greatest ethnographer, was a student of Demolins. He brought to Quebec the methods of his mentors, studied a 'typical' Quebec family in a classical Le Play-style monograph and concluded that Quebec stem families belonged to Demolins's 'quasi-patriarchal type', a collectivistic domestic environment ruled by the iron fist of a patriarch (Gérin 1898).

Horace Miner, the Chicago-trained anthropologist strongly influenced by Radcliffe-Brown (the greatest theoretician of the British school of social anthropology until the 1950s, to whose name the 'school' of structural-functionalism is linked), took over similar ideas which he cast in his master's mould (Miner 1939). Insisting on the fact that the stem family flows from the practice of impartible inheritance (also Le Play's and Gérin's theses), he saw in the French-Canadian stem family the equivalent of an African corporation. In classical ethnography, a corporation is at one and the same time a group of individuals who collectively own a given estate, and an entity transcending the lives of its individual members. As a supra-individual entity, 'a corporation never dies': the new generation takes over from the older ones and the eldest, after their death, would in Quebec have remained part of the corporation through family pictures adorning the walls of every living-room.

Despite his Radcliffe-Brownian inspiration, Miner did not push the analogy to its logical limits. He portrayed a collectivistic stem family as a corporation but balked at writing of 'corporate property': collectivism dominated household behaviour but did not extend to the ownership of property, which in the Quebec he studied was individually appropriated and did not belong to a 'house' or some other such entity. The Gérin-Miner theses dominated Quebec sociology and anthropology until the 1960s when Philippe Garigue, an Englishman of Huguenot origins, tried to puncture them (Garigue 1962). In so far as the controversy simply petered out as it led up a blind alley, it may be said that Garigue succeeded.

If the debate on the stem family subsided in France at the turn of the century, it revived with unprecedented intensity in contemporary French ethnography of the Western Pyrenees, starting with the work of Bourdieu (1962) and culminating in that of Augustins (1981; 1989). Miner had stopped short of writing of corporate property, but Augustins did not, pushing further than anyone else Demolins's collectivistic presuppositions, albeit retranslated in Radcliffe-Brown's juridical idiom of 'corporations'. In the process, he even jettisoned the classical notion of stem family, writing instead of 'House systems'.[1] Why 'House systems'? The question takes us back to Lévi-Strauss, and outside Europe.

In his lectures at the Collège de France in 1976–7, and later in various publications (1983; 1984), Lévi-Strauss studied what he was to label 'House societies', that is, North and South American, as well as Indonesian, societies where many families often live in 'long houses'. In these writings, he unequivocally equated 'Houses' with corporations owning corporeal and incorporeal property (Lamaison 1987: 34). When French ethnographers inspired by Lévi-Strauss turned their attention to southern France, they recognized in this part of their own society 'Houses' somewhat similar to what their mentor had lectured about. Thus the notion of 'House systems' was born.

According to Augustins, these European 'House systems' have reached their fullest expression in the Western Pyrenees, because the Western Pyreneans pushed to the extreme what remained a tendency elsewhere.[2] First, they evolved a form of impartible inheritance so implacable that it made a sacrosanct principle of primogeniture, and formerly of 'absolute' primogeniture,[3] and rendered it almost impossible for *cadets* or *cadettes* of one House to marry *cadets* or *cadettes* of another House (the so-called *cadets/cadettes* marriages; in French, the *aîné(e)* is the eldest child, all the others being *cadets* – boys – or *cadettes* – girls). In every House the heir or heiress would marry a *cadet* or *cadette* from another House, and a *cadet* or *cadette* from the House would marry an heir or heiress elsewhere, thanks to the dowry they were given. The Western Pyreneans thus banned the creation of new households and condemned to emigration, or to celibacy, as shepherds or quasi-servants within the House, the younger siblings who did not succeed in marrying an heir. Many of these measures were duly inscribed in the *Coutumes* in order to protect the sacrosanct integrity of the patrimony (the *Coutumes*, as their very name suggests, enshrined the traditional 'custom' and were written down around the fifteenth or sixteenth centuries to counter the advance of Roman law in the Pyrenees).

Second, the Basques and Béarnais of yore expected individuals to subordinate their destinies to that of the House which, like the corporations of classical ethnography, had to persist beyond individual lives. Individuals come and go, but the corporation remains, and the Western Pyrenean 'Houses' of the eighteenth and nineteenth century portrayed in contemporary ethnography (or perhaps, more specifically, contemporary ethnohistory) lived this corporate existence. In order for the House to persist beyond individual lives, even the heir (eldest), although head of this corporation, had to bend like his younger siblings to the collective necessity because he wielded only usufructuary rights over a family estate which he had to transmit whole and undivided to the following generation. Properly speaking, individuals owned neither the house (dwelling-unit) nor its attached land, since the House, as a corporate entity, transcended them.

Finally, Houses and people were so closely assimilated that individuals were known by House names and, at marriage, adopted the name of the House into which they married. According to this contemporary ethnohistorical literature, it is not individuals who unite in holy matrimony but Houses that exchange matrimonial partners and dowries.

Thus, behind today's Western Pyrenean 'House system' Demolins's 'quasi-communal family' and his collectivistic presuppositions still lurk. Indeed, to these same ethnographers-cum-historians, Western Pyrenean Houses would have 'naturally' formed 'patriarchal' families (that is, multiple family households) had they not been hindered in their natural development by the mountain environment in which they lived, an upland environment so difficult to exploit that it imposed severe limitations on human reproduction. In their opinion, the Pyrenees had become demographically saturated centuries ago, and this land pressure had required uncompromising and inhuman rules of transmission and marriage,[4] together with strict reproductive strategies: a very late age at first marriage, exorbitant rates of celibacy and forms of contraception (*contraception de blocage*, according to Fauve-Chamoux) that yielded a completed fertility much below national averages.[5] Without hindrances imposing impartible inheritance to the single heir, Western Pyrenean Houses would follow their natural collectivistic proclivity towards multiple family households (Augustins 1981: 99; Douglass also infers it quite explicitly for the Spanish Basques – Douglass 1988: 83).

In other words, in the most veiled and muted manner, deep-rooted evolutionist and collectivist presuppositions survive in this whole ethnography: that the closer one gets to these remote, isolated and even 'primitive' regions, the more households tend to be complex, the more they tend towards extension, lateral as well as vertical. At the primitive (and hence collectivistic) pole, multiple family households would naturally thrive if lands were plenty. Consequently, what needs to be explained are those household types, such as the Western Pyrenean House or the so-called nuclear family, which lack such extension. For both types, ethnographers seek the answer in inhibiting factors, such as demographic pressures. Such pressures would explain both the Western Pyrenean 'House systems' and their demise. On the one hand, those Houses developed because the environment did not permit partibility; on the other hand, they would have persisted indefinitely had they succeeded in stopping their demographic expansion and had they not simultaneously been undermined by the 'rise of individualism'. In this ethnographic perspective, households would thus 'nuclearize' when societies spontaneously bent towards collective practices suffer from the 'disorganizing' influences of individualism (already denounced by Le Play).

Such collectivistic assumptions also suffused German family history through the writings of Riehl (1856), a conservative but unscientific Le Play, and completely infiltrated Scandinavian family history, according to Gaunt (1987), just as they pervaded the Spanish literature on the same topic:

> At the provincial level there has been a tendency on the part of both creative writers and academics . . . to regard the isolated extended family homestead, whether *quintana*, *caserio* or *caseria*, as the ideal. At the same time they seek to show over time, that is, historically, how that ideal is being threatened by degenerating modern forces of nuclear familism and acquisitive individualism. . . .

This literate negotiation has the following consequence: the ideas are seen in terms of an evolutionary or historical perspective. The ideal of agglomeration has tended to be regarded as one ideal that was reached in a more pastoral past time. The separatist impulse is seen, in turn, to be the driving and degenerating impulse of the modern era.

(Fernandez and Fernandez 1988: 138–9)

As can be expected, collectivism also finds a strong expression in the study of multiple family households. Apart from the extremely rare French *famille taisible* (Dussourd 1979), the Serb *zadruga*, the Carelian multiple family households (Gaunt 1987) and some households found among mountain pastoralists (Montenegro, Albania and Greece), the nineteenth-century pre-emancipation Russian multiple family households rank among the largest and the most complex in Europe, and their existence has recently attracted the attention of family historians. Being among the most 'collectivistic' of multiple family households, they could not but attract collectivistic explanations in some quarters.

Collectivism and multiple family households: Russia and Eastern Europe

One of the most remarkable features of the literature on Russian peasant society, and one about which I believe there is consensus, is the corporate nature of ownership:

> The study of peasant customary law concerning heredity and succession makes it clear that property was accumulated within the common economy of a family/household not in order to eventually transmit it to individuals, but to preserve the household itself and any spin-offs from it in the predominantly prevailing complex form.
> (Aleksandrov 1979: 37–54; Czap 1982: 7)

This is a theme echoed throughout the literature (Shanin 1972: 30–31; Bohac 1985: 26; Worobec 1991: 28; Farnsworthy 1986: 55), and making the household equally a corporation of the African type: 'The Russian peasant's home was a place of worship – the worship of the family itself as an ongoing, living entity' (Matossian 1968: 19). Quoting Sir Donald Mackenzie Wallace, a nineteenth-century observer of Russian peasant households, Vucinigh brings out strikingly the classical evolutionist view of 'primitives': 'The peasants' basic social unit was not the individual but the family, developed to save the individual by suppressing him' (Wallace 1877: 8, quoted in Vucinigh 1968: xii).

It is on the question of household fission (or household partitions, that is, the fact that some of these multiple family households did now and then split to form new households), however, that collectivistic presuppositions surface most explicitly. The question of partitions is most complex, revealing simultaneously amongst many of its authors both atomistic and collectivistic sets of axioms. I shall deal with the atomistic aspect of the question in Chapter 5, and will here limit myself to isolating the collectivistic viewpoint.

As early as the nineteenth century, a vast array of Russian authors pondered the question of household divisions because, in their opinion, it flouted the most basic axioms of economic rationality (Frierson 1987: 45–6). On the one hand, these nineteenth-century authors (and more recent ones) considered partitions problematical for economic reasons; in this, as I shall argue in Chapter 5, they implicitly understood household formation in atomistic terms.[6] However, when one examines the factors adduced to account for any departure from what Russian peasants should have done rationally, we find these same authors evoking the insidious penetration of an individualist worldview gnawing at the antique and sound collectivism of the Russian peasantry (Frierson 1987: 37–8, 42). This, needless to say, betrays a wholly different set of postulates, namely the idea that Russian peasants had also developed a strongly collectivistic culture, a collectivism that sustained their large households:

> Populists viewed the phenomenon with alarm because it implied a rise in individualism and the decline of the spirit of collectivism; Marxists found in it a confirmation of the breakdown of traditional structures under the impact of the penetration of capitalism into the Russian village; to conservative bureaucrats, divisions represented the weakening of patriarchy.
>
> (Frierson 1987: 37–8)

This is a theme Frierson repeats time and time again: 'divisions came to be associated in the minds of outside observers with such developments in the countryside as migratory labor, the rise of individualism and the decline of patriarchy' (Frierson 1987: 42).[7]

It is impossible to mention the literature on Russian multiple family households without touching upon Macfarlane's sketch of 'peasant societies', drawn directly from observations made on Polish, Russian and more generally Eastern European multiple family households (Macfarlane 1978). Although my conclusions repeat Smith's on this topic, I believe the latter to have been somewhat unfair to Macfarlane.

Macfarlane wanted to prove that England had not been a peasant society since the High Middle Ages. To substantiate his thesis he depicted an ideal type of a peasant society from the works of Thomas and Znaniecki on Polish peasants, and from that of Shanin on pre-emancipation Russia (Thomas and Znaniecki 1958 [1918]; Shanin 1972). Actually, Macfarlane's demonstration stands out through its deductive character. What is to him the central feature of a peasant society? He repeats what all his sources dwell on: 'that ownership was not individualized. It was not the single individual who exclusively owned the productive resources, but rather the household' (1978: 18), a household which acted as a corporation in every possible manner. First, individuals enjoyed only usufructuary rights of the household's corporate property: 'The group dominated the individual in terms of ownership' (20), a common ownership which excluded both the idea of inheritance and the possibility of writing wills (20–1); to alienate property, the individual needed the assent of the collectivity. This feature enables him to derive 'the identification of farm and family; the household was the basic unit of production and consumption because it was also the basic unit of ownership' (21). From this basic equation he further deduces every other feature which he deems 'peasant': the peasants' abhorrence towards wage labour and, more generally, towards commercial exchanges. Peasants would thus refuse to mortgage, let alone sell, land and this, because 'a particular generation is only temporary manager of an ancestral estate that must, if at all possible, be handed down to descendants' (23). From the same premises he finally infers the patriarchal nature of peasant societies, as well as some classical demographic features: universal marriage, early age at marriage, arranged marriages linking families, not individuals, and multiple family households.

At first glance, no collectivistic presupposition seems to dwell there, since everything is very logically derived from a fundamental fact: the absence of individual ownership. But when it comes to asking 'Why should peasant societies shy away from individual ownership in favour of household ownership?', in *The Origins of English Individualism* (1978) Macfarlane sadly seems to provide no answer save an implicit: 'Because they are collectivistic!' This is never spelled out, but nonetheless comes out clearly when he contrasts his ideal-typical peasant society with England. In the end, the major difference between England and 'peasant societies' (the latter, incidentally, encompassing in his mind most of Europe, except a tiny northwestern corner) lies in the fact that the English have enjoyed individual ownership as far back as documents go. And why should they? Because of their individualism! In brief, the type of property (individual versus household) is nothing but the embodiment of individualism versus collectivism. We seem to be faced with a case of 'axiomatic dualism': individualism for the English, and collectivism for the rest of the world. We shall see that this is not exactly the case.

This same axiomatic dualism characterizes the work of another guru of the comparative study of European ethnography in France, Emmanuel Todd. Of his prolific production we shall examine one work only: his *Invention de l'Europe* (Todd 1990).

Todd's theoretical framework is distinguished by its simplicity. He supposes that 'family structures' constitute the bedrock upon which religious, economic and political phenomena stand. Family structures change slowly; so slowly, in fact, that he believes that in places they have not been modified for centuries, if not a whole millennium. And what determines a particular 'family structure'? *Sets of values*. In every society, some fundamental values organize relationships between parents and children on the one hand, and between siblings on the other. In Todd's vision, two main values mould relationships between parents and children: authoritarianism and liberalism; two also operate between siblings: equality and inequality. The first set of values manifests itself in the field of residence, through cohabitation or neolocality; the second, in the field of property transmission, through partible or impartible inheritance.

By combining these four possible values along these two axes Todd derives his typology of family structures: absolute nuclear (liberal and unequal), nuclear egalitarian (liberal and equal), stem families (authoritarian and unequal) and *familles communautaires* (multiple family households, expressing the values of authority and equality). The language may differ slightly from Macfarlane's, but the underlying assumptions are the same: some societies (the liberal ones) form nuclear households and are individualistic whereas others (the authoritarian ones – Demolins' patriarchal societies once again) form plurifamilial households and are collectivistic. As with Macfarlane, collectivistic presuppositions hold in areas of complex households, and individualistic ones in regions of nuclear households.

Such examples of collectivistic sets of axioms in the literature, both historical and anthropological, could be multiplied a dozen times, and they all reveal D.S. Smith's rather biased review of the literature. What I wish to stress, however, is that Macfarlane and Todd do not stand alone in their axiomatic dualism. I would rather state that they represent a host of family historians and ethnographers of European kinship, all of whom are, in one way or another, collectivistic *malgré eux*, even when arguing from atomistic premises. But, one may justly ask, what's wrong with collectivistic presuppositions?

When I originally contrasted collectivistic with atomistic postulates, I assumed that they represented symmetrical but inverted images of one another: the first posits a spontaneous tendency to living in complex households (within the European cultural context, it goes without saying), and the second posits a tendency to living in nuclear households. In reality, when one probes the matter deeper, no symmetry is to be found.

By espousing an atomistic set of axioms, we suppose that hindrances (e.g. becoming a widow, economic stringency, physical or psychological problems, the necessity to regroup for defence) or forces (coercing people through manipulation, mostly of inheritances), or both, can account for the formation of complex households. In a collectivist perspective, however, this distinction seems no longer to hold. Indeed, from the collectivistic literature that I have consulted, the collectivists appear unable to suggest forces when it comes to explaining the existence of less complex households (and ultimately, of nuclear ones). After pondering the question in more abstract terms, I realized that they probably could not adduce the existence of any force, for it seems to me impossible to imagine any force explaining nuclearization, except some evasive individualist pull. In other words, from what I have read, the collectivists evoke hindrances to explain the increasing lack of complexity of household (and the only hindrance they cite is demographic, as in the Pyrenean case). Otherwise, the nuclearization of households is everywhere seen as resulting from the penetration of capitalism and of its individualistic set of values.

This makes sense of the asymmetry. Whether collectivists or atomists, we all have to root our underlying assumptions about residence in something extraresidential. The collectivists cannot call economics to the rescue, for this necessarily introduces individualist or atomistic premises. They are thus left with one alternative, and one only, the very one that I shall be using myself – social-psychology. The proclivity to either collectivistic or atomistic living arrangements must stem from social-psychological predispositions. In a collectivistic perspective, however, social-psychology seems to create more problems then it solves.

Indeed, if living in large and complex households stemmed from people's very psychological predispositions, we would have to assume that this 'natural proclivity' has changed with nuclearization. From the collectivist literature, the answer seems to be in the affirmative; people have developed a taste for privacy, the collectivists argue, because their system of values, or norms, is no longer the same. Thus, whatever the guise – as values, norms, beliefs, etc. – what I have found beneath this supposed behavioural transformation is Culture. In more general terms, however, we could even go one step further. From a collectivist perspective, one conclusion seems to me unavoidable: people behave differently *because their Culture has changed*. I have examined the question from every possible angle, and I always come back to the same conclusion: all collectivism appears to lead us inevitably to culturalism or to one of its sub-species, what Bourdieu labelled *juridisme* (see Bourdieu 1980). What is culturalism? It is a type of explanation which consists in observing a patterned behaviour or a collective practice, and in accounting for its existence by invoking a set of norms, or of values, dictating this practice. In other words, it consists in summoning Culture (not specific cultural facts, but general norms, values, beliefs or a general ethos, that is, some floating, hypostatized and transcendental entity) to explain the fact that most individuals in a population act in a certain way in

21

certain circumstances (as to *juridisme*, it is but a subset of culturalism, confining itself to normative systems – see the Annex). But, to dispel any misunderstanding, I hasten to add that any attempt to explain social phenomena will of necessity include *cultural elements* (among others), and that introducing cultural phenomena in a theoretical framework is not to be confused with culturalism. To this important distinction I shall devote part of Chapter 3.

Culturalism, as a mode of explanation, is nowhere more evident than in the writings of Todd, where complex households stem from the operation of 'fundamental *values*' (a culturalist answer) or in those of Augustins, where 'House systems' derive from the 'operations of principles of legitimacy' (a euphemism for norms and hence a case of *juridisme*; Augustins 1989) ultimately rooted in the action of a 'principle of residence' or a 'principle of kinship'. (Again, on the notion of so-called 'principles of social organization' and what they really stand for, see the Annex.)

On the topic of culturalism or that of *juridisme*, one thing ought to be emphasized (and will be again at the end of Chapter 3): it is well known to a host of social scientists that Culture (once again appearing as general 'principles', or norms, or a general ethos – hence the capital 'C' when I refer to it in this manner) does not explain anything. To be more precise, I should add a very important rider: *Culture does explain one thing, namely resistance to change, that is, tradition* (see Verdon 1991). In fact, not only does Culture explain nothing, but it is precisely what we need to account for; as the philosophers of science would put it, it is the *explanandum*, not the *explanans*.

What does this mean? Let us take any case – Tuscany in the eighteenth or the nineteenth century, for instance. We could find norms 'dictating' that a son newly married stay with his new wife in his father's house, and this could even be buttressed by religious beliefs ('Obey your parents') and a general religious ethos. Do these norms and this religious superstructure account for the behaviour of individuals? Some would say 'Yes', others would say 'Up to a certain point' and others (such as Holy and Stuchlik 1983) 'No'. The question, however, is not one of individual behaviour; in a comparative perspective, the question rather is 'But why should the Tuscans behave in such a way, and the southern French or the English in a different manner?' To this question, neither norms nor religion (in the European context, where various living arrangements are found with the same set of religious beliefs) can bring an answer. On the contrary, we have to look for some elements which will plausibly account for the *emergence* of such a practice, the fact that it has been collectively embraced. Then, and only then, do norms, religion or Culture act with their full force. As I shall argue again at length below, norms or Culture evolve after the fact, so to speak, to ensure that these newly-emergent practices *endure*, persist, that they reproduce themselves and even resist changes. To that extent, in the everyday life of individuals, norms and Culture have an enormous power, no doubt, a power they unfortunately lose when it comes to explaining the emergence of collective practices. Overall, from the collectivistic literature consulted and from more general considerations, I have found all collectivistic assumptions to lead to culturalism. In this case, they cannot be said to stand as explanations of variability.

I should therefore rectify my conclusions about Macfarlane and Todd. They do not suffer from axiomatic dualism, because 'individualism', from their vantage point, shares nothing with Smith's neoindividualism, with the individualism of household economics, or with what I call 'atomism'. To Macfarlane and Todd, individualism, like collectivism, is nothing but a set of values, or a cultural code. There is nothing but Culture, here stressing the group over the individual, there the individual over the group; in the end, they both contrast collectivism and individualism as two sets of values, as two opposite cultural codes. Given their culturalist understanding of residence, we can now understand how and why D.S. Smith singled them out to illustrate what he called the 'cultural variant' in the explanations of neolocality.

Let us therefore loop the loop. If, in the study of residence, there can be two sets of underlying assumptions only, namely collectivism and atomism, if collectivism seems inescapably to lead to culturalism and if culturalism is a simple reification of the observed, there is but one choice left: we must espouse an atomistic set of axioms!

2

FAMILY, RESIDENCE, DOMESTICITY AND HOUSEHOLDS

The parameters of a conceptual morass

A set of axioms, whatever it may be, would of necessity bring us back to household history's conceptual framework and the discussions it has stimulated. This will take us on a brief survey of the relevant anthropological literature, since on the whole anthropologists have been the most forward in the critique of family history's comparative undertaking. Like any survey, the one I propose is both selective and somewhat arbitrary (as I could never do justice to this extremely vast and rich literature) but, in sketching it, I have specifically aimed at identifying and understanding the most contentious areas, in the hope, naively enough, of suggesting some elements towards a possible solution.

I have divided this sketch into three parts. In the first one, I try to follow anthropology's attempt to study domestic groups and households. In the second, I document anthropology's more recent delusion with the whole enterprise, its systematic 'deconstruction' of the very concepts upon which the whole comparative analysis is built, especially the concept of 'household'. In the third part, I try to counter the arguments and reverse the process, hoping to provide the initial foundations of a new conceptual framework which could legitimize the comparative programme which once constituted anthropology's specificity in the study of domestic groups, and now characterizes much of family history.

Towards the household: building a language for comparative analysis

As some have commented (Netting *et al.* 1984a; Roberts 1991), the notion of household came late to anthropology. At the very beginning, anthropologists did not study households, but rules of postmarital residence. The problem emerged in the context of the nineteenth-century evolutionist debate on exogamy and the priority of matrilineal descent (or matriarchy as it was then known). Since 'primitive' people commonly married outside their local group, their clan or lineage, one of the spouses had to change residence after marriage. So started the study of *rules* of postmarital residence (because of its interest in rules, let us call it the 'normative model' in the study of residence).

This understanding of residence had one immediate advantage: it was ideally suited for comparative analysis, the main methodological tool of the emerging anthropology. As two types of descent only were then identified (patrilineal and matrilineal), only two rules of residence operated (patrilocal and matrilocal). The main question was to find out whether or not there was any correspondence between descent and residence (a debate which continued to obsess American anthropology until the end of the 1960s; see Fox 1967). Such simplicity allowed easy classification and still easier theory building.

And yet, this formulation concealed profound limitations which were soon to be discovered. First, the terminology itself raised serious difficulties. N.W. Thomas was the first to label postmarital residence 'matrilocal' or 'patrilocal' (Thomas 1906). These two terms were later found to be inadequate as they did not make clear whether reference was made to the married pair's parents' settlement or domestic group (Adams 1947). This original reflection triggered off a long chain of 'revisions' which basically followed the same inspiration – should the terms used refer to the new couple's initial residence after marriage or to their later residence (if they moved from one place to another after a given period of time), should it refer to the residence of married pairs or the residence of individuals, should it refer to societies as a whole or to individual marriages, should it refer to any kinship links or to the key kinship links in the domestic groups (Murdock 1949, 1957; Goodenough 1956; Fisher 1958; Barnes 1960; Carrasco 1963; Bohannan 1957, 1963; Casselberry and Valavanes 1976)? At the end of the road, the problems besetting this type of approach meant that it more or less lapsed into disuse, despite the determination of some (Fox 1967; Ember and Ember 1971; Pasternak 1976).

Furthermore, those who focused on rules of postmarital residence never studied groups in themselves. The major step developed to overcome these shortcomings was to consider already constituted groups, those formed by people coresiding (let us provisionally call them 'domestic groups'). In this endeavour, Fortes stands as a pioneer and a major figure. In the previous approach, statistics had already raised their ugly head. When ethnographers paid more attention to the composition of groups than to mere rules of postmarital residence, they were baffled by the fact that many domestic groups in a given society do not abide by the 'rules'. Rules of postmarital residence were constantly transgressed and such ideal types as 'patrilocal' or 'virilocal' merely referred to a dominant practice. Statistics were then called upon to solve this new paradox. As a result, the 'predominant residential type' was defined as the 'statistically predominant' one, and percentages allowed comparative analysis to go on despite the uncomfortable realization that rules are not really rules, and that norms are only 'statistically' normative.

A similar problem plagued the study of constituted groups (in the study of residence, let us call this type of procedure, epitomized by Fortes's work, structural-functional): given a typology of domestic groups found in a given community, how are we to characterize this community? By singling out the most frequent type? Fortes believed, and rightly so, that conclusions based on statistical predominance led to arbitrary, and possibly contradictory, conclusions. He overcame the problem with one of the most fruitful notions in this field of study, namely that of the 'developmental cycle of domestic groups', an idea he first introduced in his Tallensi ethnography (1949a), developed in greater detail in an Ashanti study (1949b), and brought to its clearest and final formulation in the Introduction to Goody's classic *The Developmental Cycle of Domestic Groups* (1958).

In the structural-functional model, marriage and kinship figured prominently, if not universally, in the study of domestic groups, whereas residence was more or less dismissed. Thus, whereas the normative model conceived of rules of postmarital residence without isolating groups, the structural-functionalists studied constituted groups but relegated residence to a mere epiphenomenon of marriage and kinship; in their opinion, the function of domestic groups was not to bring people to live together (simple coresidence), but to have children for society to reproduce itself. This stance proved to be universal in British social anthropology (Richards 1950; Fortes 1958; Barnes 1960; Bohannan 1963; Goody 1972, 1996, among a myriad of others).

Finally, the move from domestic groups to households took place as anthropologists, and mostly Africanists, wished to remove the societies they studied from the category of 'tribal' and treat them as 'peasantries'. Inspired either by the neo-Marxists or by Chayanov and neoclassical economists, they selected the household as an easily delineated unit because of its residential dimension, because of its involvement in production and the distribution of products and, as a corollary, because it acted as a decision-making unit (for a more detailed history of the concept in anthropology, and a concomitant critique, see Guyer 1981; Guyer and Peters 1987; Roberts 1991; Russell 1993). While the household was infiltrating anthropology via 'peasant studies', it was penetrating history via 'family history'.

Individuals and processes: deconstructing our language

Households were the targets of fierce critiques as soon as they appeared in anthropology, and soon after they emerged in family history. As I have already mentioned, I merely wish to identify, amidst this increasingly vast literature, the key problems that historians, but mostly anthropologists, have perceived in the notion of household, and summarize the main objections levelled against it.

Every publication in this unfolding 'deconstruction' moves back and forth from empirical observations to more theoretical stances and, needless to say, most of the empirical obstacles seen to be in the way of households stem from specific theoretical assumptions. Furthermore, all of these theoretical presuppositions within anthropology point in the same direction: towards the dismantling of groups in order to retrieve processes and, from behind processes, individuals. For clarity of presentation, I shall mention the main empirical obstacles first, and will then evaluate their underlying theoretical substructures. In presenting this theoretical move towards individuals and processes, however, I shall limit myself to the work of Goodenough and that of his followers, to that of Wilk and Netting, as well as that of Sabean. Social historians often seek their inspiration from anthropology, but address different questions and, Sabean excepted, I shall therefore examine the theoretical attempts of Seccombe and Razi in the first pages of Chapter 7.

The more empirical critiques, denunciations and deconstructions of the household have been many and diverse (Berkner 1972, 1975; Rapp 1979; Yanagisako 1979; Chantor 1980; Creighton 1980; Harris 1981, 1984; Augustins 1981; Guyer 1981; Spiegel 1982; Hammel 1984; Guyer and Peters 1987; Martin and Breittel 1987; Murray 1987; Evans 1989; Sabean 1990; Seccombe 1992; Razi 1993; Russell 1993, to name but a few),[1] but I will try to regroup them under a few thematic headings: 1) the absence of household boundaries; 2) the absence of activities associated to households, and 3) the question of power relationships. Because of its critical importance, I will broach the last question in the next chapter.

The household and its boundaries

One of the first and main critiques addressed to the concept of household was its alleged lack of boundaries (Yanagisako 1979; Netting *et al.* 1984a; Harris 1984; Guyer and Peters 1987; Sabean 1990; Seccombe 1992; Russell 1993; Goody 1996). If households have boundaries, the argument goes, they would therefore preclude simultaneous membership in two or more households. How then are we supposed to deal with migrant labourers (Guyer 1981)? And what of the general movement of people from one household to the next in many African societies? Furthermore, how are we to consider lodgers or boarders, who move in and out at varying intervals of time? Are they members of the household or not? Because most households seem to lack boundaries, anthropologists denied them any boundaries and they, together with many family and social historians, advocated that the very notion be discarded.

Furthermore, to speak of household boundaries implied that we knew the meaning of 'coresidence'. But did we? What were we to call a group of individuals sharing the same roof but using different hearths and 'eating from different pots'? Did coresidence mean living within the same dwelling-place or in closely adjacent ones (Hammel 1984; Goody 1996)? If we failed the test on coresidence, why even bother with boundaries!

The household has no specific functions

Above all, many authors noted that coresidence never acted as the only criterion in the formation of households, and that all assemblies of coresiding individuals also shared a set of common activities commonly described as 'domestic'. This raised more unsavoury questions. Let us take some of the most common activities found in households: production, consumption and childrearing. It was obvious that, almost anywhere, people from different households could produce or eat together, or collaborate in childrearing. In brief, *no activity could be exclusively associated with households*; for some, this applied equally to families and domestic groups. In other words, within any given household many different activities overlap and, furthermore, these very same activities could also involve members of different households (Fel and Hofer 1969; Wall 1983; Goody 1996), re-emphasizing the household's lack of boundaries. Using the very Ashanti data that Fortes had analysed, some anthropologists concluded that some coresiding individuals did not do anything together; where Fortes had retained the idea of a 'domestic group', they disclaimed its usefulness, a conclusion that many others endorsed (Oppong 1981; Woodford-Berger 1981; Sanjek 1982).

In fact, this lack of activity specific to the household proved that intra-household relationships were the least important ones, a position which Sabean expressed most clearly and forcefully: the household as defined and used by Laslett and some members of the Cambridge Group was a 'decon-textualized' entity, 'a unit largely abstracted from social processes', leaving the content of social relations largely 'unexplored' (Sabean 1990: 99). As a corollary, extra-residential relationships are more diverse, richer, and in fact socially much more important. We must study the vast networks of kin linking houses together, ignoring household composition altogether (Seccombe 1992). Finally, this line of criticism led logically to deny all validity to typologies, especially typologies inspired by the Hammel–Laslett definitions (Hammel and Laslett 1974).

The theoretical obstacles to the notion of household

The questions concerning the analytical usefulness of the concept of household were in fact rooted in deeper considerations. We shall follow what I personally deem the three main theoretical avenues underpinning this deconstructivist endeavour in the study of residence.

More than thirty years ago, Goodenough argued that concepts devised for comparative analysis were extra-cultural and could not be applied to the actors' own representation of what residence really means (Goodenough 1956). He consequently advocated an emic approach to residence (where 'emic' means 'understanding from within the social actor's own set of representations'), in the hope of finding 'the ethnographic model of behaviour, . . . the set of situational, motivational and cognitive factors which precipitate a decision on the part of the actor to engage in such a behaviour' (Buchler and Selby 1968: 49).[2]

Goodenough's invitation was accepted by a number of ethnographers working in areas of fast-changing residential composition, who sought to understand the 'residential rationality' of individuals in the populations they studied (Buchler and Selby 1968; Stern 1973; Korn 1975), defining residential groups as the 'statistical outcome of multiple individual choices rather than a direct reflection of jural rules' (Leach 1960: 124, quoted in Korn 1975: 255). I shall call this the 'rational model'. In this perspective, individuals make residential choices in the same way as they make other choices: to maximize their gains and minimize their losses.

This kind of ethnography rests on the premise that there is an 'economics' or logistics of residential association. Individuals associate themselves with different residential groups at different points in time because these ties have adaptive value in their quest for wealth and prestige. From that vantage point, groups are statistical associations resulting from individual decisions. Decisions have to be taken because choices are imposed upon individuals, and choices reflect a situation of scarcity. Residence is consequently only a strategy in the allocation of scarce resources, a mere 'means to an end', an epiphenomenon of economizing. This approach looks eerily like that adopted by contemporary household economists and, in my opinion, deserves the same criticisms (see Chapter 4).

The rational approach still spoke of people inhabiting the same dwelling-place, calling their association either 'domestic groups' or 'households', despite the fact that it denied groups any reality of their own, and deflated them to being a sum of individual decisions. From the late 1970s onward, however, a more drastic appraisal emerged, one that questioned the conceptual validity of distinguishing family from household and which, in the final analysis, discarded the very notions of family, household and domestic group (Yanagisako 1979; Creighton 1980; Harris 1984; Guyer 1981; Spiegel 1982; Hammel 1984; Guyer and Peters 1987; Martin and Breittel 1987; Murray 1987; Evans 1989; Russell 1993). Of the host of such critiques, I shall select an important one; one that, feminism apart, seems to sum up most of the previous arguments and has remained a landmark in ulterior rethinking. I mean the contributions of Netting *et al.* in their voluminous collection, *Households. Comparative and Historical Studies of the Domestic Group* (Netting *et al.* 1984b; Wilk and Netting 1984a).

In the Introduction to their collection of essays, Netting *et al.* repeat in their own words the old dichotomy between structure and process. If the study of households is about types (that is, about their 'structure') and if this typology leaves us with few types, 'as dull as they are repetitive' (Netting *et al.* 1984a: xviii), what is the alternative? To jettison types and typologies altogether and approach households 'as remarkably fluid in structure and impermanent in boundaries (Wheaton 1975), [as] a "process" rather than an institution (Hammel 1972), a task-group rather than just a product of cultural rules (Carter and Merrill 1979: iii)' (Netting *et al.* 1984a: xviii). This leads them to contrast households as 'task-defined groups' (what can be termed a 'processual' view since it focuses on the processes households are involved in) with 'kinship-defined groups' (the way these authors define households when considering them as types which, in their terminology, means defining them by their 'structure'). In brief, they equate kinship with structure and claim that any approach which focuses on the so-called kinship content of households would be emphasizing their structure over the processes they are involved in.

In a following article Wilk and Netting retranslate this as a contrast between structure and *behaviour* (what was 'process' in the Introduction; Wilk and Netting 1984): kinship is structure, they assert, and household is behaviour. Thus, when classifying households (hence defining types), anthropologists and historians would do no better than classifying them 'on the basis of what kind of family lies at the core' (Wilk and Netting 1984: 3). If family is kinship only (their thesis), anthropologists and historians would consequently still be unable to distinguish households from families 'because they forsake the functional element, that is, what households do, for the tangible and observable enumeration of personnel [which, from their point of view, is structure]' (Wilk and Netting 1984: 3). This leads them to conclude that,

> as the household is in fact defined as a group sharing certain activities (residence, consumption and the like), we can argue that the elucidation of what it is that households *do* is logically prior to describing their size or composition.
>
> (Wilk and Netting 1984: 3)

In other words, behaviour (or process) precedes structure (or type, or kinship).

My reply to Wilk and Netting's critique can only be understood in the light of my definition of groups and residence. Let us therefore anticipate what is to be spelled out in more detail below. If, as I will advocate, we define groups unifunctionally (that is, we delineate a separate group for every distinct type of activity) and in terms of criteria of membership, then, by my set of definitions, groups are collections of individuals executing an activity together. Therefore, to declare that the activity is logically prior to the people executing it (Wilk and Netting's thesis) cannot mean anything since without the so-called personnel no activity will get performed; activity and personnel are but two sides of the same coin. Similarly, without an activity, any collection of individuals may form a category (if it does), but no group. The age-old structure/function, and more so the structure/process, dichotomy, then emerges as one of these 'epistemological obstacles' that Bachelard (1969) spent a lifetime tracking down in scientific thinking, obstacles that inhibit clear thinking on residence, and on social organization in general.

In my opinion, the 'processual approach' also says something else. If households are 'task-oriented', or behaviour, what will the ethnographer do? He cannot merely enumerate a sum of activities, or even describe them in detail. If households are to be perceived as behaviour, I cannot see how it can be anything else than individual behaviour. Indeed, despite some unfortunate acquired manners of speaking, all behaviour is, by definition, individual. We may speak of 'individual behaviour in a crowd context', or 'individual behaviour in the context of conjugal relationships', never literally of 'crowd behaviour' or 'conjugal behaviour', as if a social relation, or a crowd, could be endowed with a behaviour. Thus, behind the processes, we find indirectly what Goodenough was advocating, namely the rationale of individual behaviour in the context of household activities.

In my view, Sabean's (1990) theoretical stance (to use this time the case of an extremely gifted social historian) falls in the same category. We have already mentioned his critique of Laslett: the latter's 'households' are withdrawn from social processes, and he [Laslett] would be an individualist *malgré lui*:

> Social scientists whose starting point is the individual use certain concepts to sort out and label the constituents of collectivities, of groups of individual people, attitudes and values. By and large their theoretical practice is limited by this irreducible taxonomic core. A good case in point is the quixotic campaign to sort out all the world's households in a single onomatological set.
>
> (Sabean 1990: 29–30)

Against any approach resorting to notions of groups (such as households, families and the like), or rooted in individualist assumptions, he advocates starting from relationships. His 'minimal units' are not individuals, but social relations (30).

Further on, he then tackles social action theories in a similar way:

> There is a tendency in a good deal of recent sociology and anthropology to reject older structural and functional paradigms in favor

31

of analyses of raw strategy. *The problem is, there is nothing to be strategic about if there are no systematic structures which mediate social existence.*

(Sabean 1990: 184, italics added)

Despite this claim, functionalism also gets the whip for being individualistic: 'Much of the old functional school of anthropology was founded on individualistic assumptions about needs, and social forms were read off from their fulfilment' (Sabean 1990: 184).

Regardless of this failure, he nonetheless insists that we do need to introduce structures in our analyses, but structures rid of their individualistic assumptions (184–5).

This more or less sums up Sabean's key theoretical statements in his masterly book on Neckarhausen. Before dealing with the notion of relationships, however, some clarifications are needed. First, the only 'functionalist' who rooted institutions in individual needs was Malinowski, and he was completely repudiated by the 'true' functionalists, namely the structural-functionalists (Radcliffe-Brown, Fortes, and so on). In contrast, the structural-functionalists claimed that an institution can only be explained by reference to other social phenomena (thus reiterating Durkheim's celebrated 'principle of closure'; Durkheim 1967). Second, one cannot simultaneously discard groups and summon up 'nonindividualistic' structures, since 'structure' normally refers to the manner in which a society is organized into groups. This contradiction apart, let us now consider Sabean's key element, namely his 'relational' approach.

In his 1990 book on Neckarhausen, this relational approach translated itself mostly in isolating two main sets of relationships: that between husband and wife, and that between parents and children. Sabean could have usefully included that between siblings, and that between collateral kin (to name but a few relationships), but these remain either absent, or extremely peripheral.

Admittedly, when studying relationships between parents and children, and their mediation through the transmission of property, it looks as if husband and wife formed one unit, and all the children another. I say 'looks as if' because Sabean presents his cases in those terms, not because this is the manner in which relationships between parents and children are lived. Parents may be divided among themselves about what to transmit when to which of the children, as the children will be divided among themselves as to who can get what from which of the parents, and when. In fact, when we look at the other fundamental relationship he studies, that of husband and wife, the 'individualist' element comes out quite clearly: husband and wife appear set against one another, each one defending his or her own interests and claims against those of his or her marital partner, rather than acting in beatific harmony. The numerous case studies of marital relationships he documents speak for themselves, but one last 'theoretical' statement about the marital relationship has to be quoted: 'Inside the house each spouse viewed the other in terms of contending interests and conflicting loyalties and set him or her inside a configuration of character traits, blood lines, and moral force' (Sabean 1990: 143).

One could hardly be more explicit; every social relation involves at least two people, two people who, more often than not, clash over their opposite interests. And when they do act as one, it can be argued that they do so in their best *individual* interests.

It may also be of some relevance to emphasize that, in the study of social organization, the various brands of structuralism have been supplanted by theoretical postures very like those of Sabean. Like Sabean, these anti-structuralist anthropologists also reject all notion of group to focus on relationships but, interestingly enough, they also envision every social relation as a 'transaction' in which the two partners play their own individual game. For this very reason, this 'school' has been labelled 'transactionalist' and, as it happens, it defines itself as a 'social action theory' (therefore, as an individualist one).

In other words, Sabean's theoretical claims do not tally with his (admirable) practice. Behind the relationships he studies stand individuals, each defined by his or her own set of rights which dictate his or her own interests, and those interests explain the very dynamics of the relationship. Sabean's practice thus belongs to the transactionalist tradition, that is, to a clear case of social action analysis.

Overall, deep similarities run through the three theoretical vistas we have examined. In all three, groups are denied any ontological reality, either to be replaced by individual strategies (the rational model), by processes (the Wilk–Netting stance) or by relationships (Sabean). Once more, words conceal more than they reveal. Behind processes and relationships stand individuals and individual interests, so that all three theoretical stances are essentially individualistic. In the 'deconstructionist' movement, groups disappear to bring the individual back to the fore. Through individuals and processes (i.e. interactions), therefore, household boundaries have necessarily vanished.

This theoretical and empirical exercise in deconstruction has undermined the whole conceptual grid once used to study what Fortes had labelled the 'domestic domain'. In retrospect, what remains? If neither the family, nor the domestic group or the household have either identifiable functions or identifiable boundaries, what can they denote? Nothing! We are therefore left with the interesting and often extremely rich descriptions of behaviours and interactions, of bargaining and underlying decisions, such as Sabean's extraordinary work on Neckarhausen, without any hope of ever comparing them in order to reach a higher level of generality. As Goody's (1996) assault on Hajnal's theses illustrates, the very anthropological process of comparison seems to elude us. And yet, we do find comparative works of the highest quality, if not masterpieces in their own genre, such as Viazzo's *Upland Communities* (1989), directly inspired by the work done at the Cambridge Group. How can we reconcile the two?

Trying to rehabilitate the household

In one form or another, at the heart of most of these evaluations, lies the key problem of *discontinuity*. In essence, the question ought to be simple: in order to describe, compare and put forth theories, we ideally need a set of 'discontinuous' concepts or, more precisely, we need to devise our language in such a way as to delineate what appear to be discontinuous areas of social life. If the groups (families, households, kinship groups) we claim to write about are defined in such a way as to lack any boundaries (or discontinuities), it necessarily follows that everything gets blurred and any comparative venture is nipped unavoidably in the bud. With this, I utterly concur.

Unfortunately, the question is never that simple because there is a vast difference between a discontinuous *conceptual* grid, and a discontinuous world, a distinction that Foucault made quite clear long ago (Foucault 1966). Advocating the necessity of a discontinuous conceptual grid does not imply that reality itself is discontinuous, that the phenomenal world comes to us neatly packaged in prelabelled boxes. As Bachelard, Foucault and a host of epistemologists of the sciences have made clear, the problem is not so much about reality, but about the way we think and write about it. Reality is discontinuous in some of its dimensions, and not in most but, according to these epistemologists, the question we ought to raise should concern language. We should ask ourselves 'Can we impose discontinuity on our concepts and yet, still be able to write intelligently about a reality that may be continuous in many ways?' This is how I would like to broach that question.

Rehabilitating the household thus amounts to devising a discontinuous language and, in this undertaking, I shall argue that social anthropologists and historians have been unable properly to define residence because of their implicit multifunctional understanding of groups. If I am right in this assessment, we then hold the key for a possible solution: to define groups unifunctionally first, in order to grasp the notion of residence.

What is residence?

What is a 'multifunctional group'? Very simply, a group endowed with many functions.[3] It is one of those unquestioned (axiomatic) and universal assumptions in social anthropology and, to my knowledge, in the social sciences in general, and it is a direct legacy from Durkheim.

It is from Durkheim that anthropologists (and historians in their wake) have borrowed the idea that a group presupposes interaction, some community of purpose, and interests derived from the sharing of common activities. The more activities in which a community of individuals is involved, the more interaction increases as a result of this multiple involvement. As interaction increases, so does solidarity (and corporateness) (Verdon 1980b, 1991; Durkheim 1960; this is explicit in Netting *et al.* 1984a: xxv–xxvi, and in Hammel and Laslett 1974: 77). As a result, a group is declared a multifunctional entity, a conclusion which Rivers (1924) imprinted on anthropology long ago. This understanding of groups has regrettably induced social anthropologists and historians to misrepresent residence.

To understand how the multifunctional representation of groups has led to denying residence any reality of its own, let us imagine a man and a woman meeting regularly for sexual intercourse, who after a while decide to have children and to bring them up together. They may also produce and eat together. As a group, they would simultaneously be involved in five different activities. Let us now imagine that this man, woman and their children also live in the same house. The observer can legitimately ask whether they mate, reproduce and raise children as a result of having come together under the same roof, or vice versa. Phrased in this manner, the problem of residence is understandably reduced to an 'accident' of social organization; the individuals in domestic groups first came together to have children and rear them, the structural-functionalists will say, but they also had to eat (i.e. produce and consume) and house themselves in order to accomplish the prime task of social reproduction (the Marxists would declare that they first got together to produce, and the structuralists that they first got together as a result of matrimonial exchange). The domestic group is obviously multifunctional, one would argue, but residence can hardly be its prime function, in all three models.

In brief, by defining groups as multifunctional, anthropologists and historians are condemned to deflating residence to the status of a mere epiphenomenon. Goody, for instance, still denies coresidence any relevance (Goody 1996), insisting that a father living next door might impose his will on his son as much as a father coresiding with his son. If such is the case, why should anthropologists even bother to distinguish individuals coresiding from those living in completely separate dwelling-places? And why stop at the father next door? Why not assume that families (as Goody defines them – 1972) are directly amalgamated into a local group? We must conclude that people must spend money and time erecting architectural structures simply for leisure, since those structure are apparently irrelevant at both the conceptual and analytical levels!

If multifunctionality is the problem, then 'unifunctionality' must be the answer (once more, see Verdon 1991 for a full theoretical justification).

Among the many and varied meanings of 'function', as Netting *et al.* have intuited and as I have mentioned in note 3, hides the very prosaic idea of 'activity'. The multifunctional vision of groups thus boils down to stating that one and the same group performs many activities, an idea which pervades the sociological, anthropological and historical literatures. Such a representation of group is not only conceptually and analytically damaging, it is in most cases empirically false. This has often been noticed but, to my knowledge, never carried to its logical conclusion.

Indeed, anthropologists and historians have long recognized that the concept of a 'domestic group' denotes an overlapping (some write of 'nesting' – see Goody 1996) of 'functions' (activities), and that membership of any of those groups is not coterminous. Goody (1958, 1996) acknowledged this long ago when separating the various units that composed domestic groups among the LoDagaa (production, cooking, distribution, etc., albeit insisting on keeping the designation 'domestic groups' (which he has now traded for 'household', without changing its conceptualization). Wrigley (1977) expressed the same idea when he suggested using Venn diagrams to represent domestic groups. What did Goody and Wrigley imply? That units formed around the activities of production, distribution, transformation of agricultural products, childrearing and other so-called 'domestic' activities do intersect, but are rarely coterminous.

This was nowhere more striking than in the case of Abutia. Like the Ashanti, the Abutia practise duolocality (husband and wives often live in separate dwellings) so that families are scattered among diverse residential groups. But duolocality appeared as the least peculiar of their residential behaviours. In many houses, for instance, I found married men coresiding with a married sister and her young children; their spouses (of both brother and sister) lived in other houses. In houses where married brother and sister cohabited, only the sister and her older daughters would use the hearth for cooking, but the food they cooked did not feed the brother: it went to fill the mother's plate, that of her own children and of her husband living in another house. Nor could the sister count on her brother to bring her food-stuff from his farm to cook. The food that she, her husband, and her children ate came from her productive activities and those of her husband (the children being at school most of the time, the older ones helping over the weekends). In brief, brother and sister coresided but were separated in every other type of activity: in sex and procreation, in the maintenance and socialization of children, in production, transformation of products (cooking) and food consumption. Since in Abutia no cults are attached to the house, they did not even form a cult group. It made the Ashanti case pale into insignificance. And yet, such instances were to provide a most important insight.

Indeed, the Abutia arrangements acutely stirred the question: if, apart from sharing the same dwelling-place, these individuals (brothers and sisters) did not join in any activity, could they be considered to form a group at all (and, implicitly, was it relevant at all to try to understand their residential arrangements)? The answer unambiguously struck me as being in the affirmative. The Abutia live in easily identifiable architectural structures (for which, incidentally, there is a vernacular term), structures which can easily be described as houses (comprising bedrooms, a kitchen with one or many hearths, and sometimes a reception room, around an open courtyard which serves as living-room) and, above all, individuals are not distributed randomly in those houses. These coresiding individuals thus form groups, and their composition deserves our attention. Like all anthropologists I assumed that they must execute an activity together to be called a group. Did they? Yes, they performed *the activity of residence* (residence is therefore an activity and no 'principle of social organization'; on this topic, the reader is again enjoined to consult the Annex!). If residence is an activity, what does it consist in? From the Abutia case, it could clearly not be cooking, eating together or raising children together; it stood out clearly that *residence consists in occupying part or all of a dwelling-place in an exclusive manner, regularly or intermittently, for the purpose of sleeping.*[4] Groups involved in the activity of residence should thus be designated as *residential groups.*[5] From here on, therefore, I shall define a 'household' exclusively as a residential group and use the two terms synonymously.

What are groups?

The peculiarity of Abutia social organization had thus solved two conceptual problems. First, it brought into sharp focus the fact that residence should be conceived of as an activity. Second, it confirmed that groups are best defined unifunctionally if we want to move towards the desired conceptual discontinuity: one activity (or 'type of activity', what anthropologists and historians normally call 'function') – one group. No doubt, it is usually existentially true that the same set of individuals performs various activities. Analytically speaking, this multifunctional involvement can be translated as the overlapping or coterminousness of different groups engaged in different sets of activities (as coterminous intersecting Venn diagrams). It should however be noted that groups may overlap, but not activities; by definition, activities are normally discrete. Cooking is an activity different from socializing children, and from tidying up the house. Activities, therefore, are normally separate, but the individuals performing them may be the same. In other words, a mother and her eldest daughter may cook, socialize the younger children and tidy up the house together. In this example, the 'cooking group', the 'group of socialization' and the 'group of house maintenance' would overlap completely, despite the fact that the activities themselves are distinct.

This can be seen as a first step towards reconstructing what I consider a 'discontinuous' representation of groups: in order to do so, we ought first to posit that there cannot be any group without activities (to distinguish them from 'categories' or 'crowds', for instance) and that a separate group ought to be defined around every different type of activity (the 'functions' of an earlier anthropology, let us recall). And what else is needed conceptually to delineate 'discontinuous' groups? Ever since Rivers if not before, anthropologists have explicitly answered: 'Social boundaries!'

Unfortunately, the boundaries never stood out in clear relief because they were never completely disentangled from interaction. Indeed, ever since they began discussing the very notion of 'group', anthropologists have unanimously included interaction among its necessary ingredients. As I have argued and demonstrated at length elsewhere (Verdon 1991), interaction is the second most critical element inhibiting a discontinuous representation of groups.

A group presupposes the execution of an activity but, in and of itself, such a definition does not imply interaction. Interaction is altogether another dimension superimposed on activities and, once introduced, it necessarily calls up the action of *norms*. Those norms are the main culprits because they vary in intensity, thereby defining groups which vary in their very 'groupness'. By assimilating activity and interaction, anthropologists have thus confused norms and 'criteria of membership', and this amalgamation invited justifiable critiques of the notion of social boundary. From my point of view, therefore, the conclusion seems inevitable: in order to achieve a discontinuous definition of groups, it becomes imperative to dissociate activity from interaction, and to set interactions aside. This would leave us with only two elements, namely an activity, and *criteria of membership* which, from the writings of Rivers onward, were supposed to demarcate social boundaries. Activities and criteria of membership thus suffice to apprehend groups (and therefore households) in a discontinuous fashion but, as we shall see in Chapter 3, we will have to reintroduce relationships to move from a definition of household to a household typology.

Now let us examine our households (residential groups) more closely. With this new definition in hand, one can fathom the obstacles standing in the way of defining residential groups as kinship groups. Residential groups have criteria of membership, but why lump them together and label them 'kinship', assimilating residential groups to kinship groups, and equating the latter with 'structure' (a standard 'deconstructivist' practice, and one used to undermine the concept of household; see in particular Netting *et al.* 1984a; Wilk and Netting 1984)? I believe this procedure dangerously misleading. To understand why, let us take a hypothetical (European) society where residential groups never grow beyond what has been called the nuclear level. What would be the criteria giving individuals almost automatic and inalienable rights of membership to these nuclear residential groups? Shall we say marriage? This would be imprecise since only 'marriage to the *head* of the group' would qualify as such a criterion. What of filiation? Once more, similar strictures would apply: in fact, only 'filiation to the head and his or her spouse, and as long as the child is recognized as one of their dependants', would count as such a criterion. Anyone else who joins the group would do so because the head, or the head and his or her spouse, will kindly accept the request or extend the invitation.

To jump from these extremely *specific* criteria to 'kinship' is therefore most questionable. It cannot be denied that these two criteria belong to the immensely vast set of consanguineous and affinal links of all kinds called 'kinship'; nonetheless, the fact that a group recruits mostly on the basis of a few specific consanguineous and affinal links does not make it a 'kinship group'. If we follow this logic, most groups under the ethnographic sun will fall in the category of 'kinship groups' (as they unfortunately do in the ethnographic literature!) and the concept loses any validity (as it has done! see Verdon 1991). More fundamentally, it could even be argued that there are no such things as 'kinship groups' *because groups can be designated by their criteria of membership* extremely rarely (the only instance I can think of are 'age groups', although I admit that there might be a few more). The reason is simple: groups defined unifunctionally perform one activity only, while most groups have *numerous criteria of membership*. A residential group is defined around the activity of residence only, in the same way that a production group is defined around the activity of production exclusively. But as both can have many criteria of membership, most of which may be related to consanguinity and affinity, we will end up with the most disparate categories if we insist on calling them 'kinship groups'. I therefore advocate that groups be identified by their type of activity (residential groups, groups of production, of legislation, and so on), and not (or extremely rarely) by their criteria of membership. Also, we further compound the difficulties by equating the mislabelled 'kinship groups' with 'structure'. As I see it, criteria of membership do not generate any structure; they only determine a group's *composition*. As we shall see, 'structure', if it means anything at all, refers to something radically different.

Finally, some criteria delineate an assembly of individuals who, as a collectivity, are not engaged in any activity; in common parlance, this is known as a 'category' (such as all red-headed primiparous women who own a Maserati; or, more seriously, all individuals located within a given income bracket). The notion of category, as we shall see, will help solve some of the problems related to household membership.

Residential groups are not families

These definitions of group and residence also enable us to distinguish residential groups from families. I have devoted a long article to the definition of the family (Verdon 1981), I still abide by those views, but their full formulation is too abstract and complex for my immediate purpose. In this book, I shall use a highly simplified (and slightly distorted) version of my earlier definition, and refer the reader to the original for a detailed explanation.

In a unifunctional perspective, a separate group must be defined around every different type of activity and, consequently, one must be delineated around the activity of physical reproduction (or procreation). Together with some anthropologists and historians, I will therefore define the 'family' as the group formed around the socially acknowledged procreation of a woman; this group will thus consist of this woman, her socially acknowledged progeny and the individual (or individuals) socially regarded as the *pater* of this child (anthropologists distinguish the 'genitor', who is the genetic father of the child, often unknown or different from the *pater*, the socially recognized father, from whom the child derives his social identity; in some societies, the *pater* can be another woman, or even a ghost[6]), and individual(s) to whom the woman is linked through marriage (for a definition of marriage, see also Verdon 1981;[7] for the complications arising from divorces and death on family nomenclature, see Juby and Le Bourdais 1995). In accordance with this definition, I shall label differently any group including more individuals: I shall speak of 'residential groups' when 'family' refers to those living together, or the 'kinship core of a residential group' when speaking of those linked through filiation and/or marriage within a residential group, or a 'portion of kindred' if we mean those getting together at Christmas, or simply 'kindred' if we want to extend it to all of Ego's relatives, and so on and so forth.

It follows from this definition that all families are by definition 'nuclear'; a family can be monogamous, polygynous or polyandrous, but calling a family 'nuclear' or 'conjugal' seems to me tautologous, since I cannot envision what a 'non-nuclear' or 'nonconjugal' family would be (excluding monoparental families, it goes without saying, although the word family in this context is also very questionable). Furthermore, I do not understand what can be meant by 'family structure', unless one inadvertently refers to the fact that a family is monogamous, polygynous or polyandrous. Finally, marriage and filiation (once more, specifically 'marriage to the genitrix' and 'filiation to the conjugal unit formed around the physical reproduction of this genitrix') are the family's specific (and universal) criteria of membership. As with residential groups, to declare the family a 'kinship group' invites more amalgamation of disparate entities.

Families and residential groups are therefore conceptually distinct, although the family's criteria of membership are often a subset of a residential group's criteria of membership, or intersect with them. This explains why some anthropologists and historians have been led to see either the family (Laslett 1972; Hammel and Laslett 1974), or the mother–child relationship, as the 'core' or nucleus of households or residential groups (Fortes

1958; Goodenough 1970; Moore 1988). Unfortunately, such formulations lead directly, and justifiably, to the accusations levelled by Yanagisako (1979), as well as by Wilk and Netting (1984), that we deflate residential groups to families.

Families and residential groups do share one thing, however. In the anthropological literature, no term has muddled our thinking more than 'structure'. Indeed, the more I probe the literature, the more its meaning eludes me. At the end of the road, I have found no other useful meaning to the term save 'division of labour' (for details, see once more Verdon 1981, 1991). In other words, when a type of activity involves interrelated tasks, parts of which are performed exclusively by a subgroup (or different individuals), we shall say that the group is structured. Since there is no possible division of labour in the activities of residence or physical reproduction *neither family nor residential groups are structured* (incidentally, the differential contribution of the genders in copulation is no case of 'division of labour' when the activity we are referring to is procreation). In the case of residential groups one should write of their composition, not their structure.

The developmental cycle

In the deconstruction process, the 'developmental cycle' did not escape battering: it brings us back to a normative formulation, note Netting *et al.* (1984a: xvii, a claim totally supported by Hammel – Hammel 1984), and it cannot deal with change. It would also apply to homogeneous societies only, that is, societies displaying only one cycle (and would therefore preclude the study of intrasocietal variation – Netting *et al.* 1984a). I have myself emphasized that most societies do not exhibit any such cycle (Verdon 1979a). Indeed, the idea of a developmental cycle of domestic groups rests on the presupposition that most individuals in a society follow relatively similar matrimonial trajectories. It so happens that in many populations throughout the world individuals follow very different matrimonial paths and change residence rather frequently because they can opt for cohabitation with a wide range of individuals (as in Abutia, see Chapter 9), making it absolutely impossible to extrapolate any developmental cycle from a synchronic picture of domestic groups at one point in time (see also Gonzalez 1969; Stern 1973; Korn 1975).

This leaves us with one major problem. Assuming that we depict the composition of our residential groups in the manner suggested by Hammel and Laslett (1974), we must squarely confront the question: if the false problem of statistical predominance has been surmounted by that of the developmental cycle of domestic groups, how can we obviate the problems raised by the 'developmental cycle', while retaining some useful way of classifying?

There is, I believe, one solution to this difficulty. In some societies, and some of the historical cases we will be studying fall in this category, individuals did follow relatively uniform matrimonial lives so that the concept of a developmental cycle of residential groups could be used as a fair approximation. In others, and they are many, it cannot. Yet, it is possible to rephrase the question in such a way that the developmental cycle becomes but a special case of a more general concept.

Even in extreme cases like Abutia, cases which render completely meaningless the very idea of a developmental cycle of residential groups, it is nonetheless quite clear to both social actors and to observers that only some residential associations are accepted. The permutations are many, but finite. There is a boundary beyond which groups will not grow, or will grow only under exceptional, or abnormal, circumstances.[8] It is, so to speak, the maximal level of internal complexity in the composition of residential groups in a given community or population. Beyond that limit, normal groups split and form two or more residential groups, but some do not, and can be deemed 'abnormal', as when a child is born with six fingers or, worse still, with Down's Syndrome. When asked about their residential arrangements, the Abutia recognize that these abnormal, 'out of bounds' cases are irregular and they provide specific explanations for their existence. When asked about permissible combinations, however, they simply retort that this is the way they do things, or come out with platitudinous remarks, such as 'He lives with his father because he does not own a house'; we shall see later how little such a statement explains. This is exactly the type of answers I had collected in an earlier fieldwork on residence in rural French-speaking Quebec.

I therefore thought it possible to bypass the controvertible developmental cycle to focus on the 'limit of growth to residential groups', on the assumption that residential groups in a given community or region may grow in a number of ways but that, in normal circumstances, they do not grow beyond one, or very few, recognizable limits or boundaries. If one dealt with a region where a developmental cycle truly existed, and if this cycle were represented as a sinusoidal curve, this 'limit of growth' would simply represent its 'maximum', or the tangent horizontal to the summit of the curve. But any given community or region may have more than one limit of residential growth; in rural Quebec, for instance, the limit applying for lumbermen (the so-called nuclear family) differed from that for farmers (the so-called stem family). Different socioeconomic subclasses within a community or a region may thus experience different limits of residential growth, although, in my experience, such limits are normally very few in number. Furthermore, to avoid undue complications I shall use the term 'region' generically to refer to an area which can be considered homogeneous from the point of view of its limits of residential growth. Thus, 'region' may refer to a socioeconomic class dispersed over many cities, or only to the agricultural part of a given area. When I write of 'intraregional' or 'extraregional' variability, I shall therefore mean variability within or between regions thus understood.

Within Europe, extremely few regions (if any) share exactly the same limit of residential growth. Let us take the notorious 'stem family'. If we include Quebec within the compass of European ethnography, it can be shown that the precise limits of agricultural Quebec, Irish, Pyrenean, Provençal or Central European stem residential groups actually differ in some striking ways. If we add to this the fact that any geographical area (such as the Pyrenees, Quebec, Ireland or Central Europe) knows of more than one limit, it calls for a more flexible typology and detailed regional comparative analyses.

Does the notion of a limit of residential growth preclude the analysis of change? Personally, I cannot see how. At any time, the articulation (or over-lapping) of the various groups formed around the various economic and domestic activities can change: men or women can leave self-employed agri-cultural or animal production for salaried work in a factory, or vice versa; new technologies may remove women from the tasks of agricultural or animal production; schools may take children away from home for much longer periods; new services may withdraw the care of ageing parents from their children; new technologies may free individuals from some domestic tasks, and so on and so forth. Moreover, as the various groups are differently articulated, new criteria might define eligibility to any of those groups, and the whole household field would be transformed as a result, together with the limit of residential growth. In other words, any change, social, economic or demographic, has repercussions on group memberships, on the articula-tion of the various overlapping groups, as well as on the limit of residential growth and the percentage of groups of a given composition within a given region. These, in turn, have further social, economic and demographic effects, all of which can, and must, be analysed clearly. All these concepts are tools to help the analysis, no substitute for the analysis itself.

Solving some other empirical problems

I do not regard this lengthy detour through theory and a set of redefinitions as a mere academic exercise since I strongly believe that only by using a new conceptual basis, perhaps a framework like the one presented here, will it become possible to counter the 'deconstructivist' arguments. In my opinion, only within a framework which seeks to retrieve groups will we be able to solve problems branded as unsurmountable difficulties in the way of rigorous comparative analysis.

History has a strange way of repeating itself. Until 1965, anthropologists held firmly that an individual cannot belong to more than one lineage, and abhorred the idea of multiple lineage membership. Accordingly, 'cognatic lineages' (lineages the membership of which can be traced through both sexes) were deemed contradictions in terms, because one can simultaneously belong to as many lineages as there are apical ancestors traced through any combination of intermediate ancestors or ancestresses. In one of the most brilliant articles ever written in anthropology, David Schneider (1965) completely exploded this myth. Although intellectual inertia glued a number of older anthropologists to their acquired mental habits, the new generation understood the message, and cognatic lineages received their *lettres de noblesse*.

The study of households is now undergoing a similar crisis. In European history, 'households' emerged as useful units for census-taking and, to avoid double accountancy, individuals could not be listed as belonging to two households at once; hence the alleged impossibility of simultaneous membership. Historians are more constrained in this respect, but there is no reason why anthropologists should feel similarly restricted. As many of them have already remarked, exclusive residential membership does not fit reality. From the correct observation, however, why adopt a defeatist stance and deconstruct all the known concepts?

Again, Abutia presented the very same problems, and in an exaggerated form. Men and women did leave on labour migrations, some of them for up to thirty years (although they would now and then come back to the village for special events), sending money back home where they had a wife (or wives) and/or children. Were they to be excluded or included in my study of Abutia residential groups? They themselves answered the question. Despite a different architecture (see Chapter 9), I have mentioned that they had a clear concept of a 'dwelling-place', composed in part of clearly delineated bedrooms. It so happens that in many cases the migrant left many of his or her belongings in that room, which was then left untouched; it was his or her bedroom, no one else had any right to use it. When confronted with such cases, I counted the migrant as a member of the residential group, but qualified his or her membership. The term chosen is somewhat irrelevant; I then favoured 'absentee' but would now prefer Netting and Wilk's 'intermittent' member. But, intermittent or not, these individuals are part of the group's composition, since other individuals could or could not belong to the group without supposing their intermittent presence. (For instance, even if her husband's presence is completely intermittent, a woman could not live in a house a man built if she was not his wife – without his invitation, that is; thus, finding a woman living alone with her dependent children in a house owned by an absentee man only made sense if one assumed the intermittent membership of this man.)

In other instances, some individuals had inalienable rights to join a residential group, in a full or an intermittent way, but elected not to exercise it. From the point of view of the group's composition at a point in time they were irrelevant, but they could have an impact when studying changes in the composition of a residential group. Again, an easy conceptual distinction dealt adequately with this question; if someone has rights to membership but is neither a full nor an intermittent member, he or she belongs to the *category* of individuals eligible for membership. Those who activate their membership in one way or another form a residential group, but the group is only a subset of that larger entity, the residential category. Correspondingly, we can designate as 'virtual' those members of the residential category who are neither full nor intermittent members.

A modicum of terminological precision – distinguishing residential groups from residential categories, and full members from intermittent and virtual ones – can thus enable one to sidestep all the pitfalls of Abutia residence. But what of residence itself? Must members of a residential group occupy a continuous structure, or contiguous ones? Again, the answer is culturally defined and depends entirely on how individuals in a given culture define what they consider a 'dwelling-place'. From my own ethnographic experience I would be tempted to conclude that most, *but not all*, societies can identify such places (I do not consider residential groups to be universal – see note 8). In some cases, the dwelling-place will encompass contiguous structures, in others not. In European societies, I will assume that the 'house' (as distinct from the farmstead) does not spread over contiguous structures and that, in order to be members of the same residential group, Europeans have to live 'under one roof'. This is the stance taken by Hammel and Laslett in 1974 and one that I endorse, without making it a universal desideratum. It is so for most parts of Europe, it might be so for vast areas of Asia and Africa as well, but it is not universally true. Thus, a European grandmother living in a 'granny flat' at the far end of her married daughter's yard does not belong to her daughter's residential group. This may not solve cases in which whole communities move seasonally, living in a concentrated habitat (village) during a few months of the year, and in scattered (and sometimes mobile) settlements during other months (such as northern Corsicans). Here, every case must be judged on its own detailed circumstances.

Finally, what should we do with the lodgers or boarders of European ethnography and history (the so-called 'inmates' in some texts)? At a first glance, boarders (and I here include lodgers) simply sleep and eat in a given dwelling-place. They would be included in the residential group by my set of definitions. But are they? To answer this, I believe that we have to introduce yet other distinctions. Let us take a B&B. Is there any difference in the fact of boarding there for three days, a week, an academic term, an academic year, or more or less permanently? I believe there is. On the one hand, some boarders belong to other residential groups which they consider 'home', but temporarily have to stay somewhere else. The nature of that stay, I believe, makes a first difference. If they are explicitly visiting (touring, or simply on a 'business trip'), I would recommend excluding them from the residential group. If, on the contrary, they are involved in some kind of training (university course, apprenticeship, etc.) or long-term employment, we shall treat them as members of the residential group where they board for the duration of their stay, and intermittent members of the groups they left behind (if they are still considered absentee members of those groups). In contrast, other boarders have no other abode; they stay where they are, as boarders, indefinitely. They might leave in three months, in three years, when they die, when they are ejected – no one knows for sure. In such a case, they have made a given house their domicile, and I think that 'domiciled boarders' should be regarded as full members of the residential group, and of that one only. Admittedly, there are always and everywhere insoluble border cases but, as scientists emphasize, we can only progress by neglecting the negligible. As to visitors and transients, if they are domiciled somewhere else and are only 'passing through', they should also be excluded from the residential group. If they are homeless, they do not belong to any residential group. Within a given population, some individuals will belong to many residential groups, others (and they can be many) to none. Why should this trigger off any 'deconstruction'?

As anthropologists or historians (that is, as those most involved in cross-cultural comparative analysis), our task is at least twofold. On the one hand, having chosen an ethnic group, a relatively homogeneous area or a socio-professional class from the perspective of a limit of residential growth (that is, what I have called a region), one aim of comparative analysis is then to account for the existence of such limits in the different communities or regions selected, a goal which I deem completely legitimate. On the other hand, we must also account for residential variability within the community: why do some groups display a given composition, and others a different one? In brief, we must tackle both intraregional and extraregional variability, synchronically and diachronically. This book focuses mainly on the question of extraregional variability (with the exception of contemporary Canada), although the same axioms I elaborate should help equally in the study of intraregional variability.

3

AN ATOMISTIC SET OF AXIOMS FOR WESTERN RESIDENCE

As I mentioned in Chapter 2, many authors condemned the traditional notion of household because it overlooked the dimension of power relationships. Economic anthropologists had carefully constructed a notion of the household as a unitary supra-individual cell which allegedly acted as one undifferentiated entity in decision-making (we find similar assumptions among household economists). Women took no time to undermine this assumption (Harris 1981; Young *et al.* 1981; Folbre 1984, 1986; Fapohunda 1988; Moore 1988; Roberts 1988; Evans 1989). They spontaneously knew that no such beast existed in reality. First, all households are internally cleft along gender lines, with men's and women's interests conflicting more often than not, and women mostly on the weak side of the presumed economic bargain (if they wield any bargaining power at all). This was further developed into a general critique of the concept of 'domesticity', with the feminists denying that such a thing as a 'domestic domain' existed, because relationships within households were by definition power relationships, that is, political relationships (Collier 1974; Lamphere 1974; Yanagisako 1979; Guyer and Peters 1987). In family and social history, similar objections were levelled against the Laslett–Hammel vision of the household: it left no room for power relationships (Sabean 1990; Seccombe 1992).

Unfortunately, the various attempts to integrate power have all singled out interpersonal relations in one way or another. As I have already argued, it seems that we lose the household by using interpersonal relationships as our building-blocks and that, if we wish to rehabilitate the household while incorporating power relationships within our typology, we must decompose the household into its 'residential atoms', that is, into 'minimal units' defined in terms other than individuals, relationships or groups. It should nonetheless be acknowledged that power relationships between 'residential atoms' are often lived as interpersonal relationships; hence the difficulties we have encountered so far.

In fact, my earlier ethnographic work on Quebec and Abutia anticipated most of those ideas but, muddled as I was by the traditional categories, I was then blind to it. While working on Quebec, I realized that Gérin (1898) had imported more collectivistic ideology than straightforward ethnography in his portrayal of the French-Canadian stem family. From my own fieldwork in a pioneer area of Quebec, it appeared that the first generation of settlers often blackmailed their children, promising the land to one son but threatening to revoke their decisions, and at times rescinding it. There were also endemic and often bitter conflicts opposing the heir and his wife to the parents. People explained that daughters-in-law often sowed the seeds of discontent and that unfortunate parents who naively transmitted their goods and chattels *inter vivos* had sometimes been evicted by their son and left to die destitute, a theme so often invoked that it enjoyed almost mythical status (Verdon 1980a). This raised the question: if parents saw daughters-in-law as provoking dissensions that tore families apart, why did they allow the son and heir to marry and bring his wife home with him? Why did they tolerate a daughter-in-law in their household? Why did they not adopt the Welsh solution?

According to Rees, Welsh fathers transmitted the farm and the land to one heir only, but to their last son because they said a woman and her daughter-in-law cannot coreside peacefully. They thus favoured the youngest son because he would still be young enough to get married when his mother died (Rees 1961). This Welsh scenario clearly emphasized the residential dimension: land was passed on undivided to one heir who stayed with his parents but who could not bring a wife in, *so that households never grew to the point of including two coresiding couples linked by filiation* (according to my set of definitions, a minimal condition to define the stem family as a limit of residential growth).

Furthermore, the same hostilities that I recorded between families within the same residential group contradicted the traditional image of collectivism and patriarchy in Quebec; stem families appeared to arise as a reluctant agreement of cohabitation between two conjugal families who would have preferred residential separation but shared the same roof for economic reasons (Verdon 1979a). In this uneasy cohabitation, however, the family of the heir occupied a subordinate position. In brief, far from being the natural way of things (the predominant collectivistic view) the cohabitation of two couples in Quebec stem families appeared most problematical.

Inexcusable as it may seem, I was not aware at the time that this fact pervades much of the literature on complex households and that it had already been the centre of important developments in some writings (Rosaldo 1974; Lamphere 1974; but above all Collier 1974) which Yanagisako summarized excellently:

> There now appears to be a growing consensus among these anthropologists that past research tended to overlook the political consequences and motivations of women's actions in domestic

groups. . . . M. Wolf's (1972) portrayal of Taiwanese families reveals that family division is as much a result of women's attempts to advance their own interests and those of their 'uterine family' as it is an outcome of conflicts of interest between brothers. J.F. Collier (1974) and Lamphere (1974) suggest that this is a general phenomenon in societies where men gain political power by having large, cohesive bodies of coresident kin, but where women (particularly young women) gain power by breaking up these units. These authors note that the political nature of these conflicts is usually obfuscated by cultural perceptions of women as quarrelsome, selfish, and irresponsible by nature. Folk explanations of the division of patrilaterally extended joint families, for example, commonly stress women's petty jealousies, thereby masking the extent to which women's actions are politically motivated rather than generated by emotional predispositions.

(Yanagisako 1979: 190)

As Collier puts it, 'Wives are the worms within the apple of a patrilocal domestic group' (1974: 92). Needless to say, all these facts spoke of uneasy family cohabitation.

Simultaneously, my ethnographic work on Abutia led me to conclusions much more radical than the ones I had reached about the Quebec data, although I completely failed to link the two at the time. In order to account for residential composition in Abutia, I had to posit that the coresidence of dependent children with an adult is not problematical, whereas that between adults is (Verdon 1979b: 405; let us remember that I was dealing with a society practising duolocality). In retrospect, all my work was pointing towards an atomistic set of assumptions; if my conclusions on the stem family did not go far enough (for ethnographic reasons, since divorce was then forbidden in Quebec and separation was unknown in the village I studied), my work on Abutia was leading me too far in an 'individualist' direction to understand European residence. Between the two, however, stands the set of axioms that I wish to elaborate in this chapter. In those earlier writings I failed to root my intuitions in more general considerations.

Identifying our residential atoms

It was encounters with household formation and projection methods in contemporary family demography, and with feminist writings which steered me to an intermediary position, and to a theoretical justification. Family demography enabled me to delineate what can reasonably be considered as 'minimal units' in the study of residence, whereas feminist writings fed more directly into the set of axioms themselves. Let us start with the atoms.

Since the pioneering works of Brown (1951), of Glass and Davidson

(1951) and, more recently, their innovative developments in the works of Ermisch and Overton, as well as those of Juby (Ermisch 1988; Ermisch and Overton 1985; Juby 1993), the analysis of household formation has acquired a new conceptual base. Building on Glass and Davidson's idea, Ermisch and Overton introduced a major refinement. Presenting their model as a tool for the projection and analysis of households, they distinguish 'familial units' (later termed 'minimal household units' or MHUs) from households. To Ermisch and Overton, MHUs are 'but the smallest divisible, familial elements within households' (1985: 36) and their existence can be accounted for through the projection of purely demographic events (births, marriages, divorces and deaths). As to the coresidence of these MHUs, it cannot be projected from demographic events and, in so far as households often include more than one MHU, their coresidence needs to be explained and calls for the operation of social and economic variables (35). Households comprising a single MHU are called 'simple', and those encompassing two or more MHUs are called 'complex'.

In line with family demography and their own attempt to account for household composition, Ermisch and Overton thus defined as their MHUs, or what they also called their 'household irreducibles', 1) a woman with her dependent children (what I call a 'matricell'), 2) a man with his dependent children (a 'patricell' in my terminology), 3) a married couple without children (a couple, or conjugal unit), 4) a married couple with dependent children (a family), and 5) an adult.[1] Needless to say, since I have tried to rethink much of this in terms of residence, I will prefer to write of 'minimal residential units' (MRUs) instead of 'minimal household units'.

As I mentioned earlier, it would be advisable to define our building-blocks outside of any reference to individuals, interpersonal relationships or groups. When translated in purely residential terms, Ermisch and Overton's MHUs enable us to do just that. Indeed, these units are 'minimal' because the *coresidence* of individuals forming a given MRU needs no explanation (including the cohabitation of an individual with himself or herself). Why? Because it is culturally so! Indeed, most European populations stipulate that young (dependent) children ought to live with either mother or father if the latter are no longer together (either because of divorce or death), or with both if they are married, as well as psychologically and physically able to look after their children. There are obviously some exceptions, but they are negligible (as in cases of 'lending' a child to a barren sister). I also take as a given the coresidence of married individuals, again because in most European populations couples are expected to cohabit after marriage; there are notable exceptions (such as Santa Marta del Monte – Behar 1985), where husband and wife stay in their natal households for up to six to ten years after marriage. What is striking about such cases, however, is that the couple is expected eventually to coreside, and that their duolocality is explained in terms of hindrances (extreme poverty); in brief, even in those instances the couple's coresidence is taken as unproblematical, whereas their physical separation needs accounting for.

This raises a number of issues. First, our set of axioms will bear on the manner in which these MRUs relate within a residential group, and this will of necessity introduce a number of imprecise concepts. Second, after having decried culturalism and its associated *juridisme*, this definition of MRUs obviously calls for some clarification on the matter of culture, since some of the axioms are 'culturally defined'. Third, this should radically transform our understanding of household types, as a type will no longer be defined by its composition only.

If our set of axioms bears on the manner in which our 'residential atoms', or MRUs, interact to form complex households, this interaction propels us into the realm of power games, into the real stuff of social life as it is lived. There, no discontinuity is to be found and we will have to grope with the ever-elusive continuity to the best of our ability. How? By integrating some of the dynamics built into gender and intergenerational relationships, dynamics we can capture only by superimposing the 'continuous' entanglements of interactions on the discontinuous grid of groups and categories. This is because, in and of themselves, the activities of residence and physical reproduction rule out any dynamics – between MRUs, let us recall, not between individuals. If we have to look outside of residence and physical reproduction to recapture these dynamics, we cannot but examine the main activities carried out by various subsets of residential groups: economic and domestic activities. More definitions will be needed.

Let us take a residential group. Some of its members will be involved in some kind of economic activity (either primary, secondary or tertiary, or a combination of these) from which they will bring home either products if they are self-employed (as in agricultural or pastoral production, in mixed farming or agropastoralism), an income if they are salaried, or both. To simplify matters, I shall call 'economic' the following activities: self-employed 'production', income earning, income distribution or disposal, and property devolution, without assuming this list to be in the least exhaustive. Needless to say, separate groups are formed around every one of these activities, and their memberships, even if partially coterminous, are neither congruent nor confined to the same residential group.

Different groups will be defined around other activities: the transformation of products (cooking, cloth-making, and so on), their distribution and consumption, the physical maintenance of children, their socialization, the structural maintenance of the dwelling-place (woodwork, electricity and plumbing where it exists, painting) and its internal (punctual) maintenance (tidying up and cleaning), maintenance of movable property within the house (washing, mending, washing up, and so on), as well as simple rest and leisure. To delineate a group around every one of these activities would be both tedious and sterile. As the set of axioms developed below should justify,

51

it should be sufficient for our immediate purpose to concentrate only on the economic activities already mentioned, as well as on cooking, punctual house maintenance, child maintenance and childrearing, because these activities appear to be critically relevant in gender and intergenerational relations. Despite all the justified protests against the implicit male-biased connotations tainting the notion of 'domestic', I have found no better term to describe the sum of the last four activities.[2]

I have emphasized, along with those that have questioned the notion of household, that individuals outside the residential group can and will belong to any of these economic and domestic groups. In my set of definitions, therefore, it does not make sense to write of a 'domestic group' because the latter, in a European context, denotes the overlap of at least four different types of grouping which are far from congruent. In mathematics, the intersection of numerous sets defines yet another set, but I use sets as an analogy only. In the realm of social organization, if a group is defined by an activity (and one only) and specific criteria of membership, then the intersection of various groups is no group. I shall therefore avoid mentioning 'domestic groups' and will write of 'domestic activities' instead. (I would like to add that the set of activities encompassed in the category 'domestic' will change through space and time. It is one of those truly variable, culturally defined concepts.)

Let us take stock. In the wake of Ermisch and Overton, it seems apposite to identify five 'residential atoms' (MRUs). In simple MRUs composed of two adults (couples and families), there are power games played along gender lines (husband versus wife) but, from the point of view of our set of axioms (namely that of accounting for limits of residential growth) they are, at best, tangential. In the perspective of MRUs, the question of power arises with complex residential groups only. In those groups, the power relationships between adults belonging to different MRUs will emerge as the key elements to account for residential composition, and they will be central to any explanation of complex households.

As a result, our typologies for the study of European residence will no longer rest exclusively on the composition of residential groups, but upon their composition *within a given power configuration*. That configuration will be determined by a certain number of factors, but mostly by the presence or absence of force (coercion) applied internally in the relationship between MRUs (and, if so, its vector, from generationally older MRUs to younger ones or vice versa), or applied externally by extraresidential power-holders (overlords).

Finally, as Laslett (1984) and Segalen (1986) have stressed, there should not be anything in the idea of residential group or household that in any way intimates that of 'self-sufficiency' (the question of autonomy is a different one, as I shall argue below).

From atoms to axioms

In the light of these qualifications, we can now broach this new set of underlying assumptions. A complete version, one that would examine all types of relationships between all possible permutations of MRUs, would be far too complex and cumbersome a superstructure for the modest, and essentially programmatic, application I have in mind. I shall therefore sketch the main elements of what could become a more exhaustive set of axioms, one that studies specific social relationships within MRUs, without for that matter reverting to Sabean's position.

As a first simplification, I will leave aside European populations relying exclusively on pastoral production, especially mountain pastoralists (Sarakatsani, Montenegrins, Albanians and the like), or those in which pastoral activities predominate (northern Corsica, for instance). Pastoral production could be included, but at the cost of complications of dubious relevance (the mountain pastoralists could nonetheless be integrated relatively easily on the basis of Denich's article – Denich 1974).

This set of axioms rests on a first postulate which is neither psychological nor cultural, but methodological. Whatever set of axioms we elaborate in the study of residence, it seems reasonable to assume that we ought to identify our minimal units, that is, our 'residential atoms', what Ermisch and Overton called 'household irreducibles'. Logically, these 'irreducibles' should comprise those collections of individuals whose coresidence is unproblematical within a given culture. Upon this methodological desideratum I shall erect my second axiom, and the only noncultural one: that, from my knowledge of the ethnographic literature, I have never found 'normal' adults (we shall leave the case of the mentally troubled aside; we can hardly build any set of axioms on individuals with personality problems) wishing to be bossed around in the normal run of their everyday life, although, paradoxically enough, the very same individuals often relish laying down the law. Let us concentrate on one aspect only: all adults normally constituted psychologically appear to want to decide the course of their everyday life. They may be unable to do so and resign themselves to their fate but, given any choice, they will choose independence, and resent being told what to do, even if they need to consult others to make up their own mind (I put the stress on 'everyday life'; admittedly, most people prefer to leave the 'big problems' – mostly political ones, to others).

I wish to be explicit on this axiom. I do not assume that *all* adults in a given culture will prefer to have the last say on their personal matters. Indeed, some meek individuals might prefer others to decide for them, but I wish to insist that we are arguing from the point of view of a collectivity, and from that of normally constituted individuals. If we chose the alternative axiom we would have to suppose (see Chapter 1 on axioms and their implications) that all adults who are normally constituted wish others to give them orders as what to do. If such were the case, we would be involved in a rather awkward position, since such an axiom almost contains its own contradiction. Indeed, if all adults wished to depend on others' decisions, who would be the bosses? We would have to answer that they can only be those who are not normally constituted psychologically, and we would have to build a whole set of axioms on cases of psychological 'abnormality'. If, on the other hand, we assume that individuals internalize cultural norms so well that they cannot but live a life of obedience, we are again caught in some contradiction: how does the submissive subordinate daughter-in-law transmute into a dictatorial matriarch? In brief, I prefer to hold to my original axiom, even at the cost of being accused of Hobbesianism, for it remains the only one free of the contradictions plaguing the others. To phrase it more prosaically, I hold that 'adulthood' universally implies a desire for autonomy in everyday economic and domestic matters; this is the social-psychological basis of my atomistic set of underlying assumptions (always remembering that most people also delight in ordering others around . . .). These two postulates (methodological and psycho-sociological), when combined with cultural elements found in many parts of Europe over long periods of time, should yield most elements of our desired set of axioms. Because so many of these axioms revolve around the notions of 'autonomy' and 'adulthood', something first needs to be said about those concepts.

Of autonomy, residential, economic and domestic

Autonomy, being so fuzzy, is a most frustrating concept. Sabean has expressed his dissatisfaction with the notion but, in the end, he also ends up using it (Sabean 1990). In the present book, I shall speak of 'residential autonomy' when an MRU has sole occupancy of a dwelling-unit or part of a dwelling-unit that it owns, or in which (or a portion of which) it has a right to reside because it pays a rent; this is the most precise use of 'autonomy' we can make. When this MRU can decide the management of its domestic activities, I shall similarly speak of 'domestic autonomy', although in this context the idea already raises serious difficulties. It is when dealing with 'economic autonomy', however, that we encounter the most critical problems.

First, 'autonomy', be it domestic or economic, does not mean 'self-sufficiency', although the two are existentially interlinked, and therefore the source of much confusion, as many have already remarked. The world over, whatever the type of household composition, people need the assistance of kith and kin to help them out with their activities.

Second, if taken literally, 'complete autonomy' would imply that an MRU can decide every aspect of its domestic and economic activities exclusively by itself (without for that reason being self-sufficient), that it would be impervious to the power of others on its decisional process. There are few such cases in real life, where autonomy looks more like sovereignty in a

European Economic Union with a unique currency; it is, at best, a matter of degree, because autonomy has to do with decisional power, because such power varies in intensity and spills over any group boundary.

To recognize this problem, however, should not lead us to discard the notion of 'autonomy' altogether, and to ignore the fact that some circumstances favour one's power to decide whereas others hinder it. If I do not own anything and work for someone else, I can hardly be said to enjoy autonomy over decisions to do with production *stricto sensu*. If I live with my father and hand over all my wages to him, I cannot even decide the allocation of my income. If, in contrast, I own enough land to feed my family and I live next to my father, we might help one another out at critical times and, as my father and sporadic co-worker, he may try to influence my economic decisions; but, if I own property independently of him, I am in a better position to heed or ignore his advice. And the same applies to domestic matters. If a woman lives in her mother-in-law's house, she is more likely to be told what to do in the house, as well as how and when to do it, than if she lives alone with her husband and children. The mother-in-law might live next door and constantly pry into her daughter-in-law's domestic life; however, the daughter-in-law will be more likely to shut her out of her life for more of the time if she lives in her own house with her own husband.

Thus, to the extent that individuals own their own means of production or have complete control over the use of their income, and excluding serious indebtedness or complete destitution, they can be said to enjoy a certain degree of economic autonomy though they may still call for help in times of need, and those assisting may try to mingle in their affairs. In brief, one's autonomy is always relative because people are almost always and almost everywhere sporadically part of various economic groups and surrounded by individuals who help them economically. If the latters' interference does not completely dictate the behaviour of those they assist, it still makes sense to use a concept to denote the fact that one may listen to others' advice but might ignore it in the end. It is quite obvious that we cannot hope to get to any greater level of precision in delineating the notion of autonomy, but there is no greater virtue in jettisoning it altogether. Using it does inflict simplifications on the complexities of social life but, as we shall see, it also enables us to sketch a workable framework infinitely more useful and promising than the collectivistic one. *More to the point, it is the only way to move from households to a set of axioms about their composition.* I shall therefore unashamedly rely on this imprecise notion and define it as the 'power to decide for oneself, free enough of outside interference'.

If autonomy does not carry any idea of self-sufficiency and merely designates a sufficient freedom to decide, subordination obviously denotes the opposite; namely the situation in which someone's activities are more or less dictated by others. Finally, I shall define as 'equality' the situation in which MRUs who have the option of autonomy nonetheless combine in economic and domestic matters, working out as 'equally' as possible their respective shares in those activities.

It follows from this set of definitions that neither equality nor subordination can apply to the activity of residence. Residence admits of two states only: autonomy (an MRU forming its own household) or cohabitation (two or more MRUs coresiding). Subordination or equality stem from the dynamics of complex households, that is, from the relationship between MRUs.

Elusive 'adulthood'

'Adulthood' also confronts us with some of the most thorny definitional problems, as it is a process of social maturation rather than a 'state' achieved at a given point in time. In the case of adulthood (as in the case of autonomy), continuity raises its deconstructivist head. As with most processes of social maturation, we can say of adulthood that it has happened once it is achieved, but we are rarely able to point to a precise moment at which it is attained, except in some cases (such as our contemporary industrialized societies) where specific legal criteria define 'majority' and, to all practical intents and purposes, adulthood. Given married and respected citizens of forty years old, say, we would intuitively suppose that in much of historical Europe most of them would have been regarded as adults. But what of a fifteen-year-old boy or girl? Would they have been considered adults in eighteenth-century Russia, even if they were married? Probably not. In brief, in most European populations and at most times, there were rarely hard-and-fast rules clearly separating the category of adults from the non-adults. Whatever the hurdles, it is hardly a concept we can do without, and I will retain it without reconstituting its history for the societies we shall study. It is another of these culturally defined notions which evade a discontinuous representation, but I prefer to err on the side of over- or under-representation of MRUs by failing adequately to define adults, rather than scrap the concept and the whole possibility of delineating MRUs.

From autonomy to MRU relationships

Let us now go back to our point of departure, namely adulthood and autonomy, and the assumption that 'adulthood' implies a striving for economic and domestic autonomy. Inserted in the European context, it should yield the basis of our set of axioms.

To give this set of axioms wider scope and also to simplify it further, I shall ignore whether economic activities are more of a male than a female preserve in a given population at a given time, or whether both genders participate equally in those activities. No doubt the division of labour makes a vast difference in MRU relationships. If men rule over most economic activities, they will not fully express their adulthood until they feel they have gained a certain degree of economic independence, and if they depend on their father for their means of production, they will regard him as the key individual standing in the way of their achieving full adulthood. This would generate serious intergenerational conflicts over the transmission of property, but to limit ourselves to such situations would eliminate the vast majority of salaried workers, many of whom are women. I shall therefore ignore this important dimension in order to simplify my set of axioms.

The same cannot be said about domestic activities. True, modern 'liberated' couples allegedly share domestic activities but, on the whole, it is no exaggeration to say that domestic activities have been a female preserve in most places in Europe and in most periods, and that intergenerational conflicts can thrive in the domestic field as powerfully as in the economic one. To understand why, further postulates will be needed. On the basis of the available evidence, it is possible to assume that, in most cases, residential autonomy (that is, an MRU living in its own dwelling-unit) spells domestic autonomy (with all the qualifications mentioned above), *because European houses (or dispersed parts of houses or flats) are either individually owned, or provisionally treated as individual property through the payment of a rent, and because married spouses are almost everywhere expected to coreside.*[3] If the house belongs to a woman or the woman pays the rent from her own money, in her mind the house is obviously 'hers'. If the husband owns it or pays the rent out of his income, his wife normally has an inalienable right to live in it and, once more, she will treat this house as 'her house' to all practical intents and purposes. From the point of view of an argumentation in terms of MRUs this only becomes problematical when MRUs cohabit. Why? Because this possessive attitude stemming from ownership or the payment of a rent leads to the domestic subordination of one or more of the coresiding MRUs if they happen to be economically unequal.

Let us start with cases where 1) the parents 'own' (through straightforward ownership, or the payment of a rent) at least a house, but also some land (in historic Europe), and 2) where the units in presence are MRUs containing at least a conjugal unit (that is, couples or families). In those circumstances, if a woman moves to her husband's house after her marriage, and if this husband is economically subordinate to his father (or mother) and lives in a paternal house which he does not own or for which (or part of which) he does not pay a rent, the in-marrying bride will be forced into domestic subordination because the wife of the superordinate man will 'be in her own house' and will consider herself legitimately entitled to supervise domestic activities (this will be all the truer if she is the one who is also economically superordinate; needless to say, this subordination is exacerbated by the superiority that generation and age confer upon the mother-in-law).[4] Of the household dynamics, especially of the relationship between adult women in the case of multiple family households, I shall ignore the details which Wolf (1972), Collier (1974) and Lamphere (1974) have marvellously substantiated; suffice it to say that the young bride's entry and complete subordination in what they call the 'patrilocal extended family' (patrivirilocal multiple family households) sets her up directly against the mother-in-law:

> Wives are the worms within the apple of a patrilocal domestic group. They work to advance the fortunes of particular individuals – their sons or husbands – in a social system where men are taught to put group interests before private ones. In a world where men gain political power by having a large and cohesive body of co-resident kin, young women gain power by breaking up domestic units.
>
> (Collier 1974: 92)

The result is that 'old matriarchs and young mothers are doomed enemies' (Collier 1974: 93), a theme repeated by Lamphere: a young bride is a threat to the solidarity of the residential group she marries into and, '[w]omen's strategies revolve around "working through men," either their husbands or their sons. Women's interests never coincide; competition and conflict are to be expected' (Lamphere 1974: 105). In brief, mother-in-law/daughter(s)-in-law relationships are intrinsically conflictual: interests rarely converge.

Collier and Lamphere were in fact describing 'extended families'. Is the situation different in stem families? Slightly so, certainly. For one, the bride marries into a residential group where only one son (her husband) will co-reside after marriage. In a stem family, furthermore, the only heir (or the heir treated preferentially) will likely have conflictual relationships with his male siblings, as he does with the father. Why with the father, if he is privileged over his siblings of both sexes? Because the preferential heir allegedly inherits the land when he gets married but, *de facto*, his father stands in the way of his heir's economic autonomy until he (the father) dies or is incapacitated by old age. In a word, their relationship is extremely polarized. The new bride marries a man often despised by his male siblings, and in conflict with his father because of his economic subordination to the latter. Furthermore, in most regions, the bride brings in a dowry equivalent in value to the heir's inheritance. This puts her in a much stronger position to divide and rule, trying to pit her husband against his own parents; she is in a better position to make life miserable for the ageing in-laws.

This can hardly happen in cases of multiple family households, especially where the bride brings in no dowry but a meagre trousseau (as we shall see in the case of Russia, and as Denich has demonstrated for mountain pastoralists – Denich 1974). Where all married brothers stay home and inherit equally, conflicts between them are plausibly reduced since, technically, they are not divided over the inheritance. Furthermore, conflicts with the father cannot be as polarized if there are many sons and because, in these cases, property is transmitted at the father's death only. Consequently, the male agnatic core of the household can be much more solidary in a multiple family household, and the fate of the in-marrying bride corresponds more closely to the descriptions of Collier and Lamphere. When moving into such a household, the new bride does not have the weapons of her 'stem comrades' and, if she tries to set her husband against his mother and father, she is likely to be opposed by the whole residential group. She wields less power to divide in the short- to middle-term and, for this reason, must count on her own progeny and create her own little following to support her in her fights against her in-laws later in life. In brief, she might easily face fifteen to twenty years of the stick before her own sons side with her against her husband, her husband's male siblings and her parents-in-law. Here, it is the in-laws who can, and often do, make the in-marrying bride's life truly miserable.

What of uxoripatrilocal stem families (those in which the husband moves into his wife's parental house; in French, they are known as *mariages en gendre*? Although intrinsically conflictual (both daughter and son-in-law are economically and domestically subordinate), they seem to be less so, for two main reasons. First, if we are to believe Chodorow (1974) and Collier (1974), mother and daughter are much less opposed than mothers-in-law and daughters-in-law. Furthermore, although the coresiding daughter inherits the patrimonial property (she is an heiress by definition, since *mariages en gendre* always involve heiresses – see below, Chapter 6), she does not depend on this property to achieve adulthood; this she can do fully within the domestic field. As a result, property does not set mother against daughter as it does a son against his father (in fact, the daughter might be heiress while her mother is not).

As to the in-marrying son-in-law, his circumstances differ from a son's in two major ways: first he brings in a dowry at marriage (to my knowledge *mariages en gendre* are mostly found in stem family regions with dowries), something which puts him on a more equal footing with his father-in-law than the son with his father. Second, although economically subordinate to his father-in-law, he never expects to inherit from him, having to live with the idea that he will never fully achieve 'adulthood' since upon his parents-in-law's death his wife will become heiress. Thus the in-marrying son-in-law can never hope to achieve economic autonomy, as only an heir can in those regions; on the other hand, he is likely not to be as completely subordinate to his father-in-law as he would be to his own father. Is one more conflictual than the other? I find it difficult to say; if we go by the noises that conflicts make in the literature, I would conclude that the relationship between son-in-law and father-in-law is less volatile.

Now, what of 'equal cohabitation'? For instance, if the married sons in a multiple family household do not divide the land after their father's death and stay under the same roof, they are economically equal and, according to my set of axioms, this should translate as (horizontal) 'domestic equality' in cohabitation. If cohabitation in stem families and multiple family households are intrinsically conflictual because of subordination, both economic and domestic, is it substantially different with 'equal cohabitation'? It seems equally fraught with intrinsic conflicts, because both notions of 'economic equality' and 'domestic equality' seem to be very questionable, especially in the context of multiple family households. Let us first tackle the question of 'economic equality'.

While retaining the land in corporate ownership, all siblings are equal co-owners of such lands. If they do not work the land, rent it out and split the proceeds, then the alleged equality is not perturbed. But let us assume that three brothers-and-heirs collectively work the land, the usual situation in fact. If they are perfectly equal co-owners, this might not extend to two associated contexts, namely decision-making and agricultural work. Indeed, from what we know of such cases, one of the brothers will more or less step in the father's shoes by becoming 'household head' and, as such, will presumably have more weight than the others in the process of decision-making. But let us assume that it is not so, that all three brothers take an equal part in decision-making. From this point of view, they could be declared economically equal (in that they are neither autonomous nor subordinate). This equality, however, does not seem to extend to the activities themselves. On the one hand, barring the fact that the brothers might be triplets, they will differ in age and the eldest might feel he ought to wield more authority, having been associated longer with their deceased father. Second, there is no point in working collectively a piece of land owned corporately unless all the products are pooled and divided equally.[5] But, as Marx emphasized long ago in the *Capital*, individual, concrete labour is never equal, or perfectly comparable. First, brothers of dissimilar ages will also differ in physical strength, energy and speed of performance (in one word, in their productivity), and one or more will feel wronged in the deal. Second, their consumption needs will also vary; some will have more unproductive children than others and feel that they ought to receive more than a third of the harvest. In a word, collective work on corporately owned land, although dubbed 'equal' in terms of our definitions, is rarely lived as such in real life and carries its share of built-in conflicts.

The same applies to domesticity. In the most liberated contemporary couples that I know, namely those that seek to share domestic chores most equally, each spouse ends up feeling that she or he is doing more than her or his fair share. What are we then to make of coresiding but 'equal' MRUs? If one of the brothers, normally the eldest, emerges as 'household head', it is quite likely that his wife might act as if she was in a superior position within the residential group, if only because of her age and her longer association with the running of the house. Also, what obtains in economic activities applies with equal force in domestic ones: not only the variations in energy and general input will make some sisters-in-law feel cheated, but the inevitable tiffs between children of different mothers will easily escalate to the point of involving their respective mothers, pitting sister-in-law against sister-in-law. More fundamentally, the period of corporate ownership and horizontal residential extension in multiple family households is precisely the moment when wives first see the opportunity of reaching full domestic autonomy through residential separation. As a result, this is the point at which squabbles between sisters-in-law should reach their peak, each one trying to undermine the brothers' solidarity, using every trick in the trade to get her husband to demand his share of the land and build his own house for his own family, because this is the moment where sibling solidarity is at its lowest: after the father's death, they have the opportunity to claim their due share and, however equal, inheritance often divides heirs. To put it briefly, in an 'equal' domestic environment some are more equal than others, and 'domestic equality' is also intrinsically conflictual, whether horizontal or vertical (for the latter, see the Basque case in Chapter 6).

Let us remember that we have so far considered only cases where the parents own some property, where only conjugal MRUs are present and, in cases of subordination, where the parent-owners actually use the property as a form of coercion to keep married children at home, as we shall see when studying stem families and multiple family households. To give our set of axioms a wider scope, we also have to include cases of cohabitation due to hindrances (hindrances as a result of economic problems, divorce or the death of a spouse, etc.), and the problems that face lone individuals and lone parents.

Let us first consider cohabitation stemming from hindrances. In such circumstances, the situation can doubtless be much less conflictual, especially if the MRUs consist mostly of celibate individuals or 'residual families' (matricells and patricells, or individuals once married). We could consider the vast array of potential combinations due to hindrances, and we would probably find on the whole that these situations are the least conflictual, but conflictual they always potentially are, for MRUs who unite because of hindrances either hope to live autonomously or have done so in the past and, whatever the degree of intended equality, the cohabitation of once autonomous MRUs also seems to contain the seeds of conflict. Moreover, I wish to emphasize that, with the best intentions and with circumstances objectively equal, cohabiting MRUs rarely perceive their contributions as equal. When individual cases seem to belie the rule, it has more to do with personalities than organizational features (see the section 'Axioms, psychology and culture' below).

Now, what of lone individuals (either celibate, separated, divorced or widowed) and lone parents? I believe their situation calls for additional considerations, having mostly to do with marriage and companionship.

The topic of marriage would call for a whole set of axioms to itself, but I shall limit myself to general considerations. Given complete freedom from either coercion or hindrances, I believe that most individuals would prefer a harmonious marriage to celibacy, but would choose celibacy over a bad matrimonial relationship. Unfortunately, as with matters residential, there is a myriad of forces at work (among which Church, parents, and even friends), and even more hindrances (the Church again, which forbids divorce in Catholic countries, and money, together with the presence or absence of children when it comes to separation or divorce), so that many individuals tolerate a bad marriage rather than live a separation or divorce. In the light of this set of presuppositions, we should expect that lone individuals and lone parents might seek a stable relationship (or marriage), but that their inclination will be influenced by the circumstances of the time and place (also, for those who have lived a separation or divorce, by their earlier experience of the holy state of matrimony and, for lone parents, by the fact that they bring children into the relationship).

This leaves us with lone individuals and lone parents who, for one reason or another, either do not wish, or fail, to find a matrimonial partner. About them, we might assume very much what we did about marriage. Most would prefer a harmonious and fulfilling (nonsexual and, perforce, nonconjugal) companionship to living alone, but would prefer residential autonomy to a conflictual and difficult companionship, even if it means living completely alone in the case of lone parents. Admittedly, economic reasons will also come into play, but I am here arguing on the basis of psychological inclinations alone.

As I have emphasized earlier, any cohabitation based on marriage does not fall within our set of axioms, so that only the (unmarried) cohabitation of lone individuals and lone parents creates complex households. If we remove the hindrances that compel some of them to accept a cohabitation that they would rather not live, shall we conclude that lone individuals and lone parents seeking cohabitation for the sake of companionship have an easier time? I would hazard that they do if that companionship is harmonious, and that they do not in the contrary circumstances.

All things considered, therefore, whether 'intrinsic conflict' varies or not, one central element stands out unambiguously from most of the writings on the family life of European populations past and present: that save for the rare ones who seek cohabitation to evade loneliness and find an amiable and easy nonconjugal partnership, *all cohabitation of MRUs is intrinsically conflictual in the European context*, because straightforward domestic subordination contradicts the ideal of autonomy attached to adulthood, because so-called equal cohabitation is rarely perceived as such by the parties concerned, or because otherwise good friends suddenly find a host of irritants when they start living together. In other words, in so far as each MRU strives towards autonomy, both economic and domestic, within its own household, the cohabitation of MRUs, and especially of couples or families, can only be achieved at the cost of a contradiction. Upon this it now seems possible to erect an atomistic set of axioms.

Spelling out more axioms

Let us return to Ermisch and Overton's 'minimal household units'. We have already seen that, as 'household irreducibles' or 'residential atoms', the cohabitation of individuals forming an MRU needs no explanation, being culturally defined (and therefore taken as axiomatic). Nevertheless, their coresidence with other MRUs, being intrinsically conflictual in the context of European culture, must therefore be accounted for, and dictates the manner in which we will formulate the problem. If the cohabitation of two or more MRUs is problematical, save when their adult members are united through marriage[6] or an harmonious companionship (which, incidentally, has more to do with psychology than organizational features), it follows that MRUs should shun cohabitation.

In other words, if we accept the series of assumptions mentioned above, we must then logically posit that MRUs *seek residential autonomy* (they aspire to form their own separate household) or, stated otherwise, that they *resist cohabitation*; it is, so to speak, their 'inertial motion', and the coresidence of two or more MRUs calls for explanation, unless they are linked through marriage.

As in any set of axioms, moreover, MRU cohabitation will have to be explained in terms of hindrances, of forces (i.e. of coercion), or both, and their lack of cohabitation (their residential autonomy), in terms of the *absence* of these hindrances and sources of coercion (see Chapter 1). Let us dwell one last time on the necessary distinction between hindrances and forces (in the social world).

To recall our first analogy from physics, if matter's inertial motion is to retain its velocity (move at a constant speed in a straight line indefinitely) and to resist changes of velocity, there are two different ways in which such changes can occur: either because an object is hindered in its movement (as it moves through the atmosphere or water, for instance), or because it is constrained by a force (gravity, electricity, magnetism). Similarly, MRUs may either be hindered from achieving autonomy because of (mostly) economic reasons (though the reasons can also be physical or psychological), but they may also be coerced into coresidence because of the 'force' (manipulations or threats) exerted on them by another MRU or extra-residential power-holders. For the moment, let us confine ourselves to cases of intra-residential coercion. Residential phenomena, needless to say, do not behave like the movement of matter. In matters residential, in fact, coercion never operates without corresponding hindrances. When parents succeed in compelling one (or many) adult or married child(ren) into cohabitation, as we shall see, part of their coercive power stems from the fact that the child(ren) know(s) of no real economic alternative; they are hindered economically because of the absence of viable economic options, other than emigration in some cases. Given various economic opportunities, the parental powers could no longer operate and parents would have to lure their children into cohabitation if they wished them to stay at home when they reached adulthood and/or got married.

If some units are browbeaten into cohabitation, cohabitation then emerges as a matter of power relationships in which one unit lords it over the other(s); power relationships, however, depend on the strength of the protagonists, and this strength is largely determined by sex, age, and the composition (and size) of the unit.

Gender plays an important role because in most cultures the sexes are unequal in their social, economic and political entitlements and, in most of historical Europe, women were the victims of this inequality (about the near universality of this inequality, see Rosaldo 1974). As a result of women's inferior social status in much of 'traditional' Europe, we can surmise that in conditions of unequal cohabitation between MRUs, it will be easier for a minimal unit comprising a man to dominate a subordinate MRU, and easier for a minimal residential unit comprising an adult woman only to be subordinate to another MRU (such units would encompass celibate adult women, widows and divorcees without children, and matricells).

The above could also apply to age: the younger the adult member(s) of a unit, the more easily they can be kept in a subordinate position. This obviously relates to the question of adulthood. Many family historians have already emphasized that parents can more easily dominate a teenage daughter-in-law than one who is in her late twenties. This should prompt yet another rider to our set of axioms, namely that individuals who can hardly be considered adults by the standards of their own society (because they do not feel themselves ready to take their own economic and domestic decisions) might prefer temporary cohabitation if they get married. They would forbear their domestic autonomy for a short while, until they feel ready to take their own decisions on matters within their control. Once they feel they ought to be treated as adults, however, our set of axioms should apply with its full force: they will shun cohabitation, and subordinate cohabitation in particular.

Finally, the composition and size of the unit (whether an individual, a matricell, a patricell, a couple, or a family with many children) should also have some weight in this power game. Indeed, assuming the unequal cohabitation of two MRUs, it could be assumed that the superordinate MRU will more easily dominate if it consists of a couple rather than a widowed individual, especially if the subordinate MRU itself comprises a family[7] (and, by virtue of our earlier axioms, a unit comprising a man should more easily maintain its superordinate position than a unit without a man – that is, one comprising a widow, a celibate or a divorced woman only). Finally, the greater the number of children in the subordinate unit and, more particularly, the age and gender of these children (boys being more of an asset in some intergenerational fights than girls, and girls more than boys in different intergenerational struggles), the more difficult it should also be to maintain the whole unit in a state of complete subordination, and the greater the resulting conflicts between the coresiding MRUs, unless the superordinate MRU knows how to rule wisely.

This set of axioms should account for most cases of cohabitation stemming from coercion. What of hindrances? Unlike coercive action, hindrances do operate alone. In this short disquisition we will barely touch upon hindrances (most of which have already been dealt with extremely well by household economists), but we must nonetheless ask how we know that cohabitation results from hindrances rather than coercion. There is no hard-and-fast rule, especially in residential matters where domination cannot operate without hindrances, but I believe there exists a good rule of thumb which yields satisfactory approximations. Indeed, when studying residential composition over a given period of time, it is plausible to suppose that when adult or married children stay at home for a few years only, leaving as soon as they can, we are normally dealing with hindrances only (they coreside because there is as yet no house available to move into, or because they have not yet amassed enough money to buy a house, or because they are temporarily out of work, etc.). Similarly, when units who have enjoyed residential autonomy renounce it and move back to their natal home, we can also surmise that they are not coerced by their parents but pressured by their own circumstances.

This is why our household typologies should not be based on residential composition alone, but on the composition of residential groups within a given power configuration. We could, for instance, find parents cohabiting with a married son because they are destitute and because the son feels solicitude towards them. From the point of view of the household's composition we would find two couples (or a couple and a family) coresiding, two couples linked through filiation, and it would be impossible to tell this household from a stem family. In reality, the two could not be further apart. Such a group would have emerged because of the hindrances plaguing one of the couples, and its residential composition would have nothing to do with a stem family in which the parents coerce the children into cohabitation through the manipulation of inheritance. Martine Segalen long ago noticed the problem when studying Breton households (Segalen 1977).

Finally, one hindrance transcends social and cultural boundaries and affects all MRUs. If cohabitation generates tensions and conflicts, as I have inferred it does, even the superordinate couple suffers from it and its choice of coresidence also needs to be accounted for; in brief, even the couple representing the oldest generation would seek residential autonomy if it could and, if it does not, its cohabitation calls for an explanation. In most instances, I believe that it can best be accounted for by a universal hindrance called 'ageing'. In order for MRUs to realize their residential autonomy they must be physically able to do so, a fact intimately connected to the question of ageing. In so far as ageing threatens every MRU's residential autonomy it is a universal, ineluctable hindrance which can incite an MRU to cohabitation if it is incapacitated, cannot look after itself and cannot find the needed care without joining someone else's residential group. Furthermore, if forced to such a solution it will try to achieve a position of domination over the other coresiding unit rather than placing itself in a position of subordination, unless it can establish its cohabitation on a relatively equal footing. This is my last axiom but, together with the MRUs' proclivity towards residential autonomy in the context of cultural elements common to most European populations, it is a crucial one (for list of axioms, see below).

Summary of the basic postulates of an atomistic set of axioms for the study of Western living arrangements

Aim: Explaining extraregional variability in the study of residential composition in terms of limits of residential growth.

A *definition*

1 Residence is an activity around which 'residential groups' (or households) are formed;

Methodological requirements

2 In the study of residential groups, we must identify our 'residential atoms', the minimal components from which all residential groups are built;

3 Ermisch and Overton's 'minimal household units' (retranslated as 'minimal residential units', or MRUs), will constitute our residential atoms;

4 These units are minimal because the coresidence of individuals forming a given MRU needs no explanation (in most cases, is culturally dictated);

5 Hence, when studying households comprising more than one MRU, a simple description of household composition does not suffice; to get a usable typology, we need to add the dimension of interactions, or *power configuration* between coresiding MRUs;

6 This propels us out of residence into economic and domestic activities (where power games are played out);

A social-psychological axiom

7 Any adult who is normally constituted psychologically will want to run his or her everyday life; hence adulthood spells a desire for everyday economic and domestic autonomy – on the understanding that adulthood is also culturally defined and difficult to demarcate, and that autonomy is a matter of degree;

Inserted into a set of cultural axioms

8 The division of labour is of the utmost importance where men regard most economic activities as their preserve, since this can easily lead to intergenerational strife between father and sons. To give our axioms greater scope, however, we shall retain only a quasi-universal feature of division of labour in European populations, namely that women usually execute most domestic activities;

9 The individual appropriation of houses or of parts of houses, either through straightforward ownership or through the payment of a rent, means that the MRU to whom the house belongs, and especially the woman within that MRU, will feel entitled to dictate the domestic activities of all other coresiding MRUs;

10 Therefore, the economic subordination of the married son, when he has to live with his parents, translates into the domestic subordination of his wife to her mother-in-law;

11 Furthermore, economic and domestic equality, even if theoretically possible, are rarely perceived as such by the parties concerned;

12 As a result, all cohabitation of MRUs is intrinsically conflictual in the European context;

The axioms proper

13 Hence, all MRUs shun cohabitation and seek residential autonomy (the fundamental element of an atomistic set of axioms);

14 Therefore, all cohabitation of MRUs not married to one another is problematical and has to be accounted for;

15 All cohabitation of MRUs thus results either from the application of coercion, the operation of hindrances, or both;

16 Coercions result mostly from the manipulation of inheritance, but can only operate in the presence of hindrances (no viable alternative source of work);

17 The level of subordination that can be exacted from MRUs who are kept at home through coercion depends on a certain number of factors, among which are to be found the gender and age of the adult members of the MRUs, as well as the size of the MRU;

18 As to cohabitation resulting from hindrances only, it will be found when MRUs leave home soon after marriage, or return home after having been residentially autonomous;

19 One hindrance transcends any culture, however, and that is ageing. In order to fulfil their desire for autonomy, MRUs must be physically able to do so, and cannot do so as they get older. This, in fact, is one of the main reasons why parents often attempt to coerce children into staying at home after marriage;

20 Finally, there are also extraresidential forces at play to coerce MRUs into cohabitation, and these are the state, or overlords.

I have repeatedly said that this version of my atomistic set of axioms is already severely simplified and, for the applications that follow, I shall pare it down even more. I shall provisionally forget about 'minimal residential units' and write indiscriminately of 'families' or 'familial units', those units encompassing proper families, couples and lone parents. I shall thus posit that families seek residential autonomy and resist cohabitation, a resistance which has to be overcome either by coercion, hindrances, or both. Furthermore, I shall employ the terms 'autonomy', 'equality' and 'subordination' as if they could be defined with precision, and this, with the sole aim of deriving a workable and useful typology by initially distinguishing 'residential autonomy' from 'subordinate cohabitation' and 'equal cohabitation'.

Before tackling empirical cases, however, more matters have to be settled. First, in the course of presenting my axioms I mentioned the question of culture; further along, I wrote of individual psychology. The two topics still confuse many discussions, and I shall briefly touch upon them here.

Putting culture in its proper place

I will spell out again what I mentioned earlier. Once a practice has emerged and is collectively accepted and appropriated, it is then encoded in sets of norms which are built upon underlying taxonomies and are tinted by a given symbolism (which can, and often does, include religion). Together, the normative and the cognitive components (the latter encompassing taxonomy and symbolism) are analytically distinct but they make up what we call 'culture'. From my point of view, the taxonomic and symbolic aspects can be left aside (as should religion, for the cases to be examined); in the Western context they might have some relevance to residence here and there but to all practical intents and purposes I believe they can be neglected. I will therefore confine myself to the normative aspect. Once a group of individuals has collectively decided to adopt a certain type of behaviour (or, in a more neutral formulation, a set of practices), regardless of the reasons which incited them to do so, they will then invent rules to make sure that the practices are respected and survive over time (are 'reproduced', in the trendy language of today). They will equally invent all sorts of 'cultural' explanations (an ethos, a set of values, etc.) to explain those rules. Boas himself understood it all when he wrote of culture as a set of 'collective rationalizations'; what is invoked to justify those rules (let us call it the 'cultural wrapping' of the norm itself) is indeed a collective rationalization ('rationalization' understood here in its psychoanalytical sense). I shall dub this collective rationalization the 'cultural code', and also speak of cultural encoding. Once culturally encoded, therefore, these collective practices then resist change. This, as I mentioned earlier, is the only true explanatory power of Culture: in individuals' daily lives, Culture might (or might not) explain why they act as they do (something, incidentally, which psychotherapists might fiercely dispute). It explains why practices, once they have emerged and have been adopted collectively, go on being observed and even resist change (we could call this process of resistance to change the 'inertial power of Culture', known in anthropology as 'tradition').

In this perspective, most of the collective practices we come across can be described as 'cultural'. Are we then to understand that we have explained them in terms of Culture by declaring them 'cultural'? Not in the least! I have concluded earlier that culturalism and *juridisme* did not explain anything, but I never claimed that anthropological, sociological or historical analyses should rule out cultural or juridical elements. To appreciate the difference, let us take a European cultural practice, namely monogamy. If I single out this cultural phenomenon and wish to explain it (that is, put forth a theory accounting for its emergence), will I provide an answer by reporting that Europeans share a culturally determined set of norms or values forbidding polygyny and enforcing monogamy? The answer is, and should always remain, in the negative. Explaining a culturally encoded collective practice (such as monogamy) by its cultural encoding (such as the values and ethos surrounding monogamy) will always amount to a mere tautology. This is what culturalism or *juridisme* are about, a simple abstract 'translation' of the observed facts setting itself up as an explanation. But a translation is no explanation because one could immediately ask, 'But why should we find this particular set of norms or values in Europe, and not in Africa?' Jack Goody answered this question brilliantly in *Production and Reproduction* (1976), evoking a number of cultural elements (private ownership of land, improved technology, and so on) and a number of noncultural ones (demographic explosion, land scarcity) in order to build his explanatory model.

And so it is with all cultural phenomena (and with a host of noncultural ones resulting from human action): to explain them we have to summon both cultural practices and noncultural elements and articulate them as best we can into a theory (an explanatory model). When trying to account for a given limit of residential growth (a cultural phenomenon) such as stem families, have we explained anything by invoking, as Augustins does, a 'House culture', or 'principles of legitimacy', or a 'principle of residence' embodied in 'House systems'? I believe not. In other words, any sociological or anthropological explanation must of necessity include cultural elements (encompassing juridical ones) without for that reason sinking into culturalism and *juridisme* by confounding a cultural code with an explanation. In my opinion, this ought to be the proper place of culture (for further clarification, see the Annex).

But what shall we say of religion? Exactly the same as I said about culture or norms. I do not believe that religious beliefs or practices have a bearing on living arrangements in the populations that I have studied, for the simple reason that one finds extreme variability in household composition over areas of similar religious practices. To that extent, I may be accused of having ignored the role of religion in the analyses that will follow and I stand by my position until proven wrong. Were I to study Chinese or Japanese living arrangements, I might argue otherwise, for I feel that ancestral cults, common to both China and Japan, may go a long way towards explaining their limits of residential growth. Had I written a book about Far Eastern residence, I may then have been accused of giving religion too great a role!

In other words, I would like to re-emphasize that the set of axioms I have proposed applies only within a very specific set of cultural circumstances (found in most European populations or populations of European extraction). Change one or many of these cultural practices, and the set of axioms will differ correspondingly, as we shall see when studying Abutia.

Axioms, psychology and culture

When I write of the conflictual nature of cohabitation, especially that of familial units in unequal relationships, I do not imply that all the individuals involved in such cohabitation in the whole region under study and at all times have had hostile relationships. There are cohabiting mothers-in-law and daughters-in-law who get along marvellously, and coresiding mothers and daughters who heartily detest one another. There are forceful and bossy daughters-in-law who order meek mothers-in-law around. There are people who seek harmony at all costs, others who thrive on confrontation. When arguing from a comparative (or, more specifically, extraregional) vantage point, however, individual psychological idiosyncrasies should be set aside. From a comparative perspective, what matters is that some circumstances bear the intrinsic seeds of conflict. In this context, personalities might either attenuate or defuse confrontations, but the very manner in which cultural and noncultural elements intermesh is conducive to opposition and hostilities because of their internal contradictions. Personalities will merely explain why this or that household is more harmonious or more violently explosive. Thus, when writing of daughters-in-law dividing households I mean that the cohabitation of mother-in-law and daughter-in-law in the European cultural context contains all the ingredients for conflict; I do not in the least imply that all households will split because of the conflicts between the two.

Finally, I wish to stress that an atomistic set of axioms does not constitute a statement about a cultural orientation to be found in this or that part of Europe, or in Europe in general. Whatever the cultural context, I believe my first (social-psychological) axiom to be universal and, methodologically, I would everywhere approach residence in atomistic terms. The set of axioms itself is simply the set of corollaries one can derive from the impact of some cultural elements on initial axioms which, rooted in psychology, one supposes to have universal values. To that extent, the corollaries can be regarded as cultural, without resulting in a Culture. On the contrary, the Culture may postulate the opposite, as we shall see with stem families or, more so, with Russian multiple family households. In pre-emancipation peasant Russia, there undoubtedly existed a cultural orientation towards 'collectivistic attitudes', but evoking this cultural encoding does not explain this particular limit of residential growth. By supposing the very opposite and ferreting out the major sources of hindrances and coercion, in contrast, we seem to be in a better position to account for the existence of multiple family households as a limit of residential growth. A set of axioms is therefore no cultural encoding, but a tool to shape the manner in which we phrase our questions and which accordingly influences the elements we single out to answer our queries.

4

ATOMISM, NEOINDIVIDUALISM AND HOUSEHOLD ECONOMICS

At this juncture, we can appreciate the distance separating this set of axioms from Smith's position. First of all, his salvo against Laslett blinds him to the right formulation of the 'underlying philosophical assumptions' of family history, namely the opposition between collectivism and individualism. Having failed to perceive the true locus of the opposition (although culture does wriggle its way back in through collectivism, so that he does not utterly miss the point) and failing to be explicit about the relationship between a set of axioms and what we deem problematical, he cannot appreciate precisely how collectivism and individualism diverge. Second, his atoms are not minimal household units but families; from that perspective most societies studied by ethnographers, let alone our own contemporary society, would escape his underlying assumptions.

Having singled out the family as his residential atom (he should have dubbed his approach 'familistic'), he is then led to identify neolocality (of the family) as one of 'the basic tendencies that humans acquired through their biological evolutionary history' (Smith 1993: 347). As a result, residence is no phenomenon in its own right, no separate dimension of social reality, and is again deflated to being an epiphenomenon of the sociobiological proclivity towards investing in one's children (hence to child maintenance and socialization). We regress to Fortesian theses with a sociobiological twist. Without a proper definition of residence, we cannot know whether Smith's 'compounds' (i.e. households containing more than one family) should be considered as residential or domestic groups. Furthermore, Smith never broaches the question of what we are to compare in the study of residence: statistically predominant types, developmental cycles, or what exactly?

By rooting neolocality in nature Smith has no option but to translate into cultural terms all constraints leading to the formation of multiple family household, thus falling back on the old and sterile nature/culture controversy (especially sterile in the study of residence). Against such a formulation I root my set of axioms partly in nature (no longer biology but social psychology), and partly in culture, thereby averting that fruitless dichotomy. Also, I recognize that hindrances also operate in the formation of complex households, whereas Smith does not.

In the final analysis, Smith does not present us with a set of axioms, whatever his motives behind his article: he merely enunciated his first axiom, namely the family's sociobiological proclivity toward neolocality. At the end of the road, if our initial postulates vaguely seemed to converge (but for radically opposite reasons), they actually diverge on almost every point.

It is in fact the works of Ermisch and Overton, and those of household economists, that parallel most closely the atomistic assumptions that I have put forth, and it is therefore vital to appreciate the areas of disagreement between our two vantage points, despite the extremely technical aspect of the discussion (those unfamiliar with details of neoclassical microeconomics might be advised to move on directly to p. 77, 'Unfortunately . . .').

Let us look more closely at Ermisch and Overton's conceptual and analytical framework. They introduced their MHUs, it will be recalled, in the context of household projection, and added that the coresidence of MHUs cannot be projected from demographic events. To explain that coresidence, they concluded, we have to look towards social and economic variables (1985: 35). This led them 'to test hypotheses derived from an economic theory of household formation' (39). The choices leading MHUs to 'separate living' or to cohabitation would be determined, among other things, by the MHUs' desire for privacy, work sharing and economies of scale (45).

In a subsequent article, Ermisch elucidated his views further. Evoking Hajnal (1983), he defined a household as a 'consumption unit' (Ermisch 1988: 23), and a minimal household unit as a 'unit of decision making' (36); as we shall see, these are necessary suppositions to nest his analysis of household formation in the fold of neoclassical economics and to delineate units which 'attempt to maximise [their] benefits from a given set of alternatives' and which have to decide between their desires (demands) for privacy, for the sharing of domestic chores, for consumption economies of scale, and for companionship, among others (Ermisch and Overton 1985: 36). Furthermore, Ermisch and Overton overtly declare to be working within a 'household production' approach. In this perspective, the household produces 'household outputs' and MHUs have 'a preference ranking over combinations of home-produced outputs and the household grouping which can be represented by an ordinal utility function' (45). Consequently,

> an MHU chooses the household grouping, its labour supply and the purchases of goods and services which maximise this utility function subject to its budget constraint, the household production relationship and the degree of scale economies associated with certain goods.
>
> (Ermisch and Overton 1985: 45)

Here, let us emphasize the theoretical relationship binding consumption (delineating households) to decision-making (delineating MHUs). In reality, Ermisch and Overton's understanding of 'consumption' does not denote much that anthropologists or historians would recognize, as it encompasses much more than the mere sharing of meals (Hajnal's thesis); in a 'household production' perspective, individuals do not only consume food but all 'home-produced goods' such as space, leisure, companionship, love, children and the like. There is a 'demand' for those goods only in so far as they are 'consumed', and 'consuming units' must be able to decide for themselves. Hence the necessary connection linking consumption to decision-making. What these units choose, therefore, is the form of living arrangement which maximizes their joint utility function (in ordinary language, which best satisfies the manner in which they ranked their preferences, given a number of alternatives and budget constraints).

No doubt, the work of Ermisch and Overton is original in its own right, in that they at least decompose the household into minimal units. From the point of view of decision-making they treat their MHUs as one entity, but they do not make it clear whether coresiding MHUs should equally be treated as single decision-making units. I reckon they should, in so far as coresiding MHUs have reciprocally chosen the type of household composition which maximizes their joint utility function. In other words, it seems legitimate to classify Ermisch and Overton's 'household production' approach within what Alderman *et al.* (1995) have labelled the 'unitary' model of the household, an economic model viewing the household 'as having one set of preferences' (1995: 1) and acting as one. The critics of this model are many but, to my knowledge, Folbre has provided the best synthesis of those various arguments. For the sake of simplicity I shall therefore rely almost exclusively on her critique, in order to avoid a review of the literature.

In technical terms, the 'unitary' household economists

> assume that households seek to maximize exogenously given joint utility functions [that is, 'aggregated', or 'added up', sets of ranked preferences, these preferences being defined outside the household itself (exogenous), namely in the individuals' environment], and they hypothesize that differences in household behavior represent efficient responses to differences in the prices and incomes which households face.
>
> (Folbre 1984: 303)

These joint utility functions, furthermore, 'are exogenous constant over time, and vary randomly, if at all, across households' (303). As a result, these monolithic utility-maximizing units, 'motivated by stable, uniform preferences [. . . are] constrained by pooled economic resources' (Fapohunda 1988: 142).

Many economists have been prompt to denounce the model's extraordinary assumptions. First, how does one aggregate individuals' utility functions into a joint household utility function? Arrow has already demonstrated that such an aggregation is impossible if based on revealed preferences (Arrow 1963) and I have argued elsewhere that it is equally impossible if not founded on revealed preferences (Verdon 1996b). The standard (that is, Samuelson–Becker) answer is to invoke altruism. In Becker's words, 'an altruistic family can be said to have a family utility function that is voluntarily maximized by all members regardless of the distribution of family income' (Becker 1981: 191, quoted in Folbre 1984: 304). As Fapohunta and Alderman *et al.* note, this presupposition rules out any process of distribution within households, because it must presuppose pooled resources. If individual resources were not pooled, there could be no joint utility function, only individual ones.

From the strict point of view of economic analysis, these assumptions fly in the face of most of the known facts. In most of the developing world and in scores of households in more industrialized countries, pooling does not exist any more than joint utility functions. Also,

> the assumption that joint utility functions are constant and exogenously given is tantamount to the assumption that no social change takes place. It implies that the degree of 'dictatorship' and/or the degree of 'altruism' [two solutions to the joint utility function problem] in the family remain constant over time. It requires that the family itself be treated as a naturally given, ahistorical institution.
>
> (Folbre 1984: 307)

These 'natural' roots, ironically enough, Becker finds nowhere else than in sociobiology, for only in sociobiological thinking can kin-based altruism be selected by nature and have any evolutionary future (Folbre 1986: 251–2).

In fact, although 'parental authority over young children is consistent with an "altruistic dictator" theory of decision making' (Folbre 1984: 307), it cannot in any way explain relations between parents and adult children, especially when the adult children no longer live at home and yet still send their parents part of their income. Nor can it explain, argues Parsons (1984), the wish of parents to control their adult children and force them into cohabitation through manipulating wealth and inheritance. Furthermore, as Folbre so incisively puts it with regard to women and female children working more than men and receiving a reduced share of all household outputs,

The suggestion that women and female children 'voluntarily' relin-
quish leisure, education and food [in the altruistic model] would be
somewhat more persuasive if they were in a position to demand
their fair share. It is the juxtaposition of women's lack of economic
power with the unequal allocation of household resources that lends
the bargaining power approach much of its persuasive appeal.

(Folbre 1986: 251)

The assumptions of household economics also seem to contradict those of
neoclassical economics: 'There is something paradoxical about the juxtaposition of naked self-interest that presumably motivates efficient allocation of
market resources and a perfect altruism that presumably motivates equitable
allocation of family resources' (Folbre 1986: 247). Despite this internal
contradiction, 'the plausibility of the "new home economics" rests on an
analogy between the household and the firm', a strained analogy at best,
since '[i]n household production, unlike commodity production, demanders
and suppliers are often one and the same. The cost of home produced goods,
like children, is not exogenously determined' (247).

This altruism, in its classical (Becker) formulation, rules out intergenerational and gender conflicts in turn. Solutions to inequalities have no doubt
been found which do not seek to refute the classical formulation:
'Inequalities of any sort can be explained by a "taste" for altruism or volun-
tary sacrifice[!]' (Folbre 1986: 249) but, let no one be deluded, these
revisionist attempts to account for household inequalities in neoclassical
terms simply multiply the number of the model's contradictions and give it
a more striking unrealistic sheen.

The alternatives, what Alderman *et al.* call the 'collective' model of the
household, try to integrate bargaining, game theory, and mostly distribution processes within households. However, apart from hitting the nail on
the head with their critiques, the feminists or the advocates of the 'collective model' do not seem to have come up with a very successful integrated
theory. Their case studies are extremely rich and subtle, giving much
better explanations of the recorded data than the so-called unitary model,
but I have not as yet seen a new 'orthodoxy' emerging to topple the
unitary model once and for all. Parsons's (1984) excellent attempt at integrating the cohabitation of families of various generational levels leads
more to good economic sociology than standard economics. Another
attempt at an integrated theory, that of Burch and Matthews (1987), also
eloquently tells of the pitfalls threatening efforts at an integrated household economics.

Listing the very same socio-demographic developments of contemporary
societies which inspired Becker's home economics (decline of fertility,
consensual unions, rise in divorce rates and the so-called 'atomization' of

residence), Burch and Matthews propose an integrated approach which would view all these transformations 'as household formation processes in a broad sense: they result from decisions made by individuals, couples, and households in response to the general question: "With whom shall I live?" (Burch and Matthews 1987: 495), a question Burch and Matthews subsume under the notion of 'household status':

> Household status, in this perspective, may be viewed as a composite good. In choosing a particular household status, an individual or couple are in effect choosing some combination of a set of component goods, such as privacy, companionship, domestic services, and consumption economies of scale.
>
> (Burch and Matthews 1987: 496)

This assumption prompted them to comment on the hypothesis linking the rise in separate living to rising real income:

> Theoretically, this hypothesis would follow from the assumption that separate living and its associated goods (privacy, independence) are normal or superior goods, and that, with the exception of couple cohabitation, coresidence and its associated goods are inferior. Such an assumption probably is valid for the societies in question during the period at issue.
>
> (Burch and Matthews 1987: 503)

Unfortunately, Burch and Matthews's attempt at an integrated approach is as neoclassical as Ermisch and Overton's, and generates the same problems. First of all, defining households or minimal household units, or even individuals, by their ability to decide for themselves (decision-making units) does not enable us to define residence since 'decision-making units' also decide about their matrimonial status, their occupational status, and so on (and could therefore also be declared 'matrimonial units', 'occupational units', and the like). Nothing in the fact of being socially recognized as independent enough to decide for oneself leads necessarily to residence. As a result, this formulation cannot lead to any set of axioms on residence since, by their very definitions, household economists consider that every residential choice has to be explained (is problematic); Alderman *et al.* make this quite clear, despite their onslaught on the dominant unitary model. Indeed, they confess that,

> In common with the unitary model, the cooperative approach begins by noting that individuals form a household when it is more beneficial to them than remaining alone. Higher benefits could occur because forming a household is a more efficient way to

produce household goods or because some goods can be produced and shared by married couples but not by single individuals.

(Alderman *et al.* 1995: 5)

In other words, any demand, including the demand for separate living – what I have called residential autonomy – must be accounted for in the neoclassical model. Some units will choose autonomy because this living arrangement maximizes their utility function given their budget constraints, while others will opt for cohabitation. This certainly does not yield a clear formulation of the key differences between a collectivistic and an atomistic set of axioms; quite the contrary, it leads to the usual axiomatic dualism, as the following comments from Burch and Matthews testify:

Households are tending to become simpler in the sense of more homogeneous in age and sex composition, relationship structures, and sex or gender roles. This trend may be seen as a new phase in a long-term evolutionary process from corporate kinship groups to the coresidential extended family to the independent nuclear family to a system characterized by a marked increase in nongroup or nonfamily household arrangements.

(Kobrin 1976 in Burch and Matthews 1987: 498)

In fact, Becker's argument in terms of altruism also flirts with collectivism, whether the argument relies on economic 'calculations' or not. In this respect, his model should have more appropriately been dubbed 'collectivistic' since it presupposes that households are undifferentiated collectivities in which individuals have all reciprocally adjusted their behaviours so as to maximize a joint utility function. Here, culturally defined collectivistic presuppositions have been replaced by altruistic allocation of resources. The points of departure differ (culture versus nature) but the results converge strangely.

Second, such a framework makes it outright impossible to integrate the fact that some MRUs do coerce others into cohabitation. All that can be said is that some units will trade autonomy for security or some other good, autonomy or subordination being but goods among others, although possibly 'superior' or 'inferior' ones, in Burch and Matthews's formulation. But no reason is given for this superiority; it is flatly stated. No argumentation or justification links the definition of minimal household units to the superiority of the 'household good' called 'privacy' or 'separate living' (autonomy); it is exogenously given.

Third, this model engenders a nonproblem and this, at the cost of inconsistencies within the neoclassical framework itself. Let me elucidate. Where I write that MRUs seek residential autonomy and resist cohabitation, neoclassical household economists (including Burch and Matthews) write of a demand (and supply) for 'household outputs'. If some might think it possible to translate the quest for residential autonomy into a 'demand for privacy' or for 'separate living arrangement', they have misunderstood both household economics and my set of axioms.

It could be jesuitically argued that the demand for any good could be innocuously translated as a resistance against another good (my desire for a car could be thought of as resistance to public transport, my desire for a fast car as a resistance to slow ones, and so on). Within the neoclassical model, however, one does not build equations (or utility functions) on the notion of 'resistance'. Goods are either superior or inferior, as the above quotations from Burch and Matthews testify, but no demand for a good can be rephrased as a 'negative demand for another (opposite) good'. Demand, by definition, must be either positive or equal to zero, but a 'negative demand' would make it impossible to draw utility functions. Accordingly, instead of 'resistances', neoclassical economists will write of a demand 'within budget constraints': if I do not indulge in fast cars, it could be accounted for in terms of my budget constraints. Thus, instead of a resistance to be overcome they perceive a demand oscillating from nil to complete satisfaction. Demand rises and falls, and the 'demand for separate living' appears to increase with the rise in real income. This is where the problem creeps in. Unable to explain the historical link between rising real income and the 'demand for separate living' in terms of their own set of axioms, some neoclassical writers summon 'changing tastes and preferences' to account for these long-term oscillations in demand. But tastes and preferences are exogenous to neoclassical analysis; as in collectivistic assumptions, their evolution has to be accounted for, and we are then led back to culturalist explanations.

Fourth, from the point of view of the comparative analysis of residential forms in time and space, such an approach is of little use. Confronted with the comparative and historical study of residence, and having to explain why we find this or that household composition as a limit of growth here or there, the microeconomic model has little to say because it has been designed to account for household variations within our own society. By deflating relationships of subordination and group membership to a simple demand for goods (including household status) by decision-making units, the microeconomic model is handicapped when it comes to accounting for variability in time and space (across regions).

Finally, the microeconomic model presupposes on the part of its units the ability to decide, assuming that they have a choice between autonomy and cohabitation, and implying that they could achieve autonomy but some-times prefer cohabitation because it maximizes their utility function given their budget constraints. This, however, rests on an underlying assumption, namely that those decision-making units (or Ermisch and Overton's MHUs) have the power to decide. Briefly stated, it leaves little space for constraints, save 'budget constraints' (and, as an economist has already demonstrated, 'budget constraints' mean nothing other than 'fair trading opportunities' – Tsiang 1966). In other words, they argue as if their MRUs can be residentially autonomous if they so choose; then the decision to cohabit will no doubt be made on mostly economic and psychological grounds. In other words, the economic model applies best to contemporary Western situations because these represent a very special case, one in which most hindrances to autonomy have been removed for a vast majority of minimal household units. The decision to coreside may be seen as a trade-off by some, and the maximization of a joint utility function by others (the two being but one and the same to most).

In brief, a microeconomic model presenting household status as a composite good already presupposes that the question to be answered is resolved: that in order to have a demand for that good, individuals must have choices made possible by a particular set of circumstances, namely those that have permitted the expression of residential autonomy. Then, and only then, can the question of coresidence in some cases be couched in microeconomic terms. In fact, we could generalize and conclude that the most sophisticated forms of household economics designed to deal with intergenerational, as well as intragenerational and gender inequalities and conflicts, will at best provide a marvellous tool to add to a sociological set of axioms. Finally, as it stands, my set of presuppositions applies to European residence only; when we modify the cultural elements, as we shall see below when studying Abutia, we will correspondingly see the axioms change; what appeared problematical no longer will, whereas 'self-evident' elements will become problematic. Household economics does not recognize such restricting conditions. No doubt it would acknowledge that the goods comprising 'household status' in various cultures will differ and that their demand will also display divergences from what is found in contemporary Europe. However, given those goods and a given demand, household economists would claim that the same set of axioms will explain residential composition elsewhere. In short, they believe their set of presuppositions to have universal validity, with only the goods and 'tastes and preferences' changing from one setting to the next. Where household economists believe to have in hand a set of axioms of universal applicability, I contend to have created one of very limited applicability. In different cultural contexts, different sets of corollaries would have to be inferred.

This answers my earlier question: no, household economists have not developed an atomistic set of axioms, and the above should help measure the distance between what I consider a sociological set of axioms and the presuppositions of household economists.

Annex

RESIDENCE, NO 'PRINCIPLE OF SOCIAL ORGANIZATION'

Many social scientists often refer to 'principles of social organization' but, to my knowledge, no one has really fathomed what they ultimately amount to. To appreciate what lies behind such a concept, let us quickly analyse Fortes's procedure (in which he is typical of social anthropologists).

When studying the Ashanti, a matrilineal society of central Ghana, Fortes discovered a rather bewildering variety of residential arrangements. Some spouses lived together and others, although married, lived separately (duolocal residence). Some duolocally married men coresided with their sisters and their sisters' sons, and some married women, together with their children, cohabited with their mother. These, however, represented only some of the possible permutations, and they patently rendered such labelling as 'patrilocal' or 'matrilocal' useless. To counter the difficulty, Fortes resorted to statistics, though not to calculate the 'statistically predominant type'; he used them in such a way that they pointed towards a developmental cycle.

Fortes already knew that domestic groups change over time. He perceived their transformations as an 'organic process' and used statistics in order to find correlations which would bring out the key 'structural principles' at work in this organic process. Starting with the idea that different domestic arrangements have to do with 'individual maturation', he sought to find out whether age, sex and household headship were in any way correlated, whether marital coresidence, sex and age also showed some connection, and if so, why? His tables did reveal eloquent patterns; from an epistemological point of view; however, what is most striking is the way in which he explained the correlations he found.

He studied two Ashanti villages, Asokore and Agogo. Noting for instance that 'Asokore men achieve the position [of household head] more readily than Agogo men at all ages', he explained this by *the greater strength of lineage ties at Agogo than at Asokore*' (Fortes 1949b: 14, italics added), a form of explanation he repeatedly used. He called these various 'bonds' and 'ties' created by marriage or matrilineal kinship 'factors' and wrote:

> One factor is the attainment of headship of a household, another is
> marriage and parenthood, a third is matrilineal kinship; and it can
> be suggested that the type of domestic unit found in a particular
> case is a result of the balance struck between the obligations of
> marriage and parenthood on the one hand and those due to matri-
> lineal kin on the other.
>
> (Fortes 1949b: 17)

His procedure, to say the least, is peculiar. Through their link with matrilineal descent groups, Ashanti domestic groups are directly influenced by
society at large. Seen from the individual's point of view, it thus appears as if
he or she is subject to a number of 'pulls' or 'bonds' throughout his or her
life, pulls which stem from the general norms of that society (i.e. marriage,
parenthood, kinship, agnatic descent, etc.), and which often act against one
another (as marriage and matrilineal descent allegedly do among the
Ashanti). The effect of these bonds, however, is not constant throughout the
individual's life. At various times they exert a different power of attraction
and thereby generate diverse domestic arrangements. This differential
attractional or gravitational strength is expressed quantitatively by some key
demographic parameters that indicate which stage an individual has reached
in his or her life cycle. Throughout Fortes's text, however, it is stated quite
clearly that those factors – in fact social ties or bonds – are in the final analysis only values and norms, which he eventually translates as 'structural
principles'. His 'structural principles' (marriage, residence, kinship) are
nothing but the 'principles of social organization' that he, and other social
scientists, use in other texts.

Thus, behind this or that residential arrangement, Fortes observes the
'principle of matrilineal descent' or the 'principle of marriage' at work. But
what are those 'principles'? His Ashanti study makes it quite clear (as do all
his other writings, and the writings of all anthropologists conjuring 'principles'): *they are but disguised norms* – the norms of matrilineal kinship, of
agnatic descent, of marriage, of affinity, and so on – acting to bring people
together to form groups. Hence their appellation – principles of *social organization* – something they achieve through the creation of social ties and
bonds. In brief, the procedure amounts to observing a given type of
grouping – lineage, domestic group, age group – and then inventing a 'principle' to account for its existence: the principle of agnatic descent, of
residence, of age, and so on. This procedure, exceedingly common in anthropological thinking, is unfortunately no explanation whatsoever. It reminds
one of medical arguments before Claude Bernard: one observed a cancer
(supposing that one then knew of cancers) and invoked a 'carcinogenic principle' to account for its existence! Need I quote Molière on the 'sedative
virtue' accounting for the power of sleep-inducing substances?

In other words, to declare residence a 'principle of social organization' amounts to stating that a norm operates to bind individuals who share a common dwelling-place together; from all the texts in which I have seen the notion of 'principle' evoked, I have never been able to find any other meaning. In this form, the statement amounts to a mere tautology and surreptitiously invites the type of thinking we uncovered behind collectivistic axioms. Norms are but one aspect of culture, and arguing in terms of norms (*juridisme*) does not seem to explain any more than debating in terms of Culture. Culturalism or *juridisme* are merely abstract restatements of observed phenomena and as such are void of any explanatory power.

This, to some (mostly postmodernists) might seem a dead horse to flog but, sadly, it is not so. As recently as 1989, Georges Augustins who, together with Emmanuel Todd, has emerged as one of the main French gurus on the comparative ethnography of Europe, published a book which has become the bible of French Europeanists, a book replete with explanations in terms of 'principles'. To account for the diversity of household composition in Europe, that is for regions of nuclear households, of stem families (what he calls 'House systems') and of multiple family households, Augustins has identified two antagonistic 'principles': the principle of residence and that of kinship. Where residence predominates we find the supremacy of the House; where it does not we find societies organized according to a kinship principle and trying to reproduce kindreds or lineages. Here and there the two principles strike a balance and explain some intermediary forms. Needless to say, the parallels with Fortes's 1940 article on Ashanti domestic groups are manifest in the manner of argumentation. The 'principle of residence' does not explain Western Pyrenean Houses any more than the 'principle of marriage' explains the coresidence of couples in Ashanti or a 'morbigenic principle' explains a given ailment.

In fact, one of the main culprits behind this evolution from a 'principle of residence' to 'House systems' is no one other than the greatest of the structuralist pontiffs, Claude Lévi-Strauss himself. As I have already mentioned, he elaborated on the theme of the 'House' and 'House societies' in a set of lectures at the Collège de France in 1976–7, and in 1987 Pierre Lamaison, himself co-author with Elisabeth Claverie of a minor classic on southwestern French 'Houses' (Claverie and Lamaison 1982) published an interview with Lévi-Strauss entitled 'La notion de maison' (Lamaison 1987; no pun intended here on his part, I presume). In the very opening lines of the interview, Lamaison emphasizes that Lévi-Strauss has 'introduced [in his teaching] the notion of "house" as an *organizing principle* to which a number of societies resorted' (Lamaison 1987: 34, free translation, italics added). The sin, needless to say, is not exclusive to French anthropologists, nor does it originate with Lévi-Strauss.

Finally, the relationship between *juridisme* and the use of juridical elements in an argumentation is homologous to the relationship between culturalism and the use of cultural elements in the explanation of social phenomena.

If a 'principle of residence' cannot explain the Béarn or Basque types of households, one nonetheless can (and has to) evoke 'juridical elements', such as the type of property and property devolution, to name but a few, when trying to account for the Béarn and Basque limits of residential growth. Summoning juridical elements, however, has absolutely nothing to do with *juridisme*.

Part II

ATOMISM APPLIED
Some paradigmatic cases

5

AN ATOMISTIC VIEW OF THE RUSSIAN MULTIPLE FAMILY HOUSEHOLD

Let us take our bearings. In Part I we saw how much collectivistic assumptions pervade the literature on family history and that, in the end, such assumptions lead to culturalist or juridist arguments. Having argued that residence does constitute a separate plane of social reality and that residential limits of growth are a legitimate focus of comparative analysis, I then sketched the main lineaments of an atomistic set of axioms.

In Part II, I wish to illustrate the heuristic value of this new set of axioms and, for this purpose, I shall apply it to both extremes: to societies with residential limits of growth which have been openly described as 'collectivistic' – namely nineteenth-century peasant Russia and the Western Pyrenees of the *Ancien Régime* until late in the nineteenth century – as well as to areas where the residential limit of growth has been universally described as nuclear and accounted for in 'individualist' terms – namely England and contemporary industrialized countries; for the latter, I have chosen Canada, from 1971 to 1986.

Introduction

Interestingly enough, the very first Russian authors who wrote about the multiple family household in nineteenth-century Russia did partly espouse atomistic premises.[1] Indeed, as we saw earlier, an impressive body of literature on the divisions of Russian peasant households reaches back far into the nineteenth century. By definition, those who wondered why those multiple family households elected to divide, perceived partitions as abnormal and sought to understand their rationale. From an epistemological point of view, their theoretical preoccupations are most informative.

Russian authors of that era saw a problem in household fission because, in their opinion, it flouted the most basic axioms of economic rationality (Frierson 1987: 45–6). In the severely impoverished world of the peasantry, larger households were the wealthiest, and to those authors it did not make sense to jettison economic security at the risk of economic destitution, to strike out on one's own.

A clear set of presuppositions thus guided earlier Russian understanding of household partitions, namely a view of Russian peasants as primarily economic actors who, given the economic benefits of larger households, should have wished to cohabit in multiple family households. In brief, they reckoned that economic conditions were such – in other words, economic hindrances were so powerful – that individuals should have lived in large and complex households, not out of choice but out of necessity, because residential division spelled economic doom. In better economic circumstances (which included a different political economy, to use an expression of Kertzer's – 1991) it could have made economic sense for households to divide. But in the Russian circumstances of the time it did not. Their underlying assumptions were thus unquestionably atomistic but their answer, paradoxically enough, was not. In fact, it reminds me of the manner in which 'formalist' neoclassical historians dealt with Franco-Québecois economic behaviour.

Without here delving into this topic at great length, it does seem that all formalist economic explanations face the same dilemma. Let us take Franco-Québecois agricultural history in the nineteenth century. I presented the neoclassical argument as if economic 'backwardness' stemmed from market imperfections only. In Quebec as in Russia, the economic reasoning follows similar, although inverted, paths. In Quebec, the more historians examined the facts, the more they realized that ease of access to markets did not differ markedly between Franco-Québecois and Anglo-Québecois. Faced with the inability of their model to account for the fact that individuals close enough to markets to commercialize nonetheless balked at commercialization, they called upon the most classical culturalist stereotypes: the French-Canadians were backward, obstinately and irrationally attached to their tradition (needless to say, 'tradition' = culture). Thus, when neoclassical explanations fail, its devotees seem prone to invoke a different explanation: individuals are also irrational, and this irrationality has to do with their cultural values. Nineteenth-century Franco-Québecois were thus still immersed in a peasant culture.

In their own way, the nineteenth-century Russian economists, agronomists and observers of the Russian peasantry reacted in much the same way, despite the fact that they argued the opposite. In their model, partitions eluded all economic rationality; they were irrational and, it seems almost inevitably, irrationality thrusts neoclassical economists towards Culture. In the Russian case it was no longer tradition, *but the new cultural values of individualism* fostered by the incipient capitalism. Furthermore, as I insisted earlier, if the economic irrationality of Russian peasants stemmed from this new set of values, this implies that there existed a different and opposite Culture prior to these developments: collectivism.

Whether irrationally traditional (French-Canada) or irrationally 'trendy' (peasant Russia), the mode of argumentation remains the same: we slide away from economic explanations to culturalist ones, pointing to a set of values (archaic or new) which interferes with economic rationality and accounts for the irrational.

After the Revolution, the USSR was long closed to outside research. When family historians were allowed back in, most marvelled at the size and complexity of Russian multiple family households in the eighteenth and nineteenth centuries, and tried to account for their existence.[2] Logically, household historians in the wake of Laslett should have adopted an atomistic, or at least an individualist, set of presuppositions, but many failed to. Consequently, the answers to this new question, 'Why the Russian multiple family household?' have wavered between relatively atomistic stances (Worobec 1991; Czap 1982, 1983) and collectivistic (culturalist) ones (Mitterauer and Kagen 1982).

This axiomatic dualism deprived the literature on nineteenth-century Russia of the clarity and unity of focus it deserves; and what I propose in this chapter is to unify the various points of view on pre-emancipation peasant multiple family households around atomistic assumptions. In this endeavour, I will have to ignore the important variations between different categories of serfs (proprietary serfs attached to a family's domain, state serfs, the Czar's serfs, and so on), and between various regions of Russia, and will write implicitly of proprietary serfs in the agricultural centre living in communes practising repartitional tenure. (In most pre-emancipation communes – *obshchina* – household heads – *bol'shaky*, singular *bol'shak* – formed an assembly – the *mir* – which had vast decisional powers on the running of the estate. As we shall see, they collected taxes, could decide collectively whether a given household could split or not but, above all, they redistributed the land allotted to them every so many years – from six to twenty-four years, depending on the area and on the demand – according to the changing needs of households, thus ensuring equality between the producer/consumer ratio in any given household, and the amount of land it was allowed to till and, admittedly, for which it was taxed.) Before broaching this topic directly, however, we must scrutinize one universal assumption underlying all writings on pre-emancipation peasant Russia, namely the notion of corporate household property.

Family or individual property?

When applied to the Russian household, atomistic postulates immediately run into a major hurdle. Although serfs possessed only usufructuary rights of their land, all authors consulted agree that the property over which serfs had control, namely all their movable property as well as the farmstead (*dvor*), was not individually owned by the head of the residential group (the *bol'shak*) but communally owned by the family, or the household (Aleksandrov 1979: 37–54, quoted in Czap 1982: 7; Czap 1982: 6–7;

Shanin 1972: 30–2, 221–2; Bohac 1985: 25; Worobec 1991: 43; Farnsworthy 1986: 55). If Russian peasants could be assured of equal access to land (through repartitions) and did not enjoy individual ownership of their possessions, there could hardly be any domestic superiority rooted in a privileged and differential access to property. The question is vital, and explodes any atomistic set of axioms if found to be true. We must therefore probe it carefully and ask, 'Did Russian peasants truly know of family or residential group property only?'

First, what are the facts supporting such a claim? Of the authors consulted, Shanin proved to be the most exhaustive and explicit, and I shall build my argumentation around his. He first contrasts what he calls 'family property' with both individual and collective property:

> The rights of a family member 'consist of participation in the use of family property'. Unlike private property, family property limits the rights of the 'head' or 'owner'. . . . Unlike collective ownership, the rights of each member did not consist of a share, but of participation in the group-ownership of the whole property. A member of the household has no rights to the profits apart from collective consumption. In decision-making, a member was not on equal footing with the head who, within the limits imposed by custom, ruled his household.
>
> (Shanin 1972: 221)

Second, he sees in the practice of premortem fission additional proof that Russian peasants lacked any concept of inheritance, and a further corollary of 'family property'.[3] Finally, the very fact that the *mir* (the assembly of household heads in the commune) could order a *bol'shak* (household head) removed and replace him by another male member of the same household would show that he was no owner, but a mere administrator of chattels that did not belong to him individually.[4]

Before tackling the question of property, let us clearly identify the group allegedly owning it. Some authors have isolated the family, others the household. To settle the question we will have to make a detour via the transmission of property to women. Again, all authors consulted on this topic maintain that daughters were endowed upon their marriage, call this endowment a dowry, and aver that this dowry excluded them from any other claim on the property of their natal household. With these statements I beg to differ.

First, the possessions a woman brought with her upon marriage mostly amounted to a trousseau, not a dowry. One year or more before her wedding, a young woman was freed from labour in the fields and allowed to fabricate most of the items that were to make up her trousseau. She might be endowed with a few more utensils or animals but, by Worobec's own account, that so-called dowry was very modest and composed of movable property only (1991: 62–3). Moreover, no document consulted clearly stated that the possessions added on to the trousseau came from the father or the mother. In fact, women were the only ones within a household entitled to their own individual possessions, both the ones they brought with them upon marriage, and those they acquired after through various nonagricultural activities. Furthermore, in true dowry systems the mother's dowry passes on to both sons and daughters; in Russia, it was transmitted to daughters only. These facts strongly suggest that women received next to nothing from their father, and that the personal belongings they brought into their husband's household came from their trousseau and gifts from their mother; to all practical intents and purposes, they were excluded from male property transmission within their natal residential group (Mitterauer and Kagan 1982: 128). To that extent, instead of the classical dowry system of European ethnography, we find a form of devolution more akin to what Goody described as an African one, namely a nondiverging, parallel, sex-linked transmission: women's property passed on to women, and men's property to men (Goody 1973; 1976).

Consequently, we can neither write of 'family property' nor of 'household property'. On the one hand the family (husband, wife and children) did not own anything in common; on the other, adult but unmarried women had no access to the property of the residential group into which they were born. In fact, if a group owned the *dvor* (farmstead) and its attached chattels, it was mostly the male agnatic core of the household;[5] the wives had some claims on their property if they had borne sons who grew up to get married themselves, but these were claims limited to their husband's property (not to the residential group's property as such). With this proviso we can now rephrase the question: Was there a 'male household patriline property' in peasant Russia, supposing that such a property was neither individual nor corporate, as Shanin openly asserts?

The answer hinges completely upon our understanding of property. In my opinion, property is individual, or joint (owned by husband and wife but contractually) though not corporate (that is, not forming an entity outliving the husband or the wife), or corporate. In other words, the fraction of Russian peasant property which has hitherto been identified as 'family/household' property was individually owned, or it was jointly so, or the 'male household patriline' formed a corporation. Shanin himself denies this patriline the title of corporation (where Shanin speaks of 'collective property' he should have more accurately spoken of 'corporate property'). But his main argument – the fact that the members of the male household patriline 'did not assume any definable shares of the property or the profits except in terms of rights to share in collective consumption' (Shanin 1972: 30–1), and that the male agnates within the household were not on equal footing (221) – actually refers to the wrong type of corporation, for corporations come in many guises.

For our immediate purpose, let us dichotomize and distinguish 'contractual', that is, modern-type corporations, from non-contractual ones (henceforth designated as 'nonmodern'); let us furthermore use joint-stock companies as our paradigm of contractual corporations. Members of such companies gain membership through the purchase of shares and can indeed claim their 'share' of the corporation's property when leaving it (when selling their shares); from the exclusive point of view of ownership, moreover, they are also on an equal footing (all shares are of equal value, despite the fact that some individuals might own different numbers of shares). But the majority of corporations studied by ethnographers ('nonmodern corporations') – and here I have in mind the African land-owning corporations that I myself studied – differ radically from contractual ones since their membership is automatically determined by birth and, in normal circumstances, can never be stopped.

For the sake of argument, let us call such a land-owning corporation a 'lineage'. We can say that a lineage member has inalienable rights to his lineage land, whether he works the lineage land or not. If he leaves his village or homestead for a long period of time, his rights will automatically be reactivated upon his return. In such a case it is truly impossible to speak of inheritance or devolution of property. The only property transmitted are those plots that an individual has cultivated, and the products of those cultivated plots. When land left fallow has returned to a state making it impossible to tell it apart from the surrounding forest, it is open for any one to till it again. In such a context, partition is a contradiction in terms, as is inheritance and, by extension, the possibility of disinheriting.

Furthermore, although in noncontractual corporations labour gives people truly individual property of the usufructuary rights of the plot they have farmed, and of the products that grow on it, ownership of the land as such by the lineage can never be understood in terms of labour. Whether one works it or not, whether one labours industriously or loafs around, his or her rights to the corporate land are exactly the same. Birth, and birth alone, gives an individual membership of that corporation, together with inalienable and equal rights to its land. Furthermore, a man who, with his lineage head's blessing, had moved out of the village where his lineage resides and may even have signed a contract never to come back, could not claim his share of the value of the lineage land. It is simply unthinkable.

If the Russian male household patriline had been a corporation, it would have recruited its members by birth above all else (because it is above all a patriline), and should display some of the features of an African lineage; in reality it does not in the least. If it is not corporate property, is it joint (contractual) noncorporate property, as when spouses conjointly own everything they acquire after marriage? Certainly not, since all texts on Russia make it quite clear that the couple owns nothing in common, and membership of the male household patriline is not contractual. We are therefore left with one conclusion, namely that the so-called family/household property was in fact individual, despite the fact that all authors concur in denying it. By inventing a notion of 'male household patriline property', however, they have created a category to which nothing corresponds in the legal sense because of their apparently restrictive conception of 'individual property'.

The Roman legal tradition truly knows of instances of 'absolute' individual property; simultaneously, it also knows of types of property which, although individually owned, cannot be used with unhindered freedom. Mortgaged property is a case in hand; is my house not individual property because it will revert to my mortgagee if I default on payments? Let us go even further. The land on which my house is built is 35 feet wide, but four of these feet form half of a driveway, the other half of which belongs to my neighbour. I have in my possession titles declaring me individual owner of this piece of land. In reality, however, my ownership is severely restricted by *servitudes* (the word is originally French, but English-Canadian property law has adopted it; it means almost the same as easement, although seen from the opposite perspective. I shall therefore adhere to the English-Canadian usage since the very term is quite eloquent, in that *servitude* in French also means 'complete dependence', or 'bondage'). I cannot park my car in this driveway without my neighbour's permission nor can I build anything on it because it would obstruct the passage leading to the neighbour's garage at the end of the driveway. Nor can I lease out or sell that piece of land separately. In other words, this part of my individual property is conditional in so far as it is *asservie* (bonded, that is, subject to servitudes) so to speak, and I cannot dispose of it as I wish.

Interestingly enough, this is the very argument that Shanin (and others) have used in order to invent the fictional category of family/household property: the *bol'shak* could not be 'individual owner' of the farmstead and its chattels because he (and sometimes she) could not do with it as (s)he pleases. This, however, only tells of 'conditional' or 'bonded' individual property, not of some kind of group property which is neither joint, nor corporate or individual, and eludes any definition.

Furthermore, how true is it that the *bol'shak* could not dispose of the property attached to the residential group he headed? Conditions certainly varied from one region to the other, and what obtained in the agricultural centre certainly did not in the north. This may tell of varying conditions of serfdom, and of nothing else. In the European north, Vlasova informs us,

> State land ownership . . . was characterized by a juxtaposition of state land ownership, hereditary usage, and free peasant disposition of plots. In towns along the Kama with state land ownership, from

the sixteenth to the first half of the nineteenth century, the heredi-
tary homestead system of peasant land use was combined with the
right of free disposal of homestead land.

(Vlasova 1991: 9)

To which Aleksandrov echoes:

In prerevolutionary and Soviet historical literature, one continually
encounters instances which show the right of serfs to dispose of the
lands within a commune and to pass on lands to the younger generation, to exchange plots, to partition the land when undivided
families broke up, to hand over lands as part of a dowry, to buy and
sell farmsteads and allotments, and to lease out lands. Attention was
also focused on the differing status in customary law of different
kinds of lands; thus taxed allotments were regarded by the peasant
sense of law as communal lands, while ploughed lands, cleared of
timber, were seen as individual possessions.

(Aleksandrov 1985: 17)

Did household heads always consult their subordinates before engaging in
such transactions? I doubt it. For instance, if the *bol'shak* and his wife lived
with young children and some other adults who were not linked to them
through filiation (adult nephews, for instance), I do not believe that the
bol'shak would have consulted the latter before deciding to dispose of the
property attached to the household. Even if a patriarch cohabited with two
married sons, he might have acted without consulting them if they did not
themselves have grown-up sons. In a different context, Farnsworthy reports
that 'A daughter-in-law in Ziuzinskii township in Moscow province charged
her in-laws with beating her but was informed that sons and daughters did
not have the right to complain against parents' (1986: 54). Would the *mir* or
a cantonal court, especially in the agricultural centre, have received more
kindly a son's complaint that his father had not consulted him before selling
or exchanging some of the property? I would argue that the *bol'shak* probably could act according to his own wishes most of the time as long as his
handling of the property did not threaten the household's survival, and if it
did not amount to mismanagement. In reality, sons' complaints of a
mismanaging father or *bol'shak* were heard and sometimes heeded, not
because of the sons' claim on the residential property, but because the
bol'shak's behaviour threatened the whole *obshchina* (commune). We will
come back to this point later.

It is nonetheless true that the *bol'shak* could not dispose whimsically of
his property because he was bonded, first to his sons, second to the *obshchina*.
But, again, the sons' claims were much more *asservis* than was the father's
ownership.

Behind the notion of 'male household patriline property' lies the idea that a patriarch could not dispose of the *dvor*'s patrimony because it belonged equally to his children, who enjoyed equal rights to their father's property because of the labour they invested in it. Their share would somehow have amounted to wages unpaid. This 'cultural' expression of peasant property, however, reveals only part of the picture. In fact, children were much less entitled to claim their share of the property than the father was to dispose of it, since the father could elect to give his sons their share *inter vivos* and allow them to create their own separate household, or to disown them if they moved out against his wish or regularly disobeyed his commands.

In other words, I believe that the sons' entitlements were much more conditional than the *bol'shak*'s claim to property. It would in fact seem that their relationship was contractual. What were the terms of the contract? First, to work (to invest labour), unless physically or mentally unable to do so; second, to obey the *bol'shak*'s orders; third, to remain a member of the household as long as the *bol'shak* wished. If he failed to abide by the rules of the contract, whatever the amount of labour he had invested in previous years, any male member of the household save the *bol'shak* lost all claims to the property attached to the residential group. The adequation between claims to property and labour input was thus severely conditional. And even the notion of equality must be qualified.

I have hitherto written of fathers when I should have written of the *bol'shak*'s sons. In fact, writing of equal rights in this 'male household patriline property' is also misleading. Let us imagine an elderly *bol'shak* with two married sons, the elder of which has three married sons, and the younger only one. In reality, these six individuals (excluding the *bol'shak*) did not have equal rights to the *bol'shak*'s property in pre-emancipation Russia (and quite some time after). His property would be divided equally *per stirpes*: the two sons of the *bol'shak* would divide their father's property in two equal parts after his death, but their children would enjoy equal rights only to their own father's property. In this instance, one of the grandsons (the only child) would eventually inherit half of the original property after his own father's death, and the others one-sixth only. If there was equality, it could not be in terms of labour input because partibility was generational, not based on mere household membership, although household membership was a precondition for males to have access to property.

Thus, from the very outset, a man's access to ownership was conditional upon cohabitation, labour and obedience. Once he had access to it he himself became a *bol'shak*, and was in turn bound to pass on his ownership to his children, who, like their father before them, were investing their labour in the property. Since his children were normally adults when he acceded to that status, they had already worked many years under their father's orders and could claim part of his property after his death, or before if he agreed to it. He could dispose of the property, but within bounds: first, the bounds imposed by his sons' claims in the name of labour input and, second, and perhaps more importantly, the bounds imposed by his responsibility towards the *obshchina* (commune). Here, needless to say, we are speaking of the *obshchina* in areas of repartitional tenure.

The servitudes towards the *obshchina* are too famous to be examined in detail and will be mentioned in the most summary manner. By imposing a poll tax in 1718 Peter the Great transformed peasant life. The tax isolated familial units, or *tiagly* (singular *tiaglo*) as 'tax-paying units', but landowners made the commune collectively responsible for paying the tax claimed from their estates. By so doing they made sure to get the tax-money, but they also created a powerful interdependence between households. If a 'familial unit' (*tiaglo*) failed to pay (and since most *tiagly* were themselves members of multiple family households within a *dvor* or farmstead, we will argue in terms of households), the other households of the *obshchina* had to bail them out. They were collectively penalized for the failure of any one *dvor* to meet its fiscal dues. Simultaneously, however, the *obshchina* controlled access to land since it could redistribute allotments according to the changing needs of the various residential groups and thus held extraordinary powers over its member groups; it could deny a defaulting *dvor* access to land, redistributing its plots to other solvent households.

This, in my opinion, was the most oppressive servitude – and here we should register some regional variations between the types of tenures, the types of serfdom, and even the types of payments, whether in corvée labour or quit rent. Other societies also practise partible inheritance (in the Balkans for instance), and in those societies a father has a moral duty to pass on to his sons (and in many cases, to his daughters as well) a property that they helped to exploit. These societies also exercise strong moral pressures against grossly incompetent fathers so that, statistically speaking, most sons do inherit a relatively equal part of their father's property. Some fathers nonetheless dissipate their estate and incur moral ostracism. In Russia, however, and especially in regions of repartitional tenure, pressures were more than moral. Against a completely unfit *bol'shak* the *mir* (assembly of household heads, or *bol'shaky*) could apply the sternest sanctions possible: it could replace him, or deny him access to land. This is why sons could appeal against a *bol'shak* and have him replaced, thus giving the impression that he was a mere administrator of some kind of 'male household patriline property'. Removing the *bol'shak*, however, does not prove any such thing. It merely shows that the *bol'shak*'s individual property was also conditional, that he could manage his own individual property if, and only if, he did not penalize other *bol'shaky* through his mishandling of property and his wastefulness.

Bonded it certainly was, but I submit that Russian peasant property was nonetheless individual, and the ultimate proof lies in the *bol'shak*'s unique power of disinheriting sons who did not honour their contract. This extraordinary sanction – which amounted to condemning a son to destitution if not death if the latter had no alternative means of survival – is impossible in a corporation based on birth, as is it in other areas of partible inheritance, such as in western France before Napoleon, and in France since the Napoleonic code. Admittedly, French fathers of the *Ancien Régime* in the west of France were freer to alienate their property during their lifetimes but, whether or not a son or a daughter was expelled from the house and was never seen again, he or she had an inalienable right to his or her share of the father's inheritance if the latter left any property after his death. In brief, the very possibility of disinheriting a son testifies to the individual nature of property, as does the existence of the testament in pre-emancipation Russia. Worobec mentions that the *bol'shak*

> sometimes prepared a written or oral testament to prevent quarrels over property divisions or to uphold the property rights of a wife, adopted or illegitimate son, or son-in-law. A will might prevent immediate relations from encroaching upon the heir's rightful share.
>
> (Worobec 1991: 44–5)

Furthermore, he was empowered to privilege a son who stayed on to look after him in his old age (Worobec 1991: 45; Shanin 1972: 222–3). In fact, Bohac's meticulous and enlightening work on strategies of transmission has revealed scores of unequal divisions (1985: 34–5), a further proof of the individual nature of the *bol'shak*'s property. Since there was individual property there could thus be a differential access to property within the household that placed one familial unit in a superordinate position vis-à-vis the others. This is all we need to go ahead with an atomistic interpretation of Russian multiple family households.

Atomism in Russia

When reanalysing my own Quebec data, I uncovered a number of features which inspired an atomistic approach: intergenerational conflicts, particularly between mother-in-law and daughter-in-law, the accusation that daughters-in-law bring about the ruin of households by pitting the sons against their fathers, and parents afraid of being left destitute by their heir should they transmit all control over the property *inter vivos*.

Interestingly enough, recent English-speaking writings on pre-emancipation Russian peasantry have unearthed the same themes, although immensely amplified (Czap 1982; Bohac 1985; Frierson 1987; Farnsworthy 1986; Worobec 1991), revealing constant fighting within that despotic mini-state (the household) and clear evidence 'that many peasants found these conditions nearly impossible to bear' (Czap 1982: 22, 24).

Looking at it from the point of view of the young married man, Frierson recognizes that the multiple family household 'was a setting in which he remained a subordinate long into his adulthood and which fostered frequent and unpleasant dissension' (Frierson 1987: 36, repeated on 37) leading to endemic intergenerational tensions (Worobec 1991: 7). This subordination, however, weighed immensely more heavily on the in-marrying wife, especially the wife of the youngest son (Matossian 1968: 18; Frierson 1987: 47). The daughter-in-law was sometimes sexually abused by her father-in-law (Matossian 1968: 18; Worobec 1991: 82, 205) and beaten by her mother-in-law.[6] The conflicts between mother-in-law and daughter-in-law were endemic and vicious, and arguments between women were the most often invoked to account for partitions (Worobec 1991: 80, 81; Frierson 1987: 46, 47). As in francophone Quebec, the daughter-in-law was also accused of dividing her husband from his natal family:

> Even Efimenko, a sympathetic student of the peasant women's life, concurred with the general opinion that the peasant wife was a persistent, nagging strategist who used every means at her disposal to break up the extended family of her husband. She stood at his ear, constantly reminding him of every injustice she suffered, and pointing out to him any disadvantage he experienced in his position as a junior male.
>
> (Frierson 1987: 46)[7]

Furthermore, those despotic parents also feared their children, like Quebec fathers. Despite the fact that some authors do not find any evidence of premortem fission (Czap 1982; Mitterauer and Kagan 1982; we will come back to this point later), Shanin considers it natural (1972: 223) and Worobec, observing that 'a strong cultural pattern of resisting premortem household divisions in favor of postmortem fissions persisted beyond the watershed of emancipation' (1991: 89), nonetheless finds ample evidence of premortem partitions. And where she espies premortem fission she also discovers the Quebec preoccupation with keeping a son at home to be looked after in old age,[8] together with the fear of being left destitute:

> In the event of premortem fission, however, a household head sought greater safeguards. While he too may have allotted one son a larger portion of the patrimony for old age care, he might also have drawn up a will or support agreement to ensure that his sons did not default on their obligations.
>
> (Worobec 1991: 57)

Furthermore, 'In premortem transfers of property peasants could not completely trust even their blood heirs, often having to resort to the legal guarantee of support contracts' (61).

These facts should logically have led to an atomistic approach of the Russian peasant household, but did not everywhere, and consistently. Why? Because writers on Russia still phrase the question in terms of the factors explaining partition. Be it Shanin, Bohac, Frierson or Worobec, they all seek in those tensions and conflicts the cause of household divisions, thereby unwittingly inverting the terms of the problem. Let us take just two examples among many. Writing about Manuilovskoe, Bohac submits that the 'inheritance system defined relations among household members and, at the same time, created the strains that led to household divisions' (1985: 28). Against such a thesis I would rather hold that such strains always existed in rural Russia because couples seeking residential autonomy were forced to cohabit, and that the inheritance system exacerbated tensions because it acted as one of the factors thwarting their secessionist aspirations.[9]

Also concerned with explaining partitions, Frierson comments:

> It was difficult, indeed, to identify obvious economic incentives for departure. The difficulty led many observers to point to a more nebulous set of incentives which usually fell under the phrase 'the urge for independence'. More than this 'urge', however, the tension of personal relations within the extended family headed the list of reported causes for the break-up of the household.
>
> (Frierson 1987: 46)

Frierson similarly puts the cart before the horse. There is nothing nebulous about the 'urge for independence'; it is but a corollary of the desire not to live in subordinate cohabitation. Younger generations had no reason to want subordination, and sought residential autonomy. But, for reasons already alluded to and further to be examined, their ambition was frustrated and they had to suffer subordinate cohabitation. The consequence, admittedly, could only be tensions. The tensions, the dissensions and the conflicts, if not the outright physical violence, thus resulted from a blighted yearning for autonomy. In this perspective, partitions do not need explanation. They should have represented the natural course of events and what begs to be explained, in contrast, is the fact that familial units tolerated subordinate cohabitation, together with the conflicts that it engendered, if not outright brutality. When couched in those terms the answer seems obvious, partly because most of the elements already pepper the literature, albeit lightly, and partly because I have already alluded to many of them.

If partitions should have occurred frequently, then, and if ideally every couple should have formed its separate household at marriage, if not too long after, what stopped them?

Explaining the Russian peasant multiple family household

In the Introduction I briefly mentioned some of the classical explanations of the multiple family household. Culture, or collective psychology (the two synonyms in such writings), proudly lead the list, normally described as some kind of collectivistic cultural configuration related to the need for 'secure family ties', as Haxthausen put it (Haxthausen 1972 [1837], quoted in Czap 1983: 105).

Next in line follow the various economic explanations, all of them revolving in one way or another around the idea that the more *tiagly* cohabiting, the more land and the richer the household (in areas of repartitional tenure, naturally). Thus stated, the argument is erroneous. If the *mir* distributed lands according to household size (taking into account the number of active producers), a household of fifteen people would not necessarily have had more land than three households of five people; it would have depended on its producer/consumer ratio. Whatever the type of distribution, however, it remains true that larger households would in general be wealthier because of the economies of scale that cohabitation makes possible. But such domestic economies of scale hold universally and have rarely led to multiple family households in Western Europe. They explain very little outside the more general political-economic context.

Among other factors, various conditions of 'political economy' have been mentioned here and there, without being articulated into a coherent set of axioms (in this respect, 'political-economic' factors are nothing else than factors of extraresidential coercion). In a different vein, Worobec has singled out partible inheritance:

> Through partible inheritance, or the providing of equal shares to all sons, and the exclusion of endowed children from a further share of the family property, Russian peasants were able to retard the breakdown of extended families into smaller units and secure their pension rights as aged parents. Until alternative institutions could be created, the traditional extended family household was destined to remain the focal point of Russian peasant life.
>
> (Worobec 1991: 42)

Elderly parents seek to 'secure their pension rights' the world over and have achieved it without creating multiple family households; as to partible inheritance, it is also found in areas of staunch neolocality (western France). Of all the factors adduced, however, this is nonetheless the one we shall start with. Indeed, if transmission is not only partible (*per stirpes*, let us remember) but equal and *divided after death only* (excluding transfers *inter vivos* to all practical intents and purposes), the sons can hardly leave home.

The question of equality, however, is a curious one from a Russian perspective. Indeed, it may be possible to divide a property into equal parts but it is less easy to justify this, especially in terms of labour input. In western France, where the children have all left home and created their own household by the time a father's or mother's property is divided, it is not difficult to understand that the children themselves demand equality, even if they do it out of sheer greed. But in the Russian case, circumstances were different. Given what we know of the Russian household, I would spontaneously suppose that married sons would rather have inherited less than a truly equal part of the parental property and left home to create their own household;[10] in other words, I would believe 'equality' in pre-collectivization peasant Russia to have been imposed by the older generations, not the younger ones. This, together with the adequation between equality and labour input,[11] would only be cultural expressions buttressing multiple family households.[12] Underneath these nice cultural expressions, however, lay a nastier reality.

Sons could not opt for a 'less equal' part and leave home because at least three mighty *intraresidential* factors militated against it. Frederic Le Play understood the Russian multiple family household in terms of patriarchal powers (Le Play 1877–9, vol. II: 66–7, quoted in Czap 1983: 105). He hit the nail on the head, I believe. I investigated the Russian peasant customary notion of property in some detail in order to show its individual nature and the manipulations it could lend itself to on the part of the *bol'shak*. As I have emphasized, the latter could disinherit a son, a deterrent powerful enough to keep sons at home since disinheritance was almost the equivalent of death, at least in the agricultural centre where no work outside agriculture could be found.[13] But the *bol'shak*'s powers extended much further: 'A father could . . . refuse a disobedient son's request for a passport to work outside the village . . . and, until 1874, threaten with military recruitment' (Worobec 1991: 213), a sanction most awesome since military service lasted twenty-five years, a quarter of a century of a *galérien*'s life; it literally robbed a young man of the best years of his adult life and condemned his wife to a life of utter wretchedness if he was married.[14]

The *bol'shak* thus wielded truly formidable powers, on a scale not known in the sternest stem family areas, let alone in the rest of Western Europe, some parts of the Balkans excepted. In themselves, these unique and overwhelming sanctions would have enabled him to coerce some, if not all, his sons into cohabitation and, as Le Play understood, they go a long way towards explaining the multiple family household. But they operated within a much more insidious context, which further deprived sons of any bargaining power.

I earlier pointed out the quasi-African type of property devolution in pre-emancipation peasant Russia. Worobec mentions that 'Dowries were deliberately modest, as was the case among Macedonian peasants, so as not to pose "a threat to the productive capital" of the receiving family' (1991: 63), a fact unfortunately overlooked in the literature. If the dowry barely existed from the eighteenth century onward, assuming that it existed at all, husband and wife could not bring together the 'conjugal fund' that Goody (1976) associated with diverging devolution, thereby depriving the couple of an important source of solidarity and bargaining power. Had they been united through a dowry, the couple might have represented a greater threat to the parents, and have had greater incentives and means to achieve their own autonomy. They were however denied this in the most radical fashion, since husband and wife were divided through the very modalities of transmission of property, the wife bringing in next to nothing and passing it on to her daughters, and the son being completely at the mercy of his father for any fragment of property.

Dividing their sons from their wives, the powerful Russian patriarchs could rule by imposing subordination through yet another means, namely the age at marriage. Hajnal long ago identified an Eastern European pattern characterized by early age at marriage and the near absence of celibacy (Hajnal 1965, 1983), two classical features of eighteenth- and nineteenth-century peasant Russia. In some areas, the age at marriage was actually among the earliest recorded for the Western world.[15] In Mishino (an agricultural centre) in the nineteenth century, 95 per cent of women had married before their twenty-first birthday and the mean age at first marriage for women rose 'from approximately 17.5 years in the late eighteenth century to approximately 18.2 years in the mid-nineteenth. The mean age at first marriage for men increased from approximately nineteen to twenty' (Czap 1978: 112). Mishino is not Russia, but it is most likely representative of predominantly agricultural redistributional communes of proprietary serfs in the agricultural centre and, in such instances, we can truly talk of teenage marriages, of individuals, men and women, who never had the opportunity to live any part of their adult life before marriage (118).

This singularly early age at marriage in the Western context helps to explain in part how this most oppressive patriarchal domination was maintained. Admittedly, it is somewhat frightening to strike out on your own if you are eighteen and married to someone your own age. At that level, the very early age at marriage in some areas of rural Russia played a dual role in the emergence and persistence of the multiple family household. On the one hand a teenage couple could temporarily seek the 'security of family ties' before setting off on its own. On the other, from the parental point of view, it was much easier to rule over a teenage daughter-in-law and keep her in a subordinate position, even at the cost of physical violence.

The young age at marriage, however, would only explain why newly married couples should wish to stay home for a few years. It would not have generated the incidence and complexity of Russian multiple family households, especially in their most extreme expression, namely those perennial multiple family households that Czap recorded in Mishino (Czap 1982). These astounding Mishino perennial multiple family households needed more than early age at marriage and postmortem equal-partible inheritance; they also needed the appalling sanctions that the *bol'shak* wielded, as well as the fact that women were almost denied access to the property of their household patriline. These, however, represented only the intraresidential powers of coercion. The extraresidential ones were equally powerful, if not more so. They belong to the realm of 'political economy' (Kertzer 1991).

From a political-economic point of view, the facts have already been mentioned. The 1718 poll tax and the fact that landowners held the *obshchina* collectively responsible for its payment engendered a number of economic and social consequences. First, the burden of taxation was such that no *tiaglo* alone, had it formed a *dvor* (and hence a nuclear household), would have been able to meet it. It has been calculated that every *tiaglo* needed two horses to carry its agricultural work (Bohac 1985: 25–6), as well as two active adult labourers. Anything less, and they would have had to default on their fiscal dues to meet their barest subsistence needs. Only economies of scale that large households permitted ensured that taxes could be paid. Hence the complete convergence between landowners (as well as agronomists[16]), the *mir* and individual *bol'shaky*. As Czap wrote, landowners forbade, or at least controlled, the divisions of households to make sure they reaped the maximum amount of taxes (Czap 1983: 122; see also Kosven 1963: 86; Semevskii 1903, vol. I: 210–11 quoted in Czap 1982: 12–13; Aleksandrov 1976, quoted in Czap 1982: 6; Worobec 1991: 36, 84–5).[17]

The *mir* also opposed partitions for similar economic reasons: their weaker members would not be able to pay their share, and the other members would be penalized. Furthermore, building new farmsteads (*dvor*) ate away at good arable land.[18] Finally, every individual household head faced the same dilemma: if he allowed partitions he would himself slide down the economic scale and might have difficulties paying his various taxes.[19] Anthropologists report that the fiercest advocates of clitoridectomy are old women who have themselves been through it. Similarly, one could submit that the fiercest champions of that mightily oppressive patriarchal household were those who had lived a life of suffocating dependence and subordination, and had finally and painfully made it to the status of *bol'shak*. It should also be remembered that these *bol'shaky* were the very ones who constituted the *mir*, the body responsible for deciding who had how much land and where, the body responsible for permitting or forbidding partitions.[20]

If we start from the premise, openly expressed by Worobec, that peasants sought to 'secure their pension rights' (Worobec 1991: 42) and that, failing monetization and any extraresidential organization to provide the care they would need in their old age, they would want one of their children to look after them at home; if we further assume that they do not want to be at the mercy of their children, and add onto this the factors we have just isolated, we should logically find almost perennial multiple family households coupled exclusively to postmortem transmission. Even after the *bol'shak*'s death we would not necessarily expect fission,[21] except that the new *bol'shak*, being a brother, would own only his part of the estate and lack vis-à-vis his brothers the sanctions their father could brandish.[22] If brothers continued cohabiting as a *frérèche* they would most likely have done so in terms of a relatively equal cohabitation, excluding outright subordination. But if there was fission, we would also predict to find what Bohac has discovered, namely that households remained complex after division for the economic reasons already mentioned (Bohac 1985; 33–4; see also Worobec 1991: 100).

It is against this background that we can best ponder over premortem partitions without confusing sets of axioms. If, on the basis of an exclusively atomistic set of presuppositions we find circumstances leading us to expect postmortem fissions only, we can truly puzzle at the fact that some individuals did succeed in triggering off premortem partitions. The answer would follow logically from our premises but would take us in the direction of an inter-regional comparative analysis. In order to account for the multiple family household, we have implicitly used Czap's data on Mishino, a truly extreme case of multiple family households actually precluding premortem fissions. But conditions varied considerably from one area to the other, and from one type of serfdom to the other. Some landowners did not interfere as much as the Gagarins (who owned Mishino) in the domestic life of their serfs;[23] other areas did not practise redistributional tenure, and the *mir* did not everywhere enjoy the same powers; some areas offered employment outside agriculture (in the industrial centre particularly),[24] and the age at marriage was not everywhere as early as in Mishino. Where any of those factors were relaxed we can anticipate, and we do encounter, premortem partitions. Their pattern, moreover, is equally predictable. Because of the great poverty engendered by an excessive burden of taxation, the residential groups created after premortem partitions could not afford to be nuclear and were also extended, if not multifamilial. Only after the emancipation did the pattern of residential reproduction start to change significantly. I say 'start' because most of the factors yielding multiple family households were still present, and in full operation (Hivon 1990).

From 1861 until collectivization, premortem fissions thus multiplied, nuclear households greatly increased in number, and the size of households dwindled, although the various regions did not react all at once and at the same pace. The more bargaining power the new circumstances gave the sons, the more accentuated the changes were.[25] In brief, the changes that the abolition of serfdom and increasing industrialization brought about are the very ones that an atomistic set of axioms would have predicted. Moreover, this nuclearization and this reduction in the size of households did not tell of increasing individualism in the context of a collectivistic culture; they told of the fact that the constraints and hindrances that stood in the way of families' residential autonomy were being slowly removed, or relaxed, for whatever economic, demographic or political reason. Cultural explanations then emerged to crown the changes.

6

AN ATOMISTIC VIEW OF VARIOUS STEM FAMILIES

When dealing with Russian multiple family households, I have set aside the question of variability, ignoring any possible comparison between Russia and the Balkans, for example. Many reasons have inspired this decision. First, I have chosen these examples for their paradigmatic value. When analysing multiple family households (excluding the stem family and, by definition, including as a limit of residential growth the coresidence of more than one married son with the parents), it would be relatively easy to demonstrate how changes in the circumstances creating intra- and extraresidential hindrances or coercion would affect the timing and frequency of premortem and postmortem fission, as well as the timing of the development and reproduction of residential groups. Second, it appears that all multiple family households of the Russian type share one feature: in all instances, be they from Eastern or Southeastern Europe, the vector of power relationships seems always to flow from the older to the younger generations (except in the rare cases of 'deposed' *bol'shaky* and, where postmortem fission is delayed, in instances leading to the creation of *frérèches*). This, as we shall see, changes radically when contemplating so-called stem families.

Introduction

I have already emphasized how collectivistic the ethnology of Quebec and Western Pyrenean stem families was, although, if collectivism varies in degree, the Western Pyrenean ones would seemingly surpass any other. Indeed, no ethnographer of Quebec ever suggested the existence of the House as a land-owning corporation. In this, and in many other respects, Quebec and the Western Pyrenees could not be more different, so much so that one might wonder whether we should include them within the same taxon.

From around 1820 to around 1950, rural francophone Québecois transmitted most of their land intact to a single heir; they ruled out the cohabitation of two couples of the same generation but allowed residential groups to grow to the stem family level. There, however, the similarities with the Western Pyrenees end. The French pioneers who settled in Canada came from the north and west of France, and adopted the *Coutume de Paris*; they did not give their daughters dowries. In the nineteenth century, these Québecois did not choose as heirs a son of a particular rank in the group of siblings (neither primogeniture nor ultimogeniture), nor did they transmit land to daughters, even in the absence of sons. Furthermore, the parents should not be regarded as mere trustees of lands to be passed on to following generations; rather, they owned the property individually. Throughout their history, the Québecois were never obsessed with keeping a name attached to patrimonial lands, or to keeping a 'stem' grafted onto a named House. Land could be, and was, alienated. In fact, the Québecois did not show great attachment to their land, nor did they identify with any patrimonial property (or with a House). As a result, matrimonial strategies also differed: earlier age at first marriage for both sexes; lower rates of definitive celibacy; and larger family sizes. Moreover, men never married heiresses (there were none) and never left home to live with their wife's parents at marriage (the so-called French *mariage en gendre*, or uxorilocal marriage). Finally, the heir expelled his celibate adult brothers after the father's death if they were still living at home.

The dissimilarities do not end there. There is clear evidence that well into the eighteenth century land was transmitted undivided to one child, although all children inherited an equal part of its value. The child who took over the land thus accepted a mortgaged property, in that he or she had to compensate his or her siblings for their share of the inheritance, a process that could take up to twenty years (Dechêne 1972). The other siblings started clearing up new lands, or purchased lands partly deforested, and cleared up larger areas.

On the basis of this evidence and of other historical facts, I have argued elsewhere that no stem limit of residential growth was to be found in rural Quebec before the 1820s or 1830s, and that Quebec stem families arose partly because agriculture itself became threatened in some areas; more specifically, it became difficult to recruit new generations to agricultural pursuits, as increased opportunities for employment outside agriculture (in lumber camps, in the growing cities and the United States) lured many sons away from farming (Verdon 1987). As many sons displayed a greater predilection for nonagricultural occupations, fathers sought to keep at least one of their sons on the land by bequeathing the greatest part of the property to him, while nonetheless helping all their other sons to settle on the land if they showed a sincere interest for agricultural production. By the middle of the nineteenth century, however, many lands were burdened with debts and most farmers would have had to own in excess of one hundred acres of land to transmit landed property to more than one son. To keep younger generations on the land, fathers turned to preferential transmission to a single heir. The other sons inherited much less, and the daughters rarely brought more than a trousseau at marriage.

In fact, there is no evidence that stem families were then to be found as residential limits of growth throughout the whole of agricultural rural Quebec; unfortunately, the evidence on this topic is still very scarce. Finally, we must introduce further distinctions within agricultural rural Quebec itself, even in areas where stem families existed. Throughout rural Quebec, the same settlement pattern prevails: nucleated areas, called 'villages' (where artisans, professionals and retired farmers lived), are surrounded by the *rangs*, or areas of long, narrow strips of land divided by roads, with farmsteads positioned on both sides of the roads. In the *rangs*, a neighbour might live across the road, but none was to be found on the same side for a distance of five hundred to one thousand feet. The habitat was dispersed.

In the nineteenth-century *rangs*, every household was engaged in agriculture; if any household grew to a stem family level, it was in the *rangs* and the *rangs* only. In the village, matters differed considerably. There, no land was passed on, only the house and moveable property. Consequently, the older practice of equal partible inheritance continued to be applied – with one major difference: everyone would try to convince one of the daughters to remain celibate (she would often be a schoolteacher) and stay with the parents to look after them in their old age. In return for her services, she would inherit the house and a greater part of the furniture, and her siblings might help her out financially after the parents' death if she did not earn enough for her own keep.

Also, in the village, many sons married before they had amassed the wherewithal to start a separate residential group, and stayed on with their parents for a few years, until they had a first child, or until they had amassed enough money, or until the next sibling got married. In short, many married sons lived with their parents (and occasionally with the parents of their wife) for a short period of time before asserting their residential and domestic autonomy. If one took a snapshot of the composition of village households, many would have appeared multifamilial, showing all the external appearances of stem families. Yet, a close look at household development and reproduction in the village reveals that the limit of residential growth never reached a stem limit. This takes us back to the notion of 'region' I suggested earlier; we cannot speak of a stem limit of residential growth for Quebec, not even for rural Quebec, but only for the *rangs* within rural Quebec.

If we provisionally assume that impartible inheritance is intimately connected to land scarcity in the Western Pyrenees, the relationship between household composition and transmission of land obviously diverges between the two regions. Also, strictly speaking, residential groups in Quebec and the Western Pyrenees did not share exactly similar limits of residential growth. Where does all this lead us?

When discussing the Russian multiple family household, I have arbitrarily assumed that a single limit of residential growth predominated throughout the whole of pre-emancipation peasant Russia. But, as I have also emphasized, living arrangements differed over rural Russia, and a detailed comparative analysis would undoubtedly unearth slightly varying limits of residential growth. What matters, however, is that the same important core probably lodged at the heart of every limit of residential growth, a core encompassing the couple formed by the parents, as well as those formed by the married sons. The differences would easily be explained away by variations in the intraresidential and extraresidential factors already identified, as well as by others which have escaped my notice.

The same could be said about the Quebec and Western Pyrenean stem families. In fact, whether the heir or heiress allows or forbids celibate brothers to coreside, whether sons marry uxorilocally or not, these variations are easily explained. For instance, no male Québecois would marry uxorilocally because he could always clear his own land or leave agriculture altogether to work in lumber camps or in town. The same circumstances explain why heirs would not tolerate the cohabitation of their adult celibate brothers after the parents' death.[1] Similarly, the availability of land also lessened the economic burden of raising a much greater number of children, especially among French-speaking Québecois who wanted to spread as widely as possible.

Beneath all these dissimilarities, however, one fact stubbornly remains: until recently, in both the Western Pyrenees as in much of the south of France and in agricultural parts of French-speaking Quebec, an heir or heiress did not wait until the death of the mother or the father before bringing his or her spouse into the parental house. In all these areas – as in all those in which 'stem families' have been reported as a limit of growth – we also find various forms of impartible inheritance, or at least strongly preferential transmission to one heir or heiress. This, in my opinion, delineates a core of related phenomena which demarcates a sufficiently clear category to warrant comparative analysis. Ironically enough, the major taxonomic schism dividing our typology is not the one separating Quebec from the Western Pyrenees, but one that dwells within the apparently monolithic category of 'Western Pyrenean House systems' itself. Before bringing it to the surface, however, I shall continue arguing with the (now) classical view of a rather homogeneous 'Western Pyrenean House system' (let us call it the 'new orthodox' view), in an attempt to find out whether the atomism I espied in Quebec also plagues this most collectivistic type of stem families.

Many problems vitiate the new orthodox view of the Western Pyrenean stem families, three of which should be mentioned before proceeding with the analysis. First, as is the case in the Alps (convincingly demonstrated by Viazzo 1989), the standard view of Western Pyrenean House systems is derived from the study of upland communities exclusively engaged in agropastoralism. As it happens, both the Pyrenees and the Alps comprise low as well as high valleys, and the westernmost tip of the Basque country borders the sea. Of these areas little, if anything, is said.

Second, the very authors responsible for this new orthodox view never really worked in the Western Pyrenees as such; they studied villages from the *Baronnies des Pyrénées*, either in Bigorre or in areas bordering Bigorre, in what is now known as the *Département des Hautes-Pyrénées* (Central Pyrenees), whereas the Western Pyrenees belong to the *Département des Pyrénées-Atlantiques*. The Pyrénées-Atlantiques comprise both the Béarn (of Gascon origins) and the Basque country. Admittedly, the Baronnies have much more in common with the Béarn, to which the Bigorre was annexed in 1425, than with Pyrenean areas to the east. But, to my knowledge, Bourdieu's very incomplete article of 1962 remains the major new orthodox statement on the Béarn itself. Nonetheless some of the ethnohistorians-cum-historical demographers who worked in the Baronnies, paramount among whom stands Augustins, write as if they dealt with the Western Pyrenees, and sometimes the whole Pyrenees (Augustins 1986, 1989). This cannot but create some distortions since the Eastern Pyrenees are characterized by Roman law, giving fathers the right to make wills, as well as by a greater proportion of large estates. The western part of the chain, on the contrary, is famous for its *Coutumes*, that is, its codified customary law establishing primogeniture, absolute or male, and supposedly banning *cadets/cadettes* marriages, thereby forbidding the creation of new Houses; furthermore, the greatest majority of Western Pyrenean Houses own very little property, according to Soulet (Soulet 1987: 317). Despite this mingling of geographical perspectives, we will sometimes have to rely on work done in the Baronnies to argue about the Western Pyrenees.

Third, French authors writing on the Baronnies have been more concerned with ethnohistory than straightforward ethnography but, set against the work that Netting and Viazzo achieved in the Alps (Netting 1981; Viazzo 1989), their time series appears strangely dichotomized. All authors write of the demographic explosion which characterized the first half of the nineteenth century (a growth followed by a massive exodus in the second half of the century, and well into the twentieth century), but most nonetheless assume a kind of homogeneous *Ancien Régime* with a demographic pattern and social-organizational features going back for centuries.[2] Needless to say, in the light of Viazzo's brilliant reanalysis of Alpine data, this kind of 'timelessness' before the French Revolution is most debatable, but in the study of the Pyrenees the tools to dispute it seriously are missing. In other words, variations both in time and space are not often treated with the detail necessary to achieve a picture comparable to that of Netting (1981) for Törbel, or Viazzo (1989) for Alagna, not to mention a host of other authors on the Alps.

Atomism in the Pyrenees

Interestingly enough, the very literature responsible for the collectivistic representation of the Western Pyrenean House is replete with considerations unconsciously betraying atomistic postulates. In his introduction to *L'organisation de la famille* (the initial and classical statement on the stem family) Le Play argued that France could reinstate social order and stability by preserving the stem family, something it could achieve only by restoring full authority to fathers, an authority they had lost when they were refused the right to dispose freely of their property (Le Play 1907: xx–xxiii). By linking paternal authority to testamentary freedom, Le Play acknowledged that fathers used economic sanctions in order to keep children at home. He was quite explicit on the subject:

> Of their adult children, parents associate with their authority the one they believe most apt to execute with them the work of the family and to perpetuate it after their death. In order *to keep him with them* [italics added] and to make him accept a life of dependence and duty, they appoint him *heir* [italics in the original] of both the house and the workshop.
>
> (Le Play 1907: 29–30, free translation)

The message could not be more clear: if parents have to *keep* (*retiennent*, literally 'hold back') their son by handing over to him most of the patrimonial property, adult children must naturally seek to leave home and its life of dependence and duty. Adult children must resist cohabitation with the parents (implicitly a subordinate cohabitation) and, to stay home, they must need an incentive that can overpower their resistance; parents need to wield simultaneously both an incentive and a sanction. Before the Napoleonic Code they found this carrot-cum-stick in the ability to transmit a greater share of the family's wealth to one child (in French, also known as *héritage préciputaire*; for want of a more adequate term, I shall write of 'preferential transmission'). The ability to prefer a child might overcome the natural tendency to residential autonomy, and ensure that their heir fulfilled his or her responsibilities to parents and siblings. This is straightforward atomistic thinking.

Furthermore, Le Play acknowledged that tensions within families were increased on the arrival of the daughter-in-law. Wondering at the custom of 'absolute primogeniture' in France, he observed: 'the community and cohabitation are firmly maintained through successive generations. This great principle can be observed all the more easily by instituting heiresses, *thereby obviating in the most natural manner conflicts between mothers-in-laws and daughters-in-law*' (Le Play 1907: 101, free translation, italics added).

This same atomistic thinking also permeates contemporary ethnography.

In order to account for absolute primogeniture in the village of Esparros in Bigorre, Antoinette Fauve-Chamoux repeated Le Play's arguments: in-marrying sons-in-law ensure peace within households because 'between mother and daughter problems do not rankle' (Fauve-Chamoux 1993: 41), an explanation which Rolande Bonnain also invokes to explain the existence of heiresses in other parts of Bigorre (Bonnain 1986a: 170). Bonnain also remarks that mortality rates fell in the nineteenth century, as did the age at marriage of women marrying heirs. And yet, the age at first marriage of heirs remained the same. Why? Because, Bonnain explains, 'The mothers, still alive because of longer life expectancy, do not seem in a hurry to welcome a daughter-in-law into the house' (Bonnain 1986b: 98, free translation).

More generally, however, the very themes that I recorded in Quebec are echoed in the literature on the nineteenth-century Pyrenees (Soulet 1987: 385), on the Spanish Basque country (Douglass 1975: 40), and even on the Béarn of the *Ancien Régime* (Zink 1993). Everywhere we read of daughters-in-law fuelling hostilities within households and precipitating the ruin of Houses (on such implicit atomistic postulates in contemporary ethnography, see also Poumarède 1972: 313; Fine-Souriac 1977: 484; Bonnain 1986b: 98, 1986c: 134; Augustins 1981: 54).

Parents who mistrust their daughter-in-law also fear ill-treatment, especially when the son/heir has made a bad matrimonial choice. In one way or another parents seek to protect themselves against the heir himself and against the in-marrying spouse because they feel threatened, a threat mostly related to the known perils of cohabitation and property devolution; indeed, parents are well aware that they can keep the heir in subordinate cohabitation only as long as they retain control over the property. This fear is very real, especially when the parents are weakened by age:

> In some instances the ageing parents suffer persecutions clearly aiming at shortening their lives. Considered a nuisance they are insulted, ill-treated and sometimes eliminated. Such crimes can easily be concealed, given the old age of the victims and the fact that family affairs remain under the seal of the utmost secrecy.
>
> (Soulet 1987: 418, free translation)

From a series of studies carried out mostly in Provence, Languedoc and the Gévaudan, André Burguière draws the same conclusion (Castan 1971; Castan 1979; Collomp 1983):

> Studies on criminality in southern France in the eighteenth century have shown the extent to which the institution of the single heir, instead of bringing harmony and stability in the family, as Le Play had believed, maintained a climate of misunderstanding which

sometimes led to violence: misunderstanding and rivalry between brothers, resentment of the younger siblings sacrificed by an unjust father but, mostly, *the one that led to the greatest number of crimes, the misunderstanding born out of the cohabitation between the parents and the couple formed by the heir.*

(Burguière 1986: 647, free translation, italics added)

From Provence to the Western Pyrenees, distrust leaves its indelible mark on cohabitation within these allegedly collectivistic Houses. Parents look for support in old age but expect to be treated roughly, if not eliminated. They fear the baneful influence of the daughter-in-law, capable of causing the House's downfall. Bear in mind the Quebec message: cohabitation is problematic and, if it is, the stem family (as a residential group) cannot squarely be subsumed under a set of practices apparently systemic and designated as 'House systems'. From the available evidence, younger couples in this part of the world coreside with their parents because they are coerced into it, and resent both the cohabitation and the subordination. The Western Pyrenean Houses make sense only within the same set of atomistic assumptions that accounted for the Quebec stem family. The closer we examine the facts, however, the more imperative it becomes to question our own typologies.

A major typological divide

Indeed, such fear and distrust harboured by parents towards daughters-in-law seems to have characterized household life in the Béarn and to have been relatively unknown in the Basque country, especially in the eighteenth century (for this part of my argument, my sources are limited to Anne Zink's book on the Béarn and the Basque country – Zink 1993). This extraordinary fact, overlooked by ethnographers keen to accept the compelling logic of 'House systems', has recently been reported and substantiated in Anne Zink's masterful *L'héritier de la maison*, the most definitive analysis of family and devolution laws in the *Ancien Régime* in southwestern France. In fact, the contrast extends to a host of other features which Anne Zink mentions but fails to bring together. When collated, these many differences reveal a strangely systemic architecture which strongly challenges typologies (see Table 6.1). Before tackling this question, let us reflect once more upon the notion of corporate House property.

The argument in favour of corporate House property in the Western Pyrenees repeats many of those we have come across in our study of Russian households. The heir, so the argument goes, did not own the household patrimony individually (the patrimony included the dwelling and all the buildings, chattels and lands attached to it). He or she enjoyed usufructuary rights only, unable to alienate any part of the so-called *biens avitins*

Table 6.1 Main differences between *Ancien Régime Béarn* and Basque practices in matters of family and inheritance laws

Béarn	Basque country
Male primogeniture	Absolute primogeniture
Subordinate cohabitation	Equal cohabitation
Heir > in-marrying spouse	Heir = in-marrying spouse
Male in-marrying spouses less numerous	Male in-marrying spouses = female in-marrying spouses
Dowries: sons' > daughters'	Dowries: sons' = daughters'
Dowries: money > stocks	Dowries: stocks > money
Contractual institution of the heir	Binding by the dowry
No incompatibility clauses	Incompatibility clauses
Compulsory cohabitation	Optional cohabitation
No 'co-lordship' through dowry	'Co-lordship' through dowry
Heir can alienate part of the *avitins* because: • can sell one fourth • there is also a limited 'reserve'	Heir cannot alienate part of the *avitins* because: • cannot sell any part • no 'reserve'
Hence individual property of House head	Hence corporate property of parents and married heir(ess)
In-marrying spouse deprived of any right to the *acquêts*	*Acquêts* held in joint estate by the two spouses
Spouse rarely universal heir	Spouse often universal heir
Widowed in-marrying spouse has no right to the House's patrimonial property	Widowed in-marrying spouse has strong rights to the House's patrimonial property
Daughter-in-law distrusted	Daughter-in-law not distrusted
Men marry later than women	Men and women both marry younger than in Béarn, age difference between the two is less

Source: Zink (1993)

(the *biens avitins* encompassed all those possessions that had been transmitted within the House over at least three generations and which, in principle, even the heir(ess) could not alienate – although the inflexibility of this practice varied from one region to another, as we shall see). In fact, if he or she did have to alienate them in extreme circumstances, the heir(ess) could only do so with the consent of his or her own heir(ess)-designate. He or she had to transmit to his or her own heir(ess) apparent, ideally whole and undivided, what he or she had inherited. In other words, the House head and his or her own heir(ess) apparent would have been co-owners of the same patrimony.

Impartible inheritance and the existence of *biens avitins* do suggest the existence of corporate property but, if we provisionally exclude the Basque country, the case may not be as convincing as it might initially appear. In Béarn, as long as the House head lived, the heir(ess)-designate had no say about transactions regarding House property, and I can hardly imagine a teenage heir(ess) apparent opposing his or her parent's decision to alienate some land. Poumarède also writes that House heads were empowered to alienate *biens avitins* in extreme circumstances, but that lands thus sold would remain subject to the *retrait lignager* (Poumarède n.d.: 37). Augustins mentions that dividing the property was used as a last resort to compensate the younger siblings (Augustins 1981: 52). Moreover, if the House head and his or her heir(ess) formed a corporation, it involved them only, since in-marrying spouses possessed their own dowries, and the younger siblings who did not marry an heir or heiress got next to nothing, a pittance which nonetheless was their own individual property.

Let us therefore look at the relation between the House head and the child to whom he or she would bequeath the patrimonial property. If they formed a corporation, it could only be a noncontractual one and, in such a case the House head could never have disinherited his or her own child (the heir(ess)-designate). Although the greatest majority of designated heirs duly acceded to the status, the House head was actually empowered to disinherit an heir(ess) (on the power to disinherit, see Soulet 1987: 349, 412). Indeed, if the heir(ess) apparent was physically or mentally incapacitated, if he or she made a wrong matrimonial choice (one not approved by the parents), or opted for residential autonomy after marriage, he or she would have lost any claim to heirship. Furthermore, House heads could in fact dispose of part of the *biens avitins* and, in cases of extreme necessity, could alienate yet larger portions of the patrimony than permitted by the *Coutumes*. In my opinion, we are once more confronted with a case of bonded individual property (the Basques excluded, let us remember). In Béarn (and also in Bigorre), therefore, patrimonial property appears to have been bonded or conditional, but nonetheless individual, property. To understand better the logic of those practices, let us turn to Anne Zink's book.

We have already mentioned that Poumarède, one of the foremost authorities on property and family law in southwestern France, held that all Western Pyreneans practised absolute primogeniture (inheritance by the eldest, regardless of sex) five or six centuries ago (Poumarède 1972). In Béarn, absolute primogeniture had been replaced by male primogeniture relatively early (1538 according to Etchelecou – 1991: 20). Daughters inherited only in the absence of surviving sons. Heirs were formally appointed upon their marriage, through a marriage contract (the literature refers to 'contractual appointments') but the contracts did not include any 'incompatibility clauses' (clauses specifying what will obtain should the two couples be so incompatible as to make cohabitation impossible), as we shall find in the Basque country. I would argue that this was the consequence of parents retaining full control over the administration of the property until their death, despite the fact that the heir was *de jure* owner, thus making their relationship to the heir(ess)-designate fundamentally unequal (Zink 1993: 51, 189).

Towards their patrimony, including the *biens avitins*, Béarn fathers enjoyed a freedom unknown to the Basques; they could indeed alienate up to one-fourth of the *biens avitins* without asking any permission and could in general use the patrimonial property in a manner unthinkable in the Basque country (Zink 1993: 189, 389, 483). They wielded full power over the House property and the heir would be left empty-handed (and disowned) if he or she decided to live separately. Through their full authority over the inheritance, Béarn fathers could thus brandish formidable economic sanctions to impose coresidence, making cohabitation unequal.

This inequality between the coresiding couples also affected the relationship between heirs (or heiresses) and in-marrying spouses. The latter retained the right to their own dowry should the marriage terminate without issue but they were deprived of any rights to the property acquired after marriage (the so-called *acquêts*). Moreover, they were denied any share of the property of the House and, once widowed, could only claim their dowry. When the heir(ess) of the senior generation died, his or her *potestas* passed on to the junior heir(ess) whose position then rose above that of all in-marrying spouses (including his own mother in the case of an heir, or her own father in the case of an heiress inheriting from an heiress), and he or she could evict all widowed in-marrying spouses (hence his own mother in the case of an heir, or her own father in that of an heiress). Since in-marrying widows of the senior generation were completely at the mercy of the young couple of the heir or heiress, most Béarn wills (not marriage contracts) included clauses to protect them (something unheard of in the Basque country). Finally, this inequality between spouses extended to sons and daughters; since boys married in more rarely, they were more generously endowed than girls (Zink 1993: 223).

Inequality between the sexes, between the spouses within the conjugal unit and between couples within the household, imposed and subordinate cohabitation of the younger couple – all this seems very coherent (see Table 6.1). But why? Why should the Béarn parents have distrusted their daughter-in-law when the latter brought in less money and occupied the most subordinate position, inferior both to her husband and to her parents-in-law? Why should she have represented a threat? We could propose the hypothesis that the Béarn father did not tolerate residential separation for fear of his own heir(ess). But why fear him or her, and why especially be so wary of daughters-in-law who were at the bottom of the pecking order?

Some kind of perverse logic would appear to have permeated Béarn practices. For some reason, the Béarnais had erected a structure of inequality and this strong hierarchical order instilled mistrust of all underdogs. Daughters were the least endowed, in the family hierarchy daughters-in-law were pushed down to the bottom of the hierarchy, and they inspired the greatest suspicion because they had real reason to dislike their in-laws. Those in power in the senior generations feared that the very persons whom they confined to the lowest position would rebel; the unquestioning subordination exacted and firmly maintained through the control of the patrimonial property were simply ways of nipping in the bud the slightest thought of revolt. But that rebellion, however latent it was, necessarily lodged at the very heart of such a system, creating the vicious circle of this 'logic of inequality'. But why such inequality? I shall hazard a conjecture after reviewing the eighteenth-century Basque case.

If slightly diverging limits of residential growth distinguish Quebec from *Ancien Régime* Béarn stem families, I nonetheless believe that these differences can be accounted for relatively easily. Beyond their differences, the two types of stem families shared the same pivotal core: the coresidence of two families linked through filiation, i.e. the parents-owners and the heir-designate (and occasionally the heiress in Béarn). At the same time, and this is of equal importance, *the power configuration between the two families (or MRUs) displayed the same vector*: subordinate cohabitation, a subordination presumably more severe in the Béarn because the Béarnais of yore lacked some of the economic alternatives, such as the choice of clearing new land, that Québécois enjoyed from the very beginning. This would explain why the subordination within Béarnais Houses was more oppressive than in Quebec stem families. Quebec fathers maintained their own superordinate position to the end, but too authoritarian a father would have found no son to take over the estate. Quebec heirs had a certain bargaining power which inhibited a more oppressive subordination of the Béarn type, although the father retained a powerful sanction through his power over the inheritance. In both regions, heirs thus lived a subordinate cohabitation. But why insist on coresidence?

The answer is to be found in our set of axioms. I have already suggested that we can plausibly suppose that residential autonomy spelled domestic autonomy (see above, p. 57). If this is so, the Béarnais parents would have committed a major mistake by allowing residential separation. Indeed, if they maintained inequality throughout individual and MRU relationships;

if they expected care in old age from economically subordinate MRUs, they could only achieve it by ensuring domestic subordination. If residential autonomy rules out domestic subordination (by establishing domestic autonomy), Béarnais parents would have run the risk of being neglected had they allowed residential separation of the heir(ess) of the younger generation. In other words, the domestic subordination necessary for care in old age (given the built-in logic of inequality) contradicted the consequences of residential autonomy. They could not allow the residential autonomy of the heir(ess), and therefore demanded cohabitation. The same obtained with Quebec parents.

It is the Basques, however, and their extraordinary residential practices, which do challenge our typology of stem families. Unlike the Béarnais, the Basques did not rely on a formal contract to institute the heir (there was no 'contractual appointment' of the heir; heirship automatically followed the marriage of the eldest child), while their marriage contracts, unlike those found in Béarn, teemed with incompatibility clauses. Furthermore, no provisions were made for widowed in-marrying spouses in wills. We shall soon understand why.

In the Basque country, on the eve of the French Revolution, the eldest surviving child, whether male or female, inherited (absolute primogeniture). What is most surprising, however, is that upon his or her marriage the heir or heiress could refuse to cohabit with the parents (Zink 1993: 137, 181–2, 197, 264; Ott 1981: 39) and that cohabitation, whenever it was chosen, did not imply domestic subordination. This Basque peculiarity seems to flow logically from the modalities of property devolution: the coresiding couples were indeed equal in domestic matters because they enjoyed the same equality in the economic sphere. The Basque form of dowry explains this.

Elsewhere in Southern Europe the Roman-type dowry is intimately linked to the property a woman receives upon her marriage, property that she would transmit in turn to her own children; the transmission is vertical. The Basque dowry, however, differs markedly, in that its function appears to be that of facilitating the marriage of one or possibly more younger siblings, and that no part of this dowry seems to pass on to the children of the in-marrying spouse. The dowry was securely tied (*vinclée*) to a specific part of the patrimonial land, a part of equal value, to make sure that it could be returned to the spouse if the marriage terminated without any issue (Zink 1993: 127). The dowry was assimilated to the *biens avitins* which, in the Basque country, the House head himself could not alienate. It thus acted as a further guarantee that the patrimonial lands would not be divided, and it may be for that very reason that it evolved, although this remains purely conjectural.

The money (or animals) transmitted through the dowry was then given to the parents of the heir(ess), who used it to marry off a younger sibling. In the following generation the process was repeated. When the time came to endow younger children, the in-marrying spouse's dowry of the earlier generation was of no use, tied as it was to his or her spouse's land. To build up the necessary dowry, the parents had to rely on the property they acquired during their lifetime (their *acquêts*) and on the dowry brought by the in-marrying spouse of their eldest child.

Through this exchange (dowry to the parents against land of equal value set apart for the in-marrying spouse) the heir(ess) and his or her spouse gained *ipso facto* 'co-lordship' of the House (*coseigneurie*) (Zink 1993: 181–2, 187, 188, 485). This transformation of the dowry into *biens avitins* through the tying of a dowry to a specified parcel of land (*vinclage*) automatically instituted the heir(ess) without any formal contract, unlike the Béarn practices. And, unlike the Béarn contractual institution, this *vinclage* conferred on the new couple a place within the House equal to that of the parents.

The process of exchange also put the two spouses on an equal footing, an equality both economic *and social* (see Sandra Ott's interesting monograph for an ethnographic – and contemporary – demonstration of this equality – Ott 1981); husband and wife, for instance, held in joint estate the property they acquired in common (the *acquêts* – Zink 1993: 236). The eighteenth-century Basque *Coutume* emphasized the equality between spouses, and between the two couples of owners and heirs (or, in reality, of co-owners).

Paradoxically, cohabitation was optional because residential separation could not in any way threaten the physical integrity of the patrimonial property. As a matter of fact, the Basques evolved the most extreme measures to preserve patrimonies. For example, it was almost impossible to alienate any part of the *biens avitins* (whether to pay debts, or for any other purpose), giving heirs only usufructuary rights over a property that belonged to the House. The *biens avitins* could therefore be divided equally between the two couples should they wish to live apart, because the lands would automatically be re-united upon the death of one of the couples.

From this peculiarity of the Basque dowry and its accompanying *coseigneurie*, it can plausibly be submitted that most of the patrimonial property attached to the House was truly corporate among the Basques, possibly well into the nineteenth century. At its maximum extension, this corporation would have included the couple of the parents and that of the heir(ess). This corporate ownership removed all possibility of economic subordination and, since it extended to the house itself, it totally transformed the vector of power configuration between coresiding familial units, yielding equal cohabitation when cohabitation was chosen. This equal cohabitation, however, did not automatically spell harmony. Since the two couples were co-owners of equal and inalienable parts, lands could be partitioned without ever jeopardizing their legal integrity as a (corporate) patrimony; the heir(ess) and his or her spouse could opt for equal cohabitation, or reject cohabitation altogether.

Paradoxically enough, this would equally explain why Basque marriage contracts abound with incompatibility clauses. When the two couples elected to coreside, the Basque parents wished to shield themselves from possible domestic conflicts, all the more so because their children, especially their sons, had a greater say in the choice of their matrimonial partner than sons anywhere else in the Pyrenees. If cohabitation proved too stressful, the young couple could even elect to move out and as a result the parents needed to protect themselves against a potential separation. A daughter-in-law could not bring about the demise of a House but, because of the domestic equality she enjoyed through her dowry, she certainly could wreak havoc upon household solidarity, which could have left the parents in difficult circumstances. The parents sought security in incompatibility clauses. Even when equal, cohabitation can thus engender bitter conflicts. It may even be said that, the more equal the coresiding units, the less likely they will tolerate quarrels and enmity, and the more prone they will be to residential separation. Overall, the contrast with Béarn practices could not be more systemic.

But why this remarkable Basque conjugal solidarity and this extraordinary equality between the sexes? It is not implausible to connect it to absolute primogeniture. On the one hand, a long chain of causal connections seems to link the almost absurd obsession with the integrity and permanence of the House to the type of 'mortgaged dowry' and to absolute primogeniture. On the other, integral primogeniture puts sons and daughters on an equal footing in matters of inheritance, as they receive dowries of equal value (Zink 1993: 223). This equality between the sexes might be related to the equality between the spouses.

If this is so, are we to explain inequality in the Béarn in terms of male primogeniture? In the final analysis it may be that only historians of the Béarn will be in a position to answer this question fully, but I do feel that the emergence of primogeniture might have something to do with the dynamics of Béarnais MRU relationships. After all, eldest daughters could marry before the heir only if the parents pawned part of the patrimonial property (*biens avitins*) to borrow money. Male primogeniture seems to have led to increased rights over the *biens avitins*, and the two are intimately linked to the other features of this Béarn pattern. However, why should the Béarnais have introduced male primogeniture, unlike the Basque?

I have not come across many convincing responses to this question. Poumarède argues that nobles introduced it to avoid dividing their fiefs and thus inspired commoners to imitate them (Poumarède 1972: 287). Needless to say, an argument of mimicry and diffusion is unsatisfactory, especially when it concerns such a crucial mutation. Etchelecou, on the other hand, mentions that the King of Navarre simply created it by edict for the Béarn in 1538 (Etchelecou 1991: 20). Yet he is the only one to mention it and, in remote upland communities, royal decrees could easily be ignored. In the light of Alpine ethnography, it may indeed be that this royal decree was imposed on the nobility, and thus passed on to their tenants, but no evidence of this kind has come to my notice from the literature consulted, especially as all authors studied agree that upland Western Pyrenean communities acquired considerable autonomy as early as the beginning of the fourteenth century (Soulet 1987: 57; Berthe 1976: 66, 81, 139, 167). Furthermore, it is astonishing that such an important decree should have failed to attract the attention of historians and ethnographers, and we may also look elsewhere for an answer. Among the ethnographers only Rolande Bonnain has raised the question and her thesis, more sociological, appears to me more attractive.

Let us recall that Bonnain writes about the Central Pyrenees; despite this major proviso, her thesis remains most plausible for the Béarn as well. Writing about Laborde, a small village of the mountainous part of the Baronnies, she mentions that most of its inhabitants have had to supplement agriculture and sheep-raising with handicraft productions to ensure greater cashflow and make ends meet, and this for centuries (Bonnain 1986a: 167). Since all agricultural producers were simultaneously artisans, it seemed logical that the fathers wished their tools and trade to pass on to their first-born (and surviving) son, who worked as their first associate. As it happens, Bonnain found the last vestiges of absolute primogeniture in Bigorre among the wealthy families, a fact which supports her thesis since only richer families could live off their land and stocks without supplementing their income with handicraft production (Bonnain 1986a: 167, 170). The idea is quite plausible and could also apply to Béarn, where handicraft productions appeared much earlier than in the Basque country; I am not aware of a better one and I therefore accept it provisionally, though the question remains unresolved.

If indeed male primogeniture is relatively recent in the Central and Western Pyrenees, as most authorities concur, why then should this region of the Pyrenees have privileged absolute primogeniture some centuries earlier? Viazzo has brilliantly demonstrated how wary we should be of neat logical causal reconstructions to explain observed practices (Viazzo 1989), and I hesitantly submit the following as pure conjecture.

Absolute primogeniture might have been imposed by landlords during the centuries of colonization and feudal overlordship, as is evidenced for impartible inheritance and settlement patterns in the Alps (Viazzo 1989). Once more, no one, not even Poumarède, mentions any such thesis for the Western Pyrenees. It might also be that, before the advent of male primogeniture, the Béarnais also used dowries in the manner reported by Anne Zink for the Basque country at the end of the *Ancien Régime*. As we have seen, this type of dowry is intimately linked to the preservation of an undivided patrimony (by being assimilated to the *biens avitins*) and does favour absolute primogeniture. Indeed, the eldest child surviving to maturity would marry first (and therefore be heir or heiress) in order to bring in a dowry that enabled the parents to marry off younger children. As we move to male primogeniture, the parents often have to pawn or alienate property to marry off daughters before the heir's in-marrying spouse can bring a dowry in, if the oldest child to reach maturity is not a boy. This jeopardizes the integrity of the patrimony and, as I have remarked, might explain why the Béarnais eventually wielded greater power over the *biens avitins*. These considerations, no doubt, belong to the realm of pure speculation and, like so many questions, await further research.

From the point of view of an atomistic set of axioms, the Basque case is most eloquent. It tells of corporate property and of the equal or optional cohabitation that it permits, that is, of the absence of coercion within the residential field. It also tells of the conflicts built in equal cohabitation. Above all, it shows the dangers of classifying regions under a single taxon, such as 'areas of stem families'. Because the typology I advocate calls for both a limit of residential growth and a particular vector of power configuration between coresiding MRUs, we cannot include the eighteenth-century Basque case with the Béarn and Quebec ones. In Béarn and Quebec the younger couple suffered both economic and domestic subordination, whereas coresiding Basque couples enjoyed equality in both spheres. Because the very term 'stem family' belongs to the protohistory of family history, it is easier to preserve it than to jettison it, although it should no longer be used from the point of view of house composition only. From this new typological point of view, but for the sake of simplicity and convenience, let us henceforth distinguish 'downward subordinate stem families' from 'equal' ones.

Inheritance and cohabitation

We could leave the topic of stem families on this note but, once more, Viazzo's work stirs up some interesting questions. In various areas of the Alps (not to mention a host of other well-documented cases, such as areas of Germany, Russia or Tuscany), the feudal lords were the ones who imposed impartible inheritance and, often directly or indirectly, on cohabitation. What of the Western Pyrenees? Was impartible inheritance and the stem limit of residential growth imposed 'from above'?

Again, I have not come across any evidence that impartible inheritance resulted from extraresidential coercion; instead, I have found the standard explanations that Viazzo discovered for the Alps: the extreme poverty of the environment made partible inheritance impossible (Poumarède n.d.: 34), or the intense poverty and the 'vertical' ecology of the Pyrenees led to a parcelling and dispersion of plots of land so extreme that it precluded any further division (Soulet 1987: 314).

The most attractive hypothesis, however, is one that Viazzo retrieves from Rebel on the Austrian Alps (Rebel 1983, in Viazzo 1989: 265–6). In the Austrian Alps impartible inheritance was originally imposed by extraresidential power-holders during the centuries of colonization, then later by landlords, but was equally preserved by the elite of farmers that it created. In brief, its very persistence had little to do with ecology, but everything to do with external pressures and internal social stratification. For the Western Pyrenees the origins of impartible inheritance seem lost in the mists of time; I shall nonetheless argue that from the fourteenth or fifteenth century onward it could not have been maintained by extraresidential power-holders. As in the Austrian case, it could be argued that it survived because it best suited the interests of an elite of rich farmers.

As early as the end of the nineteenth century, in his study of the Vallée d'Ossau (in the Béarn), Butel contended that the key to decode upland Pyrenean social organization was not the house, but the community itself. A corporate landowner, the community (village, commune) also acted corporately in the use and management of its property, overriding in this the wishes of any one house (Butel 1894). Soulet implicitly espoused a similar stance (Soulet 1987), which resurfaces in greater detail and articulation in Anne Zink's book (1993: 270–6).

At first glance, Zink's thesis amalgamates ecological and economic arguments (a standard procedure in the study of upland communities). She views the Western Pyrenees as a finely tuned ecosystem. Western Pyrenean agriculture, she contends, depended heavily on the existence of vast areas of *landes* (heaths), covered with a host of plants (such as fern, heather, furze, gorze and others) which, regularly harvested, provided an essential source of compost. The cattle grazed and fertilized these *landes*. Furthermore, upland agriculture could not provide sufficient harvest to keep the population fed throughout the year, with the result that animal husbandry was crucial to their survival; in addition to grazing in the *landes*, the animals used forest and upland pastures. Therefore, if the community had allowed *cadets* to marry *cadettes*, or allowed the creation of new Houses, it would have had to let them cultivate lands used for pastures. Hence, according to Zink, the community's major difficulty: if more land was cultivated, more people would have practised agriculture, fewer animals could have been raised, and this would have resulted in greater and more widespread poverty (1993: 274). To Zink the outcome was inevitable: the community preferred to feed fewer people with more animals, rather than more people with greater areas of cultivated land and fewer animals. The community preferred keeping a higher standard of living for fewer people to spreading extreme poverty to a larger population (274).

Zink's thesis indirectly reminds one of Alpine Austria. Here, according to Rebel, the heirs preserved impartible inheritance because it was in their own interest to do so, long after the extraresidential power-holders had allowed partibility. I believe that a similar argument can be made for the Pyrenees of Gascon origin at least (namely the Bigorre and Béarn; the evidence collected never bears on the Basque country).

Throughout the Pyrenees, no one seems to know exactly when, how and why impartible inheritance emerged, and we have to take it as a given, certainly from the Middle Ages onward. In trying to understand it, however, invoking the 'community' as a kind of supraresidential entity, as Butel and Zink do, involves us in a circular argument, since the members of the 'community' composing the 'deciding body' regarding the use and management of communal property were none other than House heads.

In other words, we could translate matters into political terms. Where we are informed that the 'community' resisted the creation of new houses, we could in fact read that an elite of local farmers bent on keeping their standard of living opposed *cadets/cadettes* marriages (or the creation of new Houses, which amounts to the same thing). The communal will, in reality, added up to nothing other than the will of individual household heads.

Furthermore, though the corporate body of decision-makers encompassed all House heads, this does not necessarily imply that Western Pyrenean communities were stratified along an opposition between heirs (and heiresses) and *cadets*. Quite the contrary. Soulet, who emphasizes the corporate character of Pyrenean communities, also stresses the fact that their corporateness did not make these communes a democracy. He relates that upland communities were dominated by a powerful elite, an elite composed only of the most literate and the richest (those forming the 'bonnes maisons' – the 'good houses') (Soulet 1987: 130). He adds that the (external) administration always complained of the existence of factions, or 'clans', which literally 'poisoned' (*empoisonnent* in the text) communal life (173), making it clear that '[t]he "good houses" which, in those communes, most often served as the core to which those "parties" were fixed, are relatively well known . . . as the richest' (175, free translation).

The theme of the 'bonnes maisons' also dominates the ethnography of the Baronnies, otherwise utterly devoid of reference to social stratification (except for Bonnain 1981). From 1600 to 1914 in Esparros, Antoinette Fauve-Chamoux finds that only one-third of the houses managed to bequeath their property undivided, and that these are none other than the 'bonnes maisons', namely those with the best lands; she adds that the '"bonnes familles-souches", elles, occupent sans discontinuité les meilleures terres depuis des générations' (1993: 42). But this is not all; the 'bonnes maisons' are also the very ones inciting their nonheirs to celibacy (Soulet 1987: 338; Augustins 1981: 37) and, as in the Austrian Alps, rates of illegitimate births reach impressive percentages, providing cheap labour for the heirs and heiresses. Augustins mentions it with regard to the end of the eighteenth century, but without giving numerical evidence (1981: 76), while Fauve-Chamoux discovers illegitimacy rates reaching 25 per cent in the Baronnies, without however specifying the dates (1987: 250).

Overall, the richest houses were those that systematically avoided partition and condemned their nonheirs to celibacy, and yet these are the very ones that could have carved out part of their land to help establish more than one son. In contrast, the poorer ones, those that could least afford it, suffered the division of their patrimony now and then to help a son or a daughter to settle. History repeats itself to the very top of the Pyrenees. And those very same rich houses dominated the political arena, to the point of 'poisoning' communal life. The conclusion seems rather clear: as in the Austrian Alps, impartibility did not survive for ecological reasons, but because it was maintained by an elite of rich houses dominating political life, and imposing its will on the rest of the community. Whatever the distant origins of impartibility may have been, its maintenance over the last four or five hundred years seems to have to do with local stratification and politics rather than with upland ecology.

The stem family: continuity and change

Let us return to the case of rural French-speaking Quebec. From the very beginning, as we have seen, land was passed on undivided, despite the fact that the inheritance was equally divided between all the children of both sexes. The plot was evaluated, and the shares paid out over time by the one who took possession of the land. Originally, in the eighteenth century, the child who took over the 'estate' was chosen at random. In many cases, widowed parents came to some agreement with one child to look after them, privileging him or her through donations *inter vivos*, always with the agreement of their other children. The limit of residential growth might thus include a mother (rarely a father; they would work their land until their death), but the vector was reversed: the child and his or her spouse ruled the house, although the mother was not strictly speaking in a subordinate position. At any rate, the limit of residential growth never reached the stem level.

In 1784, the British political authorities granted the French-speaking Québecois the right to will, but there is no evidence that stem families suddenly appeared. In fact, we have no evidence whatsoever of the existence of stem families until much later (1860s), although historians of French Canada have never given this question much attention. The evidence we have for later dates, however, shows a major reversal. First, land was still bequeathed to one child only, always a son, and very little was used to compensate the other children. Second, the criteria used to choose an heir had completely changed, from random choice to a selection based on two major criteria: whether the son *and his bride* were committed to agriculture or not, and whether the personality of the bride made cohabitation possible or not. From these facts, I have argued elsewhere that French-Canadian stem families probably emerged in the 1820s or 1830s, when a massive rural exodus to cities and the USA threatened the very survival of agriculture and, in the minds of the clergy and the political elite, the very survival of French Canada (Verdon 1987).

I see interesting parallels between Quebec, on the one hand, and nineteenth-century Bigorre and Béarn on the other. No doubt the two areas could not be further apart in the eighteenth century; the stem family, then absent in Quebec, had existed for centuries in the Western Pyrenees, and the strategies of heirship could not have been more divergent. And yet the nineteenth century displays interesting similarities between the two areas.

Let us review some of the evidence. Although the mythical, mechanical model of the Western Pyrenees usually presents some kind of homeostatically regulated *Ancien Régime* suddenly shaken by a *cadet* rebellion (partly egged on by demographic growth and the partibility made compulsory by the Napoleonic Code), the reality is much more complex. Indeed, Etchelecou gives disturbing figures. For the localities about which censuses exist, the number of households remains remarkably stable from 1385 to 1549 but by 1770 it has often doubled, but most likely trebled or even quadrupled (Etchelecou 1991: 41, 53). In comparison with 1770, the figures for 1851 show an increase of only 40 to 60 per cent. Those figures are troubling because they belie the impression given in the literature by most authors on the Baronnies who either claim or imply that the population grew considerably (and mostly) between 1780 and 1851, not between 1550 and 1770. Etchelecou believes that this major population explosion occurred in the eighteenth century because of a sudden fall in mortality rates, accompanied by high fertility (1991: 42).

The timing and causes of this demographic boom remain a moot point, especially since much work has pointed to low fertility rates in the upland Pyrenees. To further the parallel with the Alps, Bonnain and Péron do mention the introduction of potato cultivation (one of the main causes of demographic growth in the Western Alps in the nineteenth century – see Netting 1981; Viazzo 1989) as an important factor in demographic growth before 1800 (Bonnain 1986a: 88; Péron 1986: 17). The Pyrenees might thus have followed a demographic course not unlike that of the Alps. Falling mortality rates seem to appear as a main cause of population growth in the eighteenth century, and the introduction of potato cultivation would have sustained this increased population, creating the conditions for further growth (Viazzo 1989).

Although the timing of this demographic explosion varied from one area to the other, it seems that the carrying capacity of the land had been exceeded by the early nineteenth century in some areas, and not later than

1850 in others. Concurrently, industrialization, urbanization and transformations in the means of transportation were taking place in the lowlands, and further afield on the plain. Together, these circumstances led to a massive rural exodus somewhere between 1800 and 1850 depending on conditions in the area concerned.

In the first half of the nineteenth century, the Baronnies thus experienced a drastic turnabout. Primogeniture, which until then had been automatic, more or less vanished. The heirs refused to take over the family enterprise and left the area for good (Fauve-Chamoux 1984: 523, 1993: 44, 1987: 247; Bonnain 1986b: 107), to the extent that many heiresses found it hard to find a husband, if they found one at all (Bonnain 1986b: 94, 101–2). Strategies of heirship had to change radically, and parents started selecting among their children those who were most apt to continue the family enterprise and most ready to commit themselves to an agricultural vocation, for a vocation is what it had become in the second half of the nineteenth century (Augustins 1981: 53–4; Bonnain 1986a: 170–1). Because children enjoyed more bargaining power, the fathers lost some of their former authority, and some even started retiring, handing over the farm to their children before their death, a practice unknown in the eighteenth century (Bonnain 1986a: 168).

Did the stem family disappear during this period of dramatic transformations? Not quite. Antoinette Fauve-Chamoux, whose calculations are the most thorough on this question, notes for Esparros that 'multiple family households' (stem families), comprised about 15 per cent of all households from 1793 to about 1850. After that their number dwindled to 5 per cent in 1880 (Fauve-Chamoux 1987: 245). Five per cent is a small percentage, but there is no evidence that those cases were considered abnormal; it was more that the rural exodus left some heiresses celibate and many farms abandoned. I would therefore conclude that the limit of residential growth had not yet changed, but its logic had. This time, the eldest surviving child or male did not automatically become heir, but parents had to lure one of their children into heirship, a strategy somewhat reminiscent of the Quebec situation. Although the couple formed by the heir or heiress plausibly remained in some kind of subordinate cohabitation because some children would always prefer the security of inheritance to the risks of seeking their fortune elsewhere (as in Quebec – see note 1), the parents' authority had waned, making subordination much more comparable to that observed in nineteenth-century Quebec. In brief, the Western Pyrenees witnessed a reorganization of the power configuration between coresiding MRUs as well as a change to the timing of household development and reproduction.

Thus the stem family persisted, although its incidence decreased. In terms of a typology rooted in household composition only, everything has to be translated into a statistical debate. True, the limit of residential growth remained the same, but the power configuration between MRUs in the stem family had altered, leading to a milder form of subordinate cohabitation. After 1850, the Western Pyrenean stem family (the Basque one excluded) resembled the Québecois stem family more than ever before. In other words, bringing diverse regions under the same taxon does not amount to freezing them in time. In the study of living arrangements, a typology points to convergences worthy of detailed comparative analysis, little else. Nevertheless we do need typologies and these typologies will have to take household composition as a limit of residential growth into account.

The cleavage which separates Basque stem families from those of Béarn, Bigorre or Quebec is not the only typological divide in the study of this phenomenon, but it seems to me the most eloquent. No doubt the question of Central European stem families and that of the parents' retirement would be of equal interest, but I shall nonetheless limit this chapter on stem families to the cases examined. From the little I have gleaned from the literature, however, I feel that the same axioms, if applied to Central European data, might also yield interesting results. As proof of this, I will terminate on a testimony from Mitterauer and Sieder.

According to these two authors, retirement in Central Europe had been imposed by landlords and,

> for the farming family, retirement rights always represented a great burden, at any rate for the owners of small and middle-sized properties, and were avoided when possible. The inevitable result was a relatively high marriage age. Frequently the heir had to postpone marriage until after the death of the old farmer. The causal connection between the low proportion of three-generational families and high marriage age is to be seen thus: on economic grounds, the co-residence of more than two generations was undesirable or impossible, and consequently the time of marriage was delayed.
>
> (Mitterauer and Sieder 1982: 37)

From an atomistic perspective, I would argue that coresidence was undesirable on social-psychological grounds, and that we are dealing with yet another taxon when considering Central European stem families. But that chapter is better left to those competent to write it.

7

THE WORLD WE HAVE LOST

The medieval English household

In the previous chapters we examined the most collectivistic forms of stem families and of Russian multiple family households. In the next two chapters, I shall move to the other end of the spectrum and study the most individualistic forms of household types: first, the so-called English nuclear family and, second, household types in an advanced industrialized country, namely Canada between 1971 and 1991.

These two subjects call for two different perspectives. In the English case, I will repeat the type of argumentation used for the other historical cases. When examining the Canadian data, however, the approach will be very different. Using Ermish and Overton's concepts, I will attempt to demonstrate the methodological value of an atomistic perspective in the study of contemporary aggregate national census data over a period of twenty years, a study which will involve us in intraregional variability rather than in limits of residential growth. This second part of the chapter will thus be narrowly demographic and methodological, unlike the more qualitative analyses which precede it.

The debate surrounding the misnamed 'English family' imposes an inversion of perspectives, a source of major difficulties. Whereas the origins of the Western Pyrenean stem family or of the Russian multiple family household are probably lost to knowledge for ever, a controversial question raises its head in the English case: when did the so-called nuclear English household originate, and why? The fact is, no one knows, and contemporary developments in English family history have given rise to two opposed camps: 1) the advocates of 'continuity', who see evidence of the nuclear family as far back as documents go, that is, in the Middle Ages (at least the thirteenth century; the main protagonists here are Laslett and Macfarlane – Laslett 1965; 1977; Macfarlane 1978; 1986); and 2) the advocates of 'change', some of whom claim that England had a 'stem family system' until the advent of industrial capitalism (Seccombe 1992), while others detect an 'extended family system' until the fifteenth century in vast areas of England (Razi 1993).

Not being trained as a historian, I cannot settle the question 'historically'.

It remains possible, however, to retrieve a certain number of known 'facts' about the late English Middle Ages, facts about which many historians concur, and, upon this basis, to submit my own thoughts. Unfortunately, the debate surrounding those 'facts' is so riddled with conceptual muddles and ideological biases that initial clarifications are needed before searching for some 'hard' evidence. I will therefore divide the chapter into two parts, the first assessing the reinterpretations that the 'change theorists' have put forth, the second presenting my own understanding of the evidence.

Dispelling some confusion

In this section, I shall rely exclusively on the works of Seccombe (1992, 1993) and Razi (1993), the two foremost and most influential advocates of the 'changing' English family. Despite the fact that one discerns a 'stem family system' where the other detects an 'extended family system', both share a number of common assumptions, some of which we have already come across in earlier chapters.

The first myth, and the cornerstone of most onslaughts on Laslett's position, lies in their stance on households. Paradoxically enough, both Seccombe and Razi agree that multiple family households have been exceedingly rare and exceptional in England as far as the historical evidence goes, but this does not stop them from indicting Laslett's thesis and in this their arguments follow parallel paths. Indeed, both deny almost any relevance to living arrangements, in so far as they assume that relationships outside the house far outweighed relationships within. Seccombe even goes one step further, claiming that architectural divides (that is, the fact that there are walls and houses) were completely insubstantial, so that interaction took place more often across walls than within them. He further submits that manorial organization enforced impartible inheritance and therefore unigeniture, that the heir settled on his parent'(s') holding, remaining under their authority until their death (although he admits that the case is not so strong with widows). In so far as the channels of authority based on intergenerational property transfers were responsible for closely linking parent-owner(s) and (married) heir, all of whom lived on the same holding (albeit in different houses) and collaborated closely in the management and work of the land, he concludes that the evidence points to the existence of a 'stem family system' in medieval (feudal) England (Seccombe 1992).

Studying Halesowen (West Midlands) in the pre-plague era (1270–1348), Razi also finds a custom of impartible inheritance, but one that did not eject nonheirs from the locality. On the contrary, nonheirs were given smaller plots and built their own houses on the family holding. Studying a variety of evidence (pledges, maintenance contracts), Razi further discovers that, within the village, most households were related to other households by blood, and that individuals turned to those extraresidential kin for pledges, or for maintenance in old age. From this, he concludes that Halesowen had a high 'kin density', that kin did help kin, a fact which to him proved the existence of a 'functionally extended family system' in Halesowen and many other regions of England (Razi 1993).

First, the debate seems rooted in terminological abuse. To this day, 'stem family' has to my knowledge always referred primarily to a type of household composition, one in which the heir, and only the heir, lives with his parents after his marriage. Seccombe ignores this tradition and replaces this meaning of 'stem family' with his own: a 'stem family' henceforth refers to a 'sphere of authority', that of a patriarch using his property to lord it over his heir(ess), because the two households are linked through close propinquity and intergenerational transfer of property. From this point on, the debate can no longer cover the same issues.

The case of the 'extended family' is more complicated. In the anthropological literature, it has often been used to mean 'multiple family household' or 'joint family'. Other anthropologists have also used the expression to denote a network of kin beyond Ego's lineal and primary kin, the boundary and composition of which are never defined. It is, at best, a fuzzy entity. This, presumably, is what Razi has in mind when he writes of a 'functional extended family system'. He, like Seccombe, simply does not speak Laslett's language, and cannot therefore dispute his thesis in this manner. But the two believe they refute Laslett on more fundamental grounds by denying the analytical relevance of households. Let us broach this question once more, this time by looking at it within Laslett's opponents' own frameworks.

Seccombe provides an ideal point of departure on this topic. He makes the notion of a 'family cycle' central to his argumentation, and logically concludes that a family cycle cannot be reduced to coresidence. From his first book (1992), a 'family cycle' seems to encompass intergenerational transfers of property and a medley of related phenomena, such as age at marriage, strategies of heirship, manipulation of property to ensure obedience on the part of heirs, the quality of husband–wife, sibling, and parent–children relationships, and so on.

There is no denying the importance of Seccombe's theoretical thesis, but it remains somewhat confused. There are indeed different layers of social reality. First, we can isolate such phenomena as the mean age at first marriage of men and women, rates of nuptiality and celibacy, rates of remarriage, the mean age at the first birth for women, the intergenesic interval, and a host of other demographic parameters having to do with the 'family', and which demographers describe as a 'demographic regime'. Second, we can equally focus on the modalities (or the emotional content) of relationships within the 'family': those between husband and wife, between parents and children, and between siblings, as well as between kin beyond the family, such as lineal kin of alternate generations, collateral kin, and so on. Admittedly, the modalities of those relationships, as well as the demographic parameters of the family, have a lot to do with property. This is equally the essence of my position. There is thus a 'cycle' of property transmission between generations and a division of labour, within the more political-economic context of whether land is owned individually by the producers, or conditionally in a manorial organization, or not at all; this 'cycle of property transmission' directly affects the 'demographic regime' and the 'emotional content of family relations'. These are fundamental, irreducible facts of social life, but designating them as a 'family system' subtly introduces a certain degree of confusion; indeed, one surreptitiously replaces 'household' with 'family', denying households any separate reality or even existence.

To avoid confusion, I suggest we stop writing about the 'family' when referring to a host of phenomena belonging to various (albeit somewhat interrelated) dimensions of social reality. In the anthropological tradition, one could call the combination of these various strands of social reality a 'kinship system' but, since no two anthropologists concur in their definition of the term we might as well choose another, equally fuzzy, concept, that of a 'kinship regime', one that I would favour if only because I do not believe all elements to be related in a very systemic manner in the kinship domain.

Whether we write of 'family system' or 'kinship regime', the fact remains that the two dimensions of social reality which we have hitherto identified as partly composing a kinship regime (the demographic regime and the emotional contents of relationships) are separate from residence (although intimately related to it, so that household formation would also have to be included within a 'kinship regime') both conceptually and analytically. To prove it, let us re-introduce residence within Seccombe's framework and imagine that, instead of living in separate households, parents and married heir lived in the same residential group. I claim that the absence of walls, thin or thick, separating the two couples would completely change the dynamics of household relationships (between the husband and wife of the younger generation, between father and son and, above all, between mother-in-law and daughter-in-law, not to mention the siblings), and it might plausibly affect the demographic regime as well. In other words, in so far as it does affect the modalities of relationships between spouses and primary kin, and might also have an impact on the demographic regime, coresidence is no dependent variable or, worse still, no irrelevant dimension of social reality. Quite the contrary, residence is an independent variable, a separate dimension of social reality and, as such, the development, reproduction, and limit of growth of *residential* groups is in itself a question worth asking, and any reference to 'family systems' to disprove their relevance does not bear on the question that Laslett and the Cambridge Group were asking.

Whatever the language used, we can conclude that in England, and possibly in many areas of northwestern Europe, the limit of residential growth consistently ruled out multifamilial households (in this instance, I will imply by 'family' the presence of both spouses – in other words, I shall exclude the 'residual families' which I included earlier for the ease of presentation). When considering residential groups and their history, therefore, we always come back to square one: there is indeed a noticeable absence of stem or multiple family residential groups in England, and this possibly as early as medieval times.

With these distinctions in mind, let us consider one of Razi's major theses, namely the contrast he distinguishes between areas of England with a 'functional extended family' and others with a 'nuclear' system:

> It appears that, in most of the villages of central-southern, midland and northern England, cottagers and smallholders constituted only a substantial minority, the bulk of the land was distributed through blood and marriage, despite the existence of a brisk land market; and although the peasants were by no means immobile, the majority of the landholding families had strong roots in their native villages. Consequently it is likely that kin density in these villages was high and the functionally extended family predominated. On the other hand, in the far more densely populated and economically diversified area of East Anglia, and probably also in the south-east and south-west, holdings tended to be fragmented and quite small, the land market was very intensive and the population highly mobile. Therefore, the family-land bond in these rural areas must have been rather weak, the kin density quite low and nuclear families predominant. The nuclear structure of the peasant family in these regions was probably also due to *the weakness of manorial organization and control* [italics added], which facilitated the mobility of the rural population and the early development of a peasant land-exchange system. Obviously this geographical distribution of family patterns in pre-plague England is somewhat crude. Yet none of the studies of villages in central-southern, midland and northern England provide any evidence for the existence of a nuclear rather than a functionally extended family system.
>
> (Razi 1993: 21)

What does this amount to? From considerations about the settlement pattern, the size of holdings, the number of leases and sales of land, the number of other households related through kinship in the same village, and migratory patterns, Razi concludes that in some areas the local kin density was higher, and so were kin interactions; we are therefore dealing with a 'functionally extended family system'. In other parts, more densely populated and with more fragmented holdings and greater population mobility, kin density was much lower, defining a 'nuclear family system'.

I have already dealt with the notion of 'family system', and suggested replacing it with the concept of 'kinship regime'. In this new idiom, Razi would be stating that different 'kinship regimes' characterized medieval England, quite an acceptable and tame statement. But were those differences as fundamental as he makes out? I am far from convinced, since the divergences he alludes to are differences in degrees, not in nature. Greater or lesser fragmentation of holdings, more or less active land markets, greater or lesser mobility, these are all features that simply vary in intensity. Failing nonarbitrary dividing lines that would enable us to declare that one kinship regime differs in nature from another, I remain impressed by the similarities rather than the differences: the possibility of alienating land, the possibility of migrating, the effort to pass on land to all children despite the rule of impartibility in some manors and, above all, the avoidance of the cohabitation of couples within the same dwelling-place. Overall, this is a strikingly uniform pattern given the size of the area contemplated (England), and one where variations ought to be observed. What Razi fails to mention in his contrast, however, is that impartible inheritance was practised in Halesowen, whereas customary lands were subject to partible inheritance in Redgrave. From this major difference many of the other divergences might stem.

Razi's text also illustrates another major myth of so-called family history (one not specific to him, and one particularly pronounced among some of his opponents, such as Macfarlane), namely the idea that the 'nuclearization' of households spells the weakening of kinship bonds, the demise of kinship, a move away from a kinship-based society to a 'modern' one. This representation rests on a dangerous assumption, namely that living in separate houses is almost tantamount to severing interaction. We can never state this emphatically enough: 'moving out' does not imply a 'weakening' of kinship bonds. This is an unfortunate *non sequitur*, one rooted in an old Durkheimian equation between the frequency of interaction and the 'strength' of social bonds (see Verdon 1991): the more frequent the interaction, the stronger the solidarity. First, nothing can measure the 'strength' of social bonds; but, more fundamentally, one could infer the exact opposite from the same Durkheimian premises.

To prove it, let us consider the problem within the framework of household formation and reproduction. First, if we are interested in the emotional content of relationships between kin and affines, the 'strength' of their relationship is a rather useless concept. It would be more apposite to probe their 'quality' rather than their 'strength'. In the study of coresidence, what relationship should we draw between interaction and the quality of relationships? Let us start with the obvious, namely that 'moving out' does not, and cannot, mean in and of itself the end of interaction. Those who move out might still own property in common with members of the mother-household, they might expect to inherit property from them, they might work their lands together, exchange products and services, spend all their leisure time together, to mention only the obvious. Any reader of Jane Austen will know that married sisters living far apart used every opportunity to visit one another for longish periods. Why should this belong to the world of fiction only?

If walls do not sever relationships and if we envisage the question from the angle of the quality of relationships, I would argue the opposite of the classical Durkheimian thesis: the less frequent the interaction, the greater the quality of most interpersonal relationships (except in the initial phase of 'falling in love', either with an adult of the other sex, or with one's newborn and young child). In other words, kin who have the choice not to live together under the same roof might relate better than those who are compelled by external hindrances or internal threats to share the same dwelling-place. One could thus make a strong case that the greater the nuclearization of residential groups, the greater the quality of kinship bonds. This would enable us to turn the argument around and hold that, in England, kin were too important to introduce an element of potential conflict and hostility into their relationships by bringing MRUs to live together!

Admittedly, migration does disperse kin and lessens the frequency of their interaction; but from this we cannot conclude that their relationship was of a lesser quality. Ultimately, if interaction stops altogether because of the sheer distance separating kin, then, and only then, can we make conclusions about the absence, or near absence, of kin relationships, but nothing else. Brothers who have not seen one another for twenty years might enjoy the highest quality of relationship when they meet up again. The severance of interaction between kin, therefore, does not result from the nuclearization of households, but from migration. The factors that affected the rate and pattern of migration are consequently those that most directly affected the kinship regime.

Finally, in the works of Laslett, Macfarlane and other 'continuity theorists' lives another myth, the very myth that incited the reinterpretations of Seccombe, Razi and others. From the point of view of a limit of residential growth, it is in fact erroneous to suppose that there ever was an English 'nuclear' limit of residential growth before the 1950s; even then, such a limit remains quite suspect. All the available evidence we have about English households from the Middle Ages to the twentieth century points to one inescapable fact, namely that the English limit of residential growth never seems to have been multifamilial during that period; multiple family households may have been found here and there but usually, I believe, as a result of singular and exceptional circumstances. Nonetheless, other evidence we have from the Middle Ages (mostly retirement contracts) also makes it clear that it was normal to house a widowed parent. To be precise, the limit of residential growth in England, from the Middle Ages to relatively recent times (possibly only the last four or five decades of the twentieth century and, on this issue, even questionably so) was, to use Laslett and Hammel's terminology, 'vertically extended'. Parents preferred residential autonomy – this follows from our premises – but some could not achieve it and it does not seem to have been considered singular or exceptional for those parents (normally widowed) to move back to live with a married child.

Second, when we add the dimension of power relationships between MRUs to build our typology, Seccombe's main thesis is right: there have been major changes in household types in England since the Middle Ages. The medieval evidence, mostly from retirement contracts, does not enable us to determine clearly the vector of power configuration. Did the widowed parent, through manipulations of property, dictate his or her will to the children? I have not found clear evidence of this in any of the texts consulted. On the one hand, if widowed parents went to live with a married child (rather than the married child moving in with the widowed parent), they could hardly lay down the law, and the cohabitation might have been equal, based on a trade-off, property being exchanged for care. It may nonetheless be that in cases where much property was at stake, the parent(s) did retain a superordinate position. On the other hand, some widowed parents could have lived with a child out of destitution, and suffered subordination to their own progeny.

In brief, the vector may have pointed in all directions, although the evidence suggests that most cases of coresidence involved a little property. We could therefore plausibly submit that the vector pointed downward or horizontally, but rarely upward. With the proletarianization that accompanied industrial capitalism and especially urbanization, the limit of residential growth remained vertically extended, but the power within households definitely flowed upward; on this, I accept Seccombe's thesis. Widowed parents who came to live with their children were the least endowed, and would have been subordinate in their married child's household. From this point on, we are therefore dealing with a different type of household. It is only recently, I believe, that conditions have possibly been such as to render vertical extension unusual and rather exceptional. If such is the case, we would only now be witnessing a true 'nuclear' limit of residential growth; in my opinion, however, this remains open to debate. Changes have occurred in English household history (and consequently in their kinship regimes), and major ones at that, but, in my opinion, stem families or multiple family households have never constituted limits of residential growth in England from the Middle Ages onward.

These appear as the major conceptual hurdles in the way of any discussion on early English households, and they make it difficult to separate the 'hard' facts from more controversial interpretations. Although I accept some of the reconstructions of the 'change theorists', I disagree with the manner in which they seek to impose a different typology on medieval 'family history', the only topic that interests me in this chapter.

The medieval English limit of residential growth: some conjectures

Before embarking on the most tenuous of arguments, I would like to emphasize that I do not consider England to have been the first country to display the limit of residential growth that we have defined above. In the period under consideration, some other areas, mostly in northwestern Europe, might have shared a similar limit, quite possibly from earlier centuries. But for my own linguistic reasons I could seriously consider England and France only; given that France lacks any kind of evidence comparable to English manorial court records, England imposed itself as the only choice.

Most historians would also agree that any search for the origins of the English limit of residential growth (henceforth referred to as ELRG) is, at best, a dubious undertaking. First, no set of data enables us to date its emergence even vaguely. Second, there is no evidence that it spread swiftly to the whole country once it surfaced in an area. Where did it occur first? Was it a pre-Norman feature? Even in the twelfth and thirteenth centuries, was it to be found throughout England, or were there enclaves of 'classical' ELRG interlaced with regions knowing different limits of residential growth? From the available documents, it is impossible to know. When do we first identify an ELRG? The first direct, explicit evidence is to be found in the poll taxes of 1377 and 1381. However, the fourteenth century is an awkward century to base any type of argumentation on limits of residential growth since the first part of the century reached demographic peaks that were not to be seen again for centuries, and the Black Death (1349) decimated a vast percentage of the population in the second half of the century.

The thirteenth century is no obvious choice either. Admittedly, circumstances changed from 1200 to 1300, but it was also a century of notable demographic expansion. According to recent re-evaluations, the population of England might have reached two to two-and-a-half million people at the time of the Domesday Book (1086), and much of England was still open to colonization by the beginning of the twelfth century; by 1300, however, most of it was settled and, by the time of the Black Death, it had almost reached demographic saturation. Nonetheless, the thirteenth century stands out as the best candidate because historians do not possess data of any kind on household composition for the twelfth century, but hold indirect evidence of a possible ELRG in the thirteenth century. Indeed, some manorial records reach back to the 1250s and, through the retirement and maintenance contracts they reveal, most historians have gained the strong impression that couples, and even widowed elderly persons, avoided unwelcome cohabitation if they could. In brief, we know very little about house-hold composition and about a great many other things in the thirteenth century and, as with the other limits of residential growth of historical Europe, we will have to satisfy ourselves with an approximate 'fit' between the few things we know and the not implausible fact that the ELRG might have been well established throughout much of England at that time.

There have been very few ventures to explain the ELRG. Stone (1975) places its emergence in the sixteenth century, and repeats the old-fashioned evolutionist explanation in terms of a transition from a kindred-based society to a society where the family emerges as the kingpin of social orga-nization, while the state dismantles the traditional kinship affiliations. Such thinking, needless to say, I utterly reject. Anderson (1980) has suggested some elements that I will retrieve, as did Macfarlane in a later study (1986), but Anderson failed to put forth a complete picture and Macfarlane erred on the side of his pet thesis, namely English 'individu-alism'. In contrast, I will not seek individualist elements but will rather try to identify the circumstances that enabled families to achieve residen-tial autonomy, if indeed this was the case.

Let us start with a few established facts. First, many East Anglian manors practised partibility of customary tenures; by the thirteenth century East Anglia was described as densely populated (it had a population density seven times higher than Halesowen, in the West Midlands – Razi 1993: 17), and its holdings were already fragmented (Smith 1984a: 142, 144–5). What of other areas? As we have seen, Razi divides England into two types of kinship regimes, and the one he identifies with Halesowen was much less densely populated and practised impartibility and unigeniture. These two broad areas, furthermore, seem to correspond to the distinction between two settle-ment patterns, namely 'champion' and 'woodland':[1]

> England has been broadly divided into two types of field systems, woodland and champion. The woodland had small clusters of houses (hamlets) or individual homesteads surrounded by square and rect-angular fields marked out by ditches, walls, and hedgerows. Such fields and settlement arrangements resembled our modern concep-tion of farms, although the actual divisions of labour and land usage might be among the residents rather than falling to individual families. Champion country was characterized by nucleated villages surrounded by large, open, unhedged fields. . . . There were small villages of under a thousand acres, but some were closer to five thousand. The distinction between village and hamlet is likewise flexible, and hamlets and farmsteads were mixed among the villages.
>
> (Hanawalt 1986: 20)

Two settlement patterns, two kinship regimes, and opposite rules of inheritance in the matter of tenure devolution:[2] partibility (eastern counties, and the southwest) and impartibility (Midlands and southern central England). Let us look more closely at those rules of inheritance.

First, areas of partibility were not necessarily homogeneous, as some practised partibility of customary lands (lands held in villeinage) and impartibility of free lands (such as Redgrave – Smith 1984a: 144–5). Despite these variations, all the evidence to date points to a fact: that only part of the land was divided at the death of the tenant, and much of it transferred to children *inter vivos* (Smith 1984b: 21; Smith 1984a: 153ff; Seccombe 1992: 101; Hanawalt 1986: 68). Interestingly enough, similar practices seem to have obtained in areas of impartibility. Indeed, propertied parents in champion England tried to settle all their noninheriting sons on the land before their death if they could (Razi 1980; Britton 1977; Franklin 1986; Williamson 1984; Miller and Hatcher 1978; King 1973; Hanawalt 1986: 70, 76; Seccombe 1992: 96–7), and to endow their daughters to the best of their ability; in fact, impartibility applied to the lands not transferred *inter vivos* (Smith 1984a: 15–7; Hanawalt 1986: 70, 76). Hence, the impartibility of champion England has little, if anything, to do with the harsh Western Pyrenean practices; it was a rather soft, flexible form of impartibility, one in which most male siblings received some land if the parents were propertied.

Since partible inheritance favours neolocality when much of the property is actually transferred *inter vivos* (for the most admirable description of its dynamics in eighteenth-century Swabia, see Sabean 1990), I shall therefore argue on the basis of more 'heroic' assumptions and will try to deduce the ELRG from considerations on English areas of impartible inheritance (areas which more or less correspond to champion England, that is, the Midlands and south central England, if we are to believe Razi and Hanawalt – Razi 1993; Hanawalt 1986). With impartible inheritance, as many authors would argue (for example Homans – see Homans 1941), we should find the classical circumstances favouring the emergence of a stem limit of residential growth. And yet, even those, such as Razi, who question Laslett's or Macfarlane's vision of a nuclear English 'family system', do admit that multiple family households do not seem to be a late medieval English feature. I shall therefore assume that the ELRG did exist in part of champion country in the thirteenth century and will try to deduce it from these unlikely circumstances.

If the assumption is true (for it might be plausible for Halesowen, while erroneous for champion country in general), it is most astonishing and, in an atomistic perspective, raises a number of questions: 1) did the heirs in thirteenth-century champion England have enough bargaining power to enforce residential autonomy, or 2) were the parents in a position to reject the cohabitation of their married heir(ess)? In other words, either the parents could not coerce their children into cohabitation, or their circumstances were such that they did not need to. All the elements I shall evoke have already been mentioned in the literature, and I only wish to bring them together into an overarching, atomistic framework.

First, despite important local variations, having mostly to do with population density, it now seems beyond any reasonable doubt that a land market existed throughout England by the thirteenth century (Razi 1980: 50–60; Miller and Hatcher 1978: 136–7; Williamson 1984; Smith 1981: 124). In Halesowen and similar areas, land was often transferred *inter vivos*, whether in the form of leases or sales, to kin or nonkin.[3] Whatever the variations, it seems that people could everywhere acquire land, either temporarily or for good, for the exchange of produce or money. In short, without endorsing Macfarlane's most extreme position, we can nonetheless recover one key element that both he and Anderson isolated when endeavouring to explain the existence of a medieval ELRG, namely the existence of a land market, and most likely a monetized one (Macfarlane 1978, 1986; Anderson 1980).

Second, from the incidence of widow remarriages, Richard Smith has convincingly argued in favour of a late age at first marriage for women in the thirteenth century (Smith 1981, 1983),[4] a fact that tallies remarkably well with the existing evidence concerning the incidence of domestic 'life-cycle' service during the same period. Indeed, manorial court records abundantly refer to the existence of servants (Smith 1983: 129), and Razi relates that before the Black Death, at least 40 per cent of the propertied households of Halesowen had living-in 'life-cycle' servants (Razi 1980: 90). In fact, the percentages of servants in the poll tax census of 1377 and of modern England (seventeenth and eighteenth centuries) are approximately the same (respectively 18 per cent and 20 per cent).[5] The incidence of service, furthermore, would agree with what is known of late medieval English agriculture, namely that it was marked by a significant increase in animal husbandry (Hilton 1983: 17). If agriculture requires mostly seasonal labour, animal husbandry demands sustained labour throughout the year and would explain the preference for the annual contracts of servants.

If individuals had to delay their marriage and enter service, it implies that a number of them did not inherit any land in areas of impartibility, that the same individuals left home moneyless and worked as servants in the hope of amassing enough money eventually to buy land and get married, not to give money back to their parents (Kussmaul 1981). These servants would most likely wed a wife of equally poor means, and these couples would start their conjugal life with a bare minimum. Too many children, a few bad harvests, and they would be forced to sell their belongings and, ultimately, the little land they had acquired. They were thus by definition the most vulnerable and often ended up swelling the ranks of the landless and paupers (Razi 1993: 15).

Among the poor, the women could gain a meagre income through a cottage industry but, above all, these families could sell their land because there existed an alternative to earning a living, namely wage labour; this is the other main element that Anderson and Macfarlane have isolated. No doubt, the incidence of economic diversification and of wage labour varied from one area to the next, according mostly to population density, inheritance customs, distribution of holding sizes, proportion of the landless, and many other parameters, but it seems accepted by English medievalists that a labour market did operate, be it in woodland or champion country (Razi 1980: 37, 78, 1993: 13; Raftis 1965: 92–3; Smith 1984b: 31; Hanawalt 1986: 112, 115). Finally, the countryside was dotted with marketplaces where one could obtain most consumables in exchange for money or other produce (Hanawalt 1986: 109, 116).

How did the land, labour and consumable markets accord in favouring the emergence of the ELRG? The answer, I believe, is that they concurred in freeing the parents from their distrust vis-à-vis their children.

In thirteenth-century England, as one reads throughout the literature on historical Europe, parents feared destitution and neglect from their own progeny if they transferred all their property *inter vivos*:

> Moralists not only repeated homilies about the callousness of children toward aged parents, but also warned fathers not to use their children as executors . . . [as] a persistent tension existed between the possessors of land, goods, and power and their heirs. Once the old person retired and passed on these accoutrements of adult life, he or she could be left at the mercy of the younger generation.
>
> (Hanawalt 1986: 228)

As in most places, property was constantly used and manipulated in order to ensure care in old age, and this seems to apply indiscriminately to all of thirteenth-century England:[6]

> The young were desirous of gaining control of the family resources while the old wished to secure care and comfort. In the absence of a binding cultural norm of devoting family resources to caring for the aged, such as is found in China, English peasants resorted to contracts and wills when they doubted that their families would provide adequate care.
>
> (Hanawalt 1986: 242)

No doubt, some individuals succeeded in minimizing intergenerational conflicts and received from their own children the care they deserved. But the written evidence constantly reminds us of the contractual nature of care, even between parents and children.

Within the context of impartible inheritance and of a growing population (the context of our argumentation) we should then logically expect parents to have enjoyed much more leverage; they could have demanded cohabitation even more freely than in the rest of France and most other areas of impartible inheritance. Yet, we find the very opposite. This shows blatantly the lack of necessary one-to-one correspondence between inheritance customs and living arrangements but, most importantly, it stirs the question of why the parents should avoid cohabitation with their heir(ess). We could suggest that the heir wielded great bargaining powers but the case would certainly not stand: if the father exacted coresidence and the heir refused, he would have faced the unenviable fate of the landless poor in search of wage labour, for the father could disinherit his heir, a power he could pass on to his widow (Hanawalt 1986: 222). So, we must look at the question from the opposite angle: it must be that conditions in the thirteenth century (and possibly before), in that part of England sharing most of the features of Halesowen, actually favoured parents, who preferred their own residential autonomy as long as they could (Laslett 1977; 1989) rather than suffer the conflicts of cohabitation (since elderly couples, even in a superordinate position, do have to live those conflicts, knowing that a time might come when, bedridden and incapacitated, they may have to pay for their abuse of authority, if abuse there was). For later periods (seventeenth and eighteenth century), some data gives clear, indubitable evidence of this quest for residential autonomy,[7] a quest which is also reflected in the retirement contracts:

> The aged persons showed a marked preference for staying in their own homes even if it meant that they would have to share it with nonkin. *But sharing a home was a choice imposed by economics and not by preference.*
>
> (Hanawalt 1986: 242, italics added)

As Pelling and Smith remarked, historians 'are now much less ready to assume that the needs of the elderly were being met when they are discovered co-residing with kin' (Pelling and Smith 1991: 17). Whenever they could, the parents demanded residential separation and, interestingly enough, it was the propertied and the wealthiest who made such claims, because they could afford it;[8] unfortunately, only a minority (one in twelve) could achieve it (Clark 1982: 313–14; Wall 1995). The others had to satisfy themselves with a separate room and access to the hearth.

What, then, were the circumstances that made it possible for propertied parents to enjoy their residential autonomy? No doubt, we would have to indulge in an extremely long argument were we to look at the problem from the angle of all ranges of fortune. In the two camps that Smith identified in the history of medieval England, namely the Chayanovians (stratification only reflects the household's developmental cycle) or the Leninists (there is true stratification following the accumulation of property which is not redistributed as the household contracts – Smith 1984b), I decidedly side with the Leninists. Like Hanawalt, I believe that the thirteenth century saw a growing stratification built on wealth in land, a stratification well entrenched by the end of the thirteenth century (Hanawalt 1986: 22), and I will use her classification of villagers in three categories: the primary (very rich and important) citizens, the secondary (having enough land to satisfy their household's needs and to settle most of their children on land), and the tertiary (the cottars, who eventually had to sell their land – Hanawalt 1986: 6).

Let us start with a postulate which flows from most studies of European residence: that, without property, one could hardly hope for care in old age from one's children. Either the children were themselves too poor or, if they were not, the cohabiting parent would have been experienced as a sheer burden, and suffered accordingly. Even from the parents' point of view, they were better off cohabiting with unrelated paupers than with their own children. This is explicit in England from the sixteenth century to the twentieth,[9] but there is cause to believe that it also obtained in the late Middle Ages. Although Elaine Clark studied mostly fourteenth-century East Anglian retirement contracts, she found that only one-third of the parents negotiated a contract with their own children (Clark 1982: 315), and there is no reason to presume that it was vastly different in champion country. Furthermore, microsimulations have shown that between 20 and 30 per cent of the elderly would not have had any surviving children anyway (Smith 1984b).

In brief, perhaps close to one-third of the elderly would have needed care from nonkin and, if care was often contractual, as it seems to have been, it must have been attached to property: 'There is a case historically for making a direct link between poverty, or more specifically lack of control over assets, and the *absence* [italics in the text] of retirement practices' (Pelling and Smith 1991: 23). In this perspective, the least endowed had no power to coerce children into looking after them, let alone into cohabitation. Some children might have helped, out of sheer kindness, but the vast majority might have preferred to retain their residential autonomy. To understand the existence of the ELRG in thirteenth-century champion England, therefore, we should argue from the point of view of the propertied. What were their options?

Let us compare their situation to Béarnais fathers. From the very day of his wedding, the Béarnais heir owned the House property, but did not control its management. In Chapter 6, I also mentioned that Béarn parents could disinherit the heirs or heiresses in three circumstances only: if for one reason or another they were mentally or physically incapacitated, if they made an unacceptable matrimonial choice (in other words, married against the parents' wishes), or if, once married, they decided to settle apart. Let us assume that the residential separation of the heir(ess) had been a customary practice. Assuming that the heir(ess) married according to his or her parents' will (since almost all did), such a situation would have deprived the parents of their only possibility of disinheriting the heir(ess) who, in the circumstances, was the real owner. In those conditions, as I argued earlier, the residential separation could have easily led to gross neglect of the ageing parents; when economic subordination does not translate into domestic subordination, it invites domestic insubordination (a possible course of action since the land already belonged to the heir(ess)). In brief, to allow an heir(ess) who inherits *inter vivos* to reside separately, one must be quite sure to get the needed care when desired. I believe that thirteenth-century English circumstances allowed it in a way that was not possible in upland Béarn or, for that matter, in most parts of Europe.

Let us contrast the Béarn we have described with thirteenth-century champion England. In that part of England, let us remember, the heir did not 'own' the holding; the father remained 'owner' until his death, and his widow enjoyed an unassailable right to a sizeable fraction of her late husband's property (from one-third to one-half) until her remarriage and in many cases until her death. Furthermore, the father could disinherit his heir, a power he could pass on to his widow, as we have already seen (Hanawalt 1986: 222). Also, upland Béarn was more or less free of feudal overlordship by the fourteenth century; at best we can speak of absentee overlordship for the upland Pyrenees. This was not the case for thirteenth-century champion England, where nucleated settlements were part of a strong manorial organization; there were few absentee lords, and it was in the lords' interest to make sure that their tenants, whatever their age, were well looked after (according to some, the lords were also the ones who imposed impartible inheritance and tried to inhibit an overactive land market whenever possible). More than this, these people lived within communities celebrated in the literature for their strong sense of collective responsibility for the welfare of the old (Laslett 1979; Smith 1984a: 77, 1991; Lesthaegge 1980; Hanawalt 1986: 208, 266; Thompson even argues most convincingly that early seventeenth-century England was already a welfare state on the scale witnessed in the 1960s and 1970s and that there are certainly grounds to believe that this sense of collective responsibility for the poor and aged did exist in the late Middle Ages – Thompson 1991). Finally, propertied fathers lived in an environment where land, labour and commodities were marketed.

It must be remembered that retirement contracts were a minority of intergenerational transfers (approximately 10 per cent of manorial records of land transfers), and they may be more characteristic of wood-pasture than champion England.[10] The lower incidence of retirement contracts in champion England would substantiate Razi's thesis of its distinctive 'kinship regime', one of higher local kin density, where elderly parents were surrounded by two or more children in the same settlement. But what do we find in Halesowen? Instead of insisting on the cohabitation of their married heir, the wealthier parents seemed to insist that they settle separately but on the same holding, or close to the parents' holding.

To explain this residential separation, we could invoke one of Hanawalt's themes, namely the plasticity and cheapness of the wattle and daub houses of medieval England, and what this implied: that houses did not last more than twenty years, that sons preferred to build than inherit the parental house, that houses and village sites were often moved, and so on and so forth (Hanawalt 1986: 24ff.). Admittedly, as we shall see in the case of contemporary societies (see Chapter 8), the availability of a cheap housing market does help residential autonomy, but is this enough by itself? The type of medieval architecture might have eased the building of separate cottages, but one cannot rest the emergence of ELRG on architecture alone, for the point remains that when combined with residential autonomy, economic subordination does not necessarily translate into adequate care for elderly parents. In other words, parents must have had the opportunity to find the care they needed from individuals other than their own children or even kin, should the case arise. And they did.

Despite the higher kin density of champion England, the settlements were on the whole small, and rates of local exogamy high (Hanawalt 1986: 81); migration in general was high (Smith 1983: 138, 1984b: 31; Razi 1993: 10; Hallam 1958; Dewindt 1972; Britton 1977; Raftis 1964). If we add to this a relatively high degree of genealogical amnesia (Hanawalt 1986: 81), we get a combination which might have been found in few places indeed. Within a given community, the propertied would have been surrounded by a substantial number of unrelated individuals, many of them poor; many of the elderly propertied, moreover, had no surviving children. Simultaneously, there operated a market for land, labour and consumables. Thus propertied parents in thirteenth-century champion England (and *a fortiori* more so in wood-pasture England) had a major lever: if they did not get the care they wanted from their own children, and on their own terms (i.e. without cohabitation), they could disinherit the designated heir, lease the land or sell part of it, and buy the services of a poor person who would look after them. Precisely this is part of Macfarlane's thesis (although he implies the monetization of these markets – Macfarlane 1986: 115–16), a thesis that Blanchard had already put forth for the post-plague period (Blanchard 1984) but that could apply equally well before the Black Death, whether we invoke the existence of cash or not.

In other words, a combination of factors, such as the housing situation, the existence of a market in land, labour and consumables, the greater number of kith than kin in any given settlement, the existence of a class of landless poor, or of paupers with very little land, as well as community support, gave propertied parents the assurance that there was always someone, ideally even someone unrelated and poor, who would come and live with them, someone subordinate who would not import the hostility of sons who expect to inherit, someone who would look after them in old age with more devotion than their own children, if they had any. From the poor's point of view, this simultaneously constituted a way of earning a living, if not of inheriting some movable and immovable property in the end. Furthermore, *pace* Macfarlane (1986: 115–16), these retiring individuals lived within a manorial organization where the lord made sure that they were treated well and where contracts were respected (Smith 1991: 46, 56; Hanawalt 1986: 208, 233; Raftis 1965: 42–6), and within a community which played a similar role (Hanawalt 1986: 258–60; Smith 1984b: 75, 77). Hence these parents could enforce what most parents in Europe could rarely do: they could oblige the son to buy or build his own house nearby, and to look after them from his separate residence; when they cohabited with a married child, it was in most cases plausibly more out of necessity than out of choice. The residential separation of the ageing parents and the married heir meant that both parties simultaneously gained from the deal: each could achieve residential autonomy and reduce the level of antagonism with the other. So it may be that thirteenth-century English parents, if they could afford residential separation, valued kinship too much to allow cohabitation to undermine it. The mobility and the architectural divide might have served to keep a better quality of relationship between parents and children.

Many children certainly looked after their parents without resort to retirement contracts, but retirement contracts made sure that the more callous children (perhaps the progeny of more callous parents) did so with obvious interests in mind. If the residential separation of the heir did not lessen intergenerational conflicts, it seems to have heightened the quality of one relationship at least, namely that between husband and wife. Indeed, Hanawalt strongly emphasizes the relative peacefulness of conjugal relationships, the trust that bound husbands and wives (1986: 218ff.): without mother-in-law or sisters-in-law to sour relationships, couples could live in relative peace. From this point of view, English circumstances in champion country, and as early as the thirteenth century, may have removed for the wealthier one of the greatest constraints to the residential autonomy of older generations, and the main cause of parents coercing their children into cohabitation: the fear of being left destitute and neglected in old age. As a result, one can logically deduce the ELRG: elderly couples would try to live autonomously, as long as they could, and widowers, but mostly old widowed mothers, would often end up living with a child (Razi 1993: 12–13), often a celibate daughter (Pelling and Smith 1991: 14). On the whole, as long as they were married, parents sought to preserve their own residential autonomy as much as their own married children cherished theirs (assuming that they had the property to do so).

So if we have been able to derive an ELRG from the more 'heroic' assumptions of champion England, assuming that such an ELRG did exist in thirteenth-century England, the conclusions apply still more forcefully to areas of partibility, especially to the eastern counties where there was greater economic diversification, much greater mobility among the labouring population, and a much more active and monetized land and labour market.

8

THE WORLD WE HAVE GAINED

Canada 1971–1986[†]

If thirteenth-century England displayed some important regional variations, what are we to say of a country like Canada in the latest decades of the twentieth century? By including this example, my aims are twofold. First, from a purely methodological point of view, we wish to show the superiority of Ermisch and Overton's orientation over that of headship rates, still the most common approach to the analysis of households in contemporary societies. Second, our findings are intended as a contribution in their own right to the vast debate on household developments in Canada and other Western industrialized countries.

The mounting dissatisfaction towards the traditional headship approach is evident in Statistics Canada's treatment of household data in the published census tables over the 1970s and 1980s. Until 1971, almost all published census information on Canadian households referred to the characteristics of household heads, according to their sex, age, matrimonial status, and some other features. Direct information on household composition was not presented on the assumption that this could be reliably inferred from the characteristics of household heads. Under conditions of relative marital stability, such a premise was justifiable. However, the drastic transformation of matrimonial behaviour from the late 1960s onward made this proposition quite untenable. Consequently, by 1986, information relating to household composition (family structure, presence or absence of nonfamily individuals, and so on) had virtually replaced that of household heads in published census tables.

Not all statistical organizations responded with Statistics Canada's efficiency to the radical changes in family norms, largely due to the problems raised: problems of household classification, of how best to describe household composition (see, for instance, Wall 1996; Duchêne 1987; Norris and Knighton 1995; Mulder and Manting 1993). As a result, researchers still tend to fall back on headship rates when it comes to analysing household formation

---

† This chapter was co-authored with Heather Juby.

and change, overlooking (or unaware of) the potential of Ermisch and Overton's framework. We have already advocated the latters' approach in the study of household formation as a promising alternative, and we will employ it in this analysis.

Before going ahead with any application, however, we need to introduce another one of their concepts, namely that of the 'loneship ratio'. Just as the headship rate measures the proportion of household heads within a given subgroup, so the loneship ratio represents the proportion of MRUs within any subgroup that do not share living accommodation with other MRUs, in other words, the proportion of MRUs that are residentially autonomous. Our aim, therefore, is to demonstrate the potential of the loneship ratio in the analysis of changes in household formation, as well as in that of intraregional variability.

An already vast and expanding literature has documented the recent trends in household formation in advanced industrialized countries, including Canada. However, the unprecedented fertility decline, the rapid growth of consensual unions, the steep increase in divorce rates and the concomitant number of one-parent families mean that family (or MRU) formation issues have predominated. The nuclearization of households, as households shed members who are not directly part of a family, and as three-generational households become increasingly uncommon, has not gone unnoticed (Aquilino 1990; Buck and Scott 1993; Goldscheider and Goldscheider 1992; Keirnan 1986; Peron *et al.* 1986; Ward *et al.* 1992; Weinick 1995, to mention but a few), though most contributions focus on the phenomenal growth of solitaries and children leaving home (Keilman 1987; Kerckhoff and Macrae 1992; Avery *et al.* 1992; Goldscheider and Goldscheider 1992; Buck and Scott 1993; Goldscheider *et al.* 1993; Kramarow 1995; van Hoorn 1994; Heaton and Hoppe 1987; Kobrin 1976; Michael *et al.* 1980; Lehrhaupt *et al.* 1993; Baanders 1993; Glick 1993; Wall 1983, 1988, 1995). Two categories have attracted particular attention, namely changes in the home-leaving process as more children leave home earlier to live independently, and the growing number of elderly widows. More recently, a number of studies have examined the coresidence of parents and adult children (Chudacoff and Hareven 1979; Fengler *et al.* 1983; Goldscheider and Goldscheider 1993; Wolf and Soldo 1988).

No doubt, there is a direct link between the phenomenal increase in the percentage of elderly widows living alone and the decrease of three-generational households, but we wish to widen the discussion by showing a general trend among all MRU types to live alone. In brief, we wish to widen the discussion from solitaries to the residential autonomy of MRUs, for this is the way we envision the phenomenon.

Some preliminary considerations

To simplify an already complex presentation, we shall further reduce our MRUs to the following categories:

U1 Lone adults (or 'nonfamily individuals', namely individuals living with neither partner nor children);

U2 Single parents with children (monoparental families);

U3 Couples without children (whether childless, or without any child living with them); and

U4 Couples with children.

In this framework, any household which includes one or any combination of U2, U3 and U4 units will be called a 'family household'; accordingly, 'nonfamily households' will designate those composed exclusively of one or more U1s. Each unit either lives independently in a 'simple' household, or shares with other units in 'complex' households. Thus, Ermisch and Overton's framework enables us to omit reference to household heads, and has the added advantage of discarding the term 'family', a term so often confused, or used interchangeably with that of 'household' in the current demographic literature.

As we have seen in Chapter 4, Ermisch and Overton drew a clear distinction between the formation of households and that of MHUs (our MRUs) at the explanatory level. They view *demographic* decisions or events, such as marriages, divorces, childbearing or deaths, as the principal determinants of MHU formation, and perceive the sharing patterns of these units primarily as the result of socio-economic factors, thereby separating two different fields of study. First, one which focuses on the formation of MHUs, examining such issues as increasing numbers of single parents or reconstituted families, decreasing family size, and such other phenomena. Second, one which places the emphasis on patterns of coresidence between these units. As mentioned earlier, most publications on household formation fail to make this distinction, describing in detail changes in family formation while touching on household formation only in so far as nonfamily individuals are concerned, or to mention in passing that fewer households contain two generations of adults. As the transformation of the family in Canada is relatively well researched and documented, this part of the chapter is devoted uniquely to household formation, that is, to changes in the sharing patterns of MRUs in Canada from 1971 to 1986.

By distinguishing MRU formation from household formation in this manner, one can better appreciate the different ways in which MRUs and households have evolved over the last twenty years. On the one hand, the striking transformation of family-related behaviours, such as marriage, divorce and fertility, has led both to changes in the distribution of MRUs, such as increasing proportions of nonfamily individuals (U1) and single parent units (U2), and to an increasing heterogeneity of individual life histories within any given unit, resulting, for example, in greater numbers of reconstituted families. On the other hand, residential groups have become increasingly homogeneous, in that fewer households now contain more than

150

one MRU. Although in Western societies conjugal and parent/child ties have been the principal criteria dictating coresidence, secondary criteria, such as more extended kinship ties, also played an important role in the past. In recent years, however, these secondary links have gradually lost their traditional role, resulting in a situation where most family households contain only family members; furthermore, the majority of nonfamily households contain only one person. In other words, an increasing number of households include a single MRU; in Canada, for example, the proportion of complex households dropped from 19 to 12 per cent between 1961 and 1981, with the greatest difference registered among nonfamily households.

This analysis draws on published census data and the Public User Sample Tapes of the four censuses taken between 1971 and 1986. Two aspects of this data create difficulties for the approach to household formation used here. The first concerns the organization of household and family data in the Public User Sample Tapes. Statistics Canada's preference for household composition rather than headship, so evident in the published census tables, is unfortunately not reflected in the presentation of the Public User Sample Tapes (those of 1981 excepted), from which one can glean very little information on the minimal units who share households. In the household tape, one cannot even identify the MRUs, as the family unit used is the 'economic family', which by definition may include more than one MRU; the family micro-data, on the other hand, provides no information on the household to which the MRUs belong, thus rendering impossible any analysis of sharing patterns. Paradoxically, the tape describing characteristics of individuals is the greatest source of data on sharing patterns of families and nonfamily persons within households. It allows one to establish loneship ratios for the different types of unit, as well as providing a limited analysis of the characteristics of units within complex households and the relationship which exists between them.

The second issue concerns the allocation of independent MRU status to unmarried young people living with their parents. Ermisch and Overton argue that all children over the age of 16 should be counted as independent MRUs because, able to leave school and earn their own living, they are potentially in a position to make their own decisions about living arrangements. Unlike Ermisch and Overton we would choose the age of majority in Canada (eighteen years). Whether we set the limit of 'adulthood' in contemporary industrialized societies at sixteen or eighteen years old, or at any other age, is irrelevant. What matters is that such a decision makes sense, both conceptually and analytically, in terms of the society under study.

However, this is purely hypothetical, given the fact that Statistics Canada defines all unmarried individuals living with their parents as children in the census family of their parents, irrespective of age. This definition may have been acceptable in the past, but it is becoming increasingly difficult to accept the residence of adult single children in the parental home as the norm;

furthermore, such a definition blurs the analytical distinction between once-married and never-married children. With the increasing incidence of premarital residential independence, cohabitation and returns to the parental home, the assumption that a celibate adult living with parents has experienced neither conjugal life nor residential independence is no longer tenable (Desrosiers *et al.* forthcoming).

An additional inconvenience is that the group of lone parent families defined in this way includes residential groups which hardly conform to the current meaning of a lone parent family (such as the 85-year-old widowed mother living with her 60-year-old unmarried daughter, classified in census tables as a lone mother family). By our definition, the ageing mother and single daughter household would join the ranks of complex households containing two nonfamily individuals – a more appropriate classification. Since it is impossible to identify MRUs according to this definition in the census data, we have retained the definitions of Statistics Canada within the compass of this chapter and included all unmarried children living at home in the MHU of their parents, whatever impact this had on the calculations.

Now, with these tools in hand, what can we discern in the evolution of autonomous living for the different MRU types during the period 1971–1986?

Loneship ratios: 1971–1986

Loneship ratios of nonfamily adults (U1)

Table 8.1 gives us a breakdown of the loneship ratios of nonfamily adults. The steep rise in autonomous living for both men and women is striking. From 1971 to 1986, the proportion of nonfamily men living alone increased from 29 to 52 per cent, and the loneship ratios of nonfamily women rose from 37 to 62 per cent during the same period. Around 90 per cent of this growth, however, occurred during the first decade for men and women alike, and the slowing down of this trend between 1981 and 1986 is quite as dramatic as its increase in the earlier period.

The fact that nonfamily adult women tend to live alone more often than do men in similar circumstances – this is consistent through time and for all age groups – is the main difference between male and female U1s. Otherwise, they share a similar pattern of distribution between age groups, and the evolution of their loneship ratios from one census to the next follows closely parallel paths.

As we move from the younger to the older age groups for any given year, we notice that the ratios rise steeply for young adults, and more slowly with advancing age. If we look across time, however, different patterns emerge. Indeed, if we exclude the youngest age group (fifteen to twenty-four), all others display the steepest increases between 1971 and 1976. Between 1981

Table 8.1 Loneship ratios of nonfamily persons (U1), by sex and age, Canada 1971, 1976, 1981, 1986

Age group	Loneship ratios			
	1971	*1976*	*1981*	*1986*
Male				
Total 15+	29	41	50	51
15–24	12	20	28	24
25–34	28	44	52	48
35–44	34	51	59	60
45–54	37	53	60	62
55–64	40	54	61	65
65+	41	54	61	66
Female				
Total 15+	37	50	58	60
15–24	13	22	32	27
25–34	30	48	57	53
35–44	36	53	60	61
45–54	41	56	63	64
55–64	46	60	67	69
65+	46	61	68	72

Sources: Canadian censuses

and 1986, however, differences in their evolution begin to appear according to age: loneship ratios continue augmenting for the two oldest groups, while this tendency is considerably mitigated in the two central age groups, and is entirely reversed for those aged under thirty-five years. We will discuss the implications of these results, and those given in the two following sections, later in the chapter.

Loneship ratios of lone parent units (U2)

Although the general level of loneship ratios is higher among single parents than lone adults (Table 8.2), the evolution of the rates between 1971 and 1986 is similar: within any given year, the ratios increase with age, and they also augment over time, and more so during the first decade than between 1981 and 1986. However, the decline in rates between 1981 and 1986 for those under thirty-five years of age, so evident among nonfamily individuals, is either totally absent or greatly mitigated for single parents. Between 1981 and 1986, it is rather among those between the ages of thirty-five to forty-four that the ratios decrease slightly for both fathers and mothers.

Except for the patricells included in the 15–34 age bracket, the increase in loneship ratios in the 1970s affected the younger parents, those who can truly be described as single parent families.[1] These rose so steeply that, by 1986, for mothers at least, the ratios were similar for all age groups, resembling more closely the age pattern for couples (as we will see in the following section) than for nonfamily units. By 1986, nearly four out of five young lone mothers lived autonomously for all age groups compounded as opposed to 70 per cent for men. For the youngest age group, the discrepancy is most startling: 78 per cent of matricells lived on their own, as opposed to only 50 per cent of patricells.

Loneship ratios of couples and families (U3 and U4)

The two types of unit containing couples, with and without children, are presented together (Table 8.3), as the loneship ratios of these two groups are very similar. Once again, one can identify the pattern of increasing loneship ratios during the 1970s, with a slowing down between 1981 and 1986, except for the youngest age group (fifteen to twenty-four) which displays a slight decline. The evolution is less pronounced than for the other types of MRUs because of the already high levels of residential autonomy among couples in 1971 (86 per cent). Unlike the other types of unit, however, the ratios do not increase with age; throughout the period, couples aged from twenty-five to forty-four years enjoy the highest level of residential autonomy.

Income and household formation

Household transformations, especially their nuclearization and the exponential increase in the number of one-person households, have been explained in terms of three sets of factors: cultural, demographic and economic ones. The cultural explanations are the most elusive and revolve mostly around two supposedly related phenomena: the rise of individualism and the concomitant decline in family-centred values, or the emergence of a propensity to live alone, i.e. changes in living preferences revealing this increasing individualism and rejection of family values (on the changes in living preferences, see note 2; for cultural explanations, see Beresford and Rivlin 1966; Kobrin 1976; Roussel 1983; Pampel 1983; Ruggles 1991, 1994). We have already made our position clear vis-à-vis this type of explanation in earlier chapters, stressing its tautological character; we shall therefore ignore it.

Table 8.2 Loneship ratios of lone parents (U2), by sex and age, Canada 1971, 1976, 1981, 1986

Age group	Loneship ratios			
	1971	*1976*	*1981*	*1986*
Fathers				
Total 15+	56	62	70	70
15–34	38	32	46	49
35–44	45	57	73	72
45–54	59	69	73	72
55–64	69	73	72	76
65+	74	76	77	78
Mothers				
Total 15+	71	77	80	80
15–24	50	63	69	78
25–34	66	74	79	79
35–44	72	78	83	81
45–54	74	79	81	82
55–64	75	78	77	79
65+	78	81	82	83

Sources: Canadian censuses

As to the demographic factors they are *prima facie* more convincing. Indeed, many authors have emphasized the role of escalating divorce rates, of delayed marriage among young people, of a longer life expectancy as well as a differential life expectancy between men and women, together with falling fertility rates, in explaining the decline of three-generational households and the rise in the overall number of households, many of them composed of solitaries or lone parents (Hall 1986; Heaton and Hoppe 1987; Schmid 1988; Schwarz 1988; Kramarow 1995). Despite their appeal, however, these arguments are somewhat flawed because the demographic factors cited account for the sizeable increase in the number of *MRUs*, not of households.

Let us take escalating divorce rates. They might account for the swelling number of lone parents and solitaries but do not explain the manner in which

Table 8.3 Loneship ratios of couples (U3 + U4), by sex and age, Canada 1971, 1976, 1981, 1986

Age group	Loneship ratios			
	1971	*1976*	*1981*	*1986*
Total 15+	86	89	91	91
15–24	84	90	90	89
25–34	88	91	92	92
35–44	88	90	92	92
45–54	86	88	89	90
55–64	84	87	89	89
65+	85	88	90	92

Sources: Canadian censuses

these MRUs share dwelling-places. In other words, there is nothing that intrinsically links soaring divorce rates to a greater number of households of smaller size. Theoretically, one could imagine all kinds of new residential groupings resulting from high levels of divorce, such as lone parent families coresiding for mutual child-care and to benefit from economies of scale, not to mention lone parents coresiding with related nonfamily individuals for similar reasons. And the same can be said about the elderly: fewer children, the greater longevity of women as well as a longer life expectancy in general do not explain the swelling number of elderly solitaries, since elderly widowed people, like lone parents, could also have formed complex households, as they are occasionally seen to do. Yet, such new household forms remain the exception rather than the rule. To the question of why so many lone parents and elderly people increasingly choose to establish or retain their own households, rather than share them with others, demography alone gives no answer, and we most therefore look elsewhere.

We are thus left with economic factors, the list of which is by far the longest and most complex. One theme nonetheless dominates most discussions: that the rise in income levels and the emergence of state welfare, together with a more favourable housing market, have 'enabled the elderly to "purchase" more privacy in the form of living alone' (Kramarow 1995: 336; for the economic argument, see, among others, Burch and Matthews 1987; Brouwer 1988; Duchêne 1987; Miron 1988; Schwarz 1988; Goldscheider *et al.* 1993). As Kramarow astutely remarks, 'These arguments [linking rising income levels to the "purchase" of privacy] imply that privacy has always been a desired good' (1995: 337).[2] As expected, this is exactly our position, but only when inserted in the set of axioms we have elaborated; indeed, we believe that a favourable economic climate, state welfare and a more accessible housing market (which marked the 1960s and 1970s in Canada, but also in the USA and many parts of Europe) do have a predominant explanatory power in so far as they can be interpreted as a means of allowing people a greater choice in living arrangements, and make possible the expression of MRU residential autonomy. Despite their great significance, however, it would be naive and erroneous to assume that economic factors alone account for living arrangements.

In Chapter 4, we mentioned that in the circumstances of our industrialized countries economic models gain greater relevance, and we will call upon a certain number of economic considerations to argue that something has been gained in this household atomization, namely residential autonomy. Unfortunately, because of the nature of the data in hand, we will not be able to go much beyond documenting this move, and offering the simplest of correlations. Furthermore, we will take as given the existence of state welfare and a more accessible housing market to focus uniquely on the dimension of income.

The previous pages have documented the growth of residential autonomy during the 1970s, not only among the solitaries but among all MRU types, a trend which not only slowed down considerably from 1981 to 1986 but was even reversed in certain subgroups. Moreover, for any given year, we also observe heightening loneship ratios as we move up from younger to older age groups, except for couples. These, and many other facts, point to a relationship between income levels and contemporary household transformations.

A more complete understanding of the link between income and household formation would require an in-depth multivariant analysis, one which furthermore would compare the characteristics of MRUs within simple and complex households; this, unfortunately, is both technically difficult, and falls beyond the narrow compass of this chapter. While MRUs lend themselves very well to this form of analysis, the census data are rather less accommodating because, as we have already mentioned, the Public User Sample Tape data prevent us from distinguishing the characteristics of MRUs residing autonomously from those living in complex households. In addition, most information allowing us to compare real income across time relates to economic family income rather than MRU income, further inhibiting the desired comparison. Nonetheless, published census data can provide a limited insight into the relevance of income to household formation.

For instance, data on low incomes for family units and nonfamily individuals throw some light on trends in loneship ratios (Table 8.4). This table shows the percentages of economic families and nonfamily individuals whose income fell below the poverty line in the years under study (1971, 1981 and

157

1986), according to their age. If we focus on the changes in the percentages between 1971 and 1981, on the one hand, and those witnessed between 1981 and 1986, on the other (the bottom two lines of each series of figures), we first find confirmation of rising incomes during the 1970s, which permitted MRUs not only to establish independent households but also to do so in comfort. Despite this household 'atomization', the proportion of all .MRU types living below the low income threshold had declined considerably by the end of the decade. Also in evidence are the worsening economic conditions from 1981 onward. The percentage of economic families with incomes below the poverty line increased across the board, and did so substantially for most. Overall, the rise and fall in incomes more or less reflects the evolution of loneship ratios during the period under consideration. No doubt, there is no one-to-one correspondence between the two, nor should we look for one, for more than sheer economic considerations are at play; the parallels between income levels and loneship ratios are nonetheless too striking to be dismissed.

Most conspicuous is the relation between income and autonomy in the oldest (sixty-five years and above) and youngest (fifteen to twenty-four years) age groups. With the exception of lone parents, all MRU types in the youngest age group experienced a decline in residential autonomy between 1981 and 1986;[3] these youngsters also registered the sharpest reduction in income during the same period. At the other extreme, those in the oldest groups were the only ones protected from the deteriorating economic conditions, with substantial drops in the proportion below the low income threshold (Table 8.4). Predictably, loneship ratios of elderly MRUs were still on the rise in 1986. In between we note that on the whole MRUs between the ages of twenty-five and thirty-four display rates of residential autonomy not unlike those of younger cohorts. For all the other intermediate age groups, the rates sometimes oscillate a little, registering a slight fall or rise in places, and remaining more or less stable in others.

Let us focus on the two extremes, and their clear pattern of behaviour. For the youngest, it stands to reason that they rank amongst the most vulnerable in times of economic difficulties; if able to find work at all, they are often the most unstably employed. They have the advantage, however, of being most easily able to adapt their living arrangements to changes in income. Returning to the parental home, where their bedroom may still await them, is often a possibility, since they might have left not very long ago; alternatively, young nonfamily individuals will easily find among their peer group a great many unattached individuals with whom to share living accommodation.

At the other extreme, the elderly's incomes increased, and the reduction in the proportion of elderly with low incomes might not tell the whole story. For one, many of those elderly will be recently widowed, living alone on an income which previously supported two. Furthermore, not only are the elderly enjoying higher incomes, but their economic commitments are concurrently

Table 8.4 Low income economic families and unattached individuals (in percentages), 1971, 1981, 1986

		Total	*15–24*	*25–34*	*35–44*	*45–54*	*55–64*	*65+*
Unattached males	1971	36	42	18	21	28	38	41
	1981	30	38	19	19	27	33	47
	1986	33	50	25	25	32	40	34
% change	1971/1981	-15	-9	-5	-10	-3	-12	13
	1981/1986	9	32	32	28	17	21	26
Unattached females	1971	51	56	26	33	36	47	67
	1981	45	52	21	25	34	41	57
	1986	42	62	26	26	37	46	45
% change	1971/1981	-12	-7	-18	-24	-6	-12	-15
	1981/1986	7	20	21	6	7	13	20
Lone fathers	1971	24	–	–	–	–	–	–
	1981	16	24	15	15	14	14	16
	1986	18	31	20	20	16	18	13
% change	1971/1981	-36	–	–	–	–	–	–
	1981/1986	17	31	32	35	15	28	18
Lone mothers	1971	43	–	–	–	–	–	–
	1981	40	72	60	45	32	27	19
	1986	42	79	63	45	32	27	15
% change	1971/1981	-6	–	–	–	–	–	–
	1981/1986	4	10	4	0	0	0	17
Couples (by age of husband)	1971	17	–	–	–	–	–	–
	1981	10	16	10	9	7	8	11
	1986	10	23	12	10	8	11	7
% change	1971/1981	-42	–	–	–	–	–	–
	1981/1986	7	43	20	5	15	35	34

Sources: Canadian censuses

reduced. With the house paid for and the children educated, often with reduced consumption needs and with a national health service providing free care, they are indeed well off both in relative and in real terms. At the extremes (the youngest and the oldest), the links between economic conditions and household formation appear to be at their strongest.

At the ages in between, as already mentioned, the situations vary. Couples, with or without coresiding children, display a rise throughout the period, one somewhat attenuated between 1981 and 1986, no doubt partly due to the fact that they already enjoyed both the highest incomes and the greatest residential independence of all MRU types in 1971. As to the others, only one fact needs to be emphatically stressed, namely that lone mothers between the ages of thirty-five and sixty-four retain roughly the same proclivity to live alone, with the lowest incomes of all economic families. This, in our opinion, says something of the utmost importance about psychology and living arrangements: that lone mothers would rather live alone and in poverty than cohabit with another MRU and benefit from economies of scale and other trade-offs. Their extremely high loneship ratios, only exceeded by those of couples, eloquently upholds our main thesis, namely that MRUs seek residential autonomy, and often at substantial economic costs.

On the topic of lone mothers, one last feature ought to be discussed. Indeed, even if we take into consideration the under-representation of the youngest cohort (see note 3), the fact remains that lone mothers between the ages of fifteen and twenty-four maintained a strong desire for residential autonomy between 1981 and 1986, when they were rated as the poorest among all MRUs of all ages. Why should this be so? Most plausibly because their very poverty entitled them to supplementary benefits, and because part of those supplementary benefits were meant to defray the cost of housing. Thus, it would appear that the welfare state gave them a chance to retain their residential autonomy, despite the poverty attached to it, and also that they preferred a life of relative destitution and autonomous residence to cohabitation.

As the case of lone mothers makes quite clear, economic considerations are not the sole determinant in the choice of living arrangement. While the favourable economic climate of the 1970s certainly contributed to the overall trend towards heightened loneship ratios for all types of MRUs, other aspects of living arrangements escape this form of explanation, for example the fact that female U1s and single mothers enjoy a much higher degree of residential autonomy than their male counterparts, despite much lower incomes. This, one may argue, may have something to do with survivals from a traditional division of labour which made it easier for women than men to manage daily life, to look after themselves and their children, and also perhaps to make their pennies go further. Nowadays many men, particular older ones, still depend on women for most domestic activities. Since the ability to live alone depends greatly on the ability to execute daily domestic activities, it stands to reason that most women still find it easier than most men to live alone, although the differences might diminish, and even disappear, in future generations.

Overall, however, we believe that the condition of the Canadian economy and the evolution of loneship ratios in contemporary Canada tell us something about the world we have gained. If we find so few complex households, if so many nonfamily individuals and many more monoparental families elect not to coreside with other MRUs, it is because the economic circumstances of postwar Canada have gradually removed all the coercive forces and most of the hindrances to residential autonomy, and made it possible for most MRUs to achieve what they aspired to. In other words, what the figures clearly point to is an overwhelming desire to shun cohabitation, as well as economic circumstances which allow most people to exercise this decision freely; in the contemporary Canadian case, it could be argued that economic circumstances explain the limit of residential growth. When it comes to intraregional variability, however, many other parameters have to be introduced, although real income remains predominant.

Where are the others? Complex households in contemporary Canada

However great the number of MRUs expressing their residential autonomy, and however favourable the economic circumstances in the country, no MRU type reached a loneship ratio of 100 per cent. By definition, those who have not achieved residential autonomy coreside with other MRUs, and this necessarily begs the question of complex households in contemporary industrialized societies ('complex' according to Ermisch and Overton's definitions, let us recall). No doubt, the number of complex households is on the decline (19 per cent in 1971); by 1981, they comprised only 12 per cent, but also 12 per cent in 1991, of all private households in Canada. Interestingly enough, this small minority of households nonetheless contained no less than a quarter of all MRUs: half of the male and two-fifths of the female nonfamily units; almost one in three lone fathers and one in five lone mothers; and close to one couple out of ten, with or without children. In fact, the percentages would be more had we been able to apply the definitions of Ermisch and Overton; indeed, treating all adult individuals as independent MRUs would considerably boost the number of complex households, adding all those in which adult unmarried individuals reside with their parent(s). If loneship ratios tell the story of an evolving freedom from coercion and hindrances in living arrangements, complex households remind us that the evolution might not have reached its term. But can it ever be complete?

Complex households fall into three general categories: multiple family households, which contain at least two family units; households in which a family unit will share with one or more U1s, and households with no family unit in which two or more U1s coreside.

Multiple family households

In 1971, multiple family households accounted for only 2 per cent of the total number of Canadian households and contained 5 per cent of all family units. Ten years later these proportions had declined by half, leaving 2.8 per cent of family units living in 1 per cent of the households – the complete eradication of multiple family households seemed well on its way and, following the scientists' motto to neglect the negligible, it is tempting to ignore this marginal form of living arrangement; this is what we shall do here.[4]

Multiple family households may or may not include nonfamily units (individuals living without partner and children); all other types of complex households, however, contain at least one such individual. This individual may be living with one (or more) nonfamily individual(s), with a family unit (U2, U3 or U4), or with both. Let us therefore approach complex households in terms of the sharing patterns of nonfamily adults.

Nonfamily adults in complex households

In 1986, three out of five nonfamily individuals in complex households lived exclusively with individuals in similar circumstances (Table 8.5). Of the two in five who lived in family households, just over a quarter shared with single parent units (U2), another quarter with couples without children (U3), and almost a half with couples with children (U4); only 3 per cent lived in multi-family households.

In general, the type of unit with which U1s coreside seems to vary little according to sex or age, with slightly more men than women living with other nonfamily persons. Only with advancing age does a preference for sharing with families begin to emerge; over the age of fifty-five the proportion of women living with 'complete families' (couple and their nonadult children) increases more quickly than that of men but, by the age of sixty-five, about 50 per cent of lone individuals live with family units, up from 30 to 40 per cent at younger ages.

But who are the relatives with whom nonfamily individuals or lone parents choose to cohabit? The data made it difficult to isolate family MRUs, so that the following considerations stem from computations made on lone individuals. Below the age of forty-four, they either live with a parent or with nonrelatives. But when studying the kinship affiliations of lone individuals above the age of forty-five in complex households, one fact is striking: they increasingly share with relatives. The majority of those once married live with children though, interestingly enough, a substantial number coreside with siblings, as does the overwhelmingly majority of elderly who have never married.

Our previous conclusions should therefore not give the wrong impression.

Table 8.5 Distribution of nonfamily men and women in complex households, according to the type of MRUs with which they cohabit, 1986

Age group	U2	U3	U4	MFH	NFH	Total
U1 Women						
15–24	10	9	19	1	61	100.00
25–34	12	7	10	1	70	100.00
35–44	16	7	10	0	67	100.00
45–54	13	9	12	1	65	100.00
55–64	10	8	22	1	59	100.00
65+	8	13	30	1	48	100.00
Total	10	10	20	1	59	100.00
U1 Men						
15–24	8	11	19	1	61	100.00
25–34	10	9	13	1	67	100.00
35–44	17	10	10	1	62	100.00
45–54	19	8	10	1	62	100.00
55–64	11	8	13	2	66	100.00
65+	9	12	25	1	53	100.00
Total	11	10	15	1	63	100.00

Sources: Canadian censuses

Notes:
MFH = multiple family households
NFH = nonfamily households

Despite an almost completely nuclear limit of residential growth, complex households are still part of the Canadian residential landscape, and are probably there to stay. Undoubtedly, much of that cohabitation results from hindrances, and will be short-lived. Indeed, while the poverty of single parent households created by marital breakdown is well documented, studies of these financial constraints on the residential choices immediately after a separation are few and far between (Festy 1988; Sullivan 1986). Nonetheless, research in the Netherlands has shown that the separation or divorce of couples leads to an increase in complex households, in that the majority of individuals who leave the conjugal home temporarily stay with parents, relatives or friends, or in some other kind of shared housing, for an average of six months or so after the separation (Dieleman 1989).

Similar considerations also apply to some nonfamily individuals. Indeed, if economic circumstances have become predominant in the choice of living arrangements in advanced industrialized countries, one could expect a return to a greater proportion of complex households in a period of recession (such as the year 1986, from which our data is drawn). As it happens, studies indicate that the trend towards early age at leaving home, so apparent in the 1970s, was reversed during the 1980s in Europe and in North America, with young people delaying the move towards residential autonomy (Glick and Lin 1986; Keilman 1987; Miron 1988). In Oslo, 45 per cent of unmarried persons between the ages of twenty and twenty-one lived with their parents in 1982, and 60 per cent in 1986 (Gulbrandsen and Hansen 1986, quoted in Keilman 1987: 304–5); 'most of these persons gave financial considerations as a major reason for still being a member of the parental household' (Keilman 1987: 305).

On the other hand, it would be implausible to argue that all cases of cohabitation result from economic hindrances, especially among elderly nonfamily individuals. In their case, psychological motivations may be paramount, such as the desire to escape loneliness and enjoy companionship, as well as the quest for mutual physical care.

Overall, this brief glance at complex households in Canada has revealed the types of unit most likely to be found coresiding: nonfamily individuals and lone parents, particularly when young and male and, among the elderly, unmarried individuals. If the former are more likely to resign themselves to coresidence mostly because of economic hindrances, the latter may seek it positively for psychological and physical reasons and, if this is so, complex households may be here to stay, forming a ceiling beyond which loneship ratios may never go, for we find the same percentages both in 1981 and 1991, which mark a decade of economic difficulties.

On the other hand, with falling fertility rates, most lone elderly individuals will have no siblings to live with, once the baby boom generations have passed away. Without siblings, the elderly might have little choice but to opt for solitary residence or new residential arrangements with nonrelatives. Loneship ratios might be pushed to their extreme limit, one in which complex households result from economic hindrances only. Alternatively, people may shake off old habits and form new types of households, keeping complex households very much around the 10 per cent mark, if not more. It is this human creativity that makes predicting future household formation impossible and which forbids us to herald the complete disappearance of complex households.[5]

9

ABUTIA

A different residential logic

Abutia is a confederation of three Ewe-speaking villages located in the Volta Region, in eastern Ghana. I conducted fieldwork in one of its villages, Kloe, from March 1971 to November 1973 and, by definition, what follows applies to observations made during fieldwork. As far as I can tell, Kloe was perfectly representative of the two other villages.

Abutia villages are nucleated and surrounded by their farmlands. They are also relatively large; at the time of the fieldwork, Kloe could boast of 1200 inhabitants (1500 in the 1960 census), and the smallest village, Agove, counted no less than 1000 inhabitants. Their size has favoured village endogamy, which covered approximately 70 per cent of all marriages.

At the time I collected my own census, between September 1971 and February 1972, I identified 172 houses in Kloe, with their respective residential groups. Altogether, 137 (80 per cent) of them were surveyed in detail. My intimate knowledge of all the other groups not surveyed convinces me that none of them differed significantly from the ones described here. I therefore believe this sample to be representative of the population of Kloe and, by extension, of that of Abutia.

The Abutia dwelling-place and its transmission

The Abutia designate their habitations as *xonu*, some kind of 'residential complex', or more simply 'house', which comprises three types of buildings, namely: 1) a rectangular building (*xo*) internally divided into bedrooms which are not interconnected since their only door opens onto the outside courtyard (let us call this the 'bedroom wing'); 2) a kitchen which faces the bedrooms across an open space and shelters one to three hearths; and 3) a 'bathroom-cum-urinal' which stands behind the kitchen or next to the bedrooms. These three buildings are positioned on both sides of, or around, an open space which also forms an integral part of the *xonu*, rather like an open room (or courtyard). When at home, women spend most of their time in this open space, either busy with the care of young children, or absorbed in the preparation of meals (peeling or pounding vegetables; only the actual cooking takes place on the hearth). The open space is diligently swept every day, and kept as neat and tidy as the floor of an actual room, since it is in fact the place where food is processed.

Three main types of house can be observed in Abutia, their sizes directly reflecting the wealth of the builder. The smallest ones, with thatched roofs, are two-room buildings with a kitchen facing towards the house (the 'bedroom wing' is reduced to a partitioned bedroom only). Larger dwelling-places boast of a greater number of bedrooms (a proper wing), whereas the largest comprise two separate bedroom wings built at a right angle to form an L-shaped structure, each side of which being subdivided into three or four bedrooms (the largest number of bedrooms I recorded in the village I studied was thirteen). A large kitchen faces one of the wings, thereby giving these large residential complexes a U shape.

A dwelling-place rarely has more than one 'kitchen'. Kitchens in the largest houses can be mistaken for a 'bedroom wing' because of their cement walls; kitchen floors, however, are never cemented (whereas bedroom ones are). Large kitchens have two to three hearths, without any dividing walls, whereas the poorer ones simply consist of a hearth sheltered by a palm-branch roof, supported by four poles.

The Abutia dwellings are not enclosed by either fences or walls, but are positioned in such a way as to be half-enclosed by the back walls of surrounding buildings. The intervening spaces between houses are mainly made up of the network of paths used to reach them, or of the ditches into which dirty water is thrown. The house, however, is no 'compound'. Once built, the owner rarely adds another building to it. 'Building' means erecting a completely separate and distinct *xonu*, not adding an extension to an already existing one.

Two houses may have adjacent kitchens and their respective open spaces may form one continuous floor. Merged houses like these seem to form a compound, but are in fact referred to by their dwellers as distinct houses with their separate kitchens and bathrooms, despite the exchange of services which may take place between the two. Such (rare) situations tend to arise when brothers build their houses with the bedroom wings facing one another across the open space and not back to back, as is the normal practice. I have recorded only four such cases in Kloe. These facts thus suggest that the Abutia abode is a discrete and clearly delineated unit, a unit also explicitly named in the Ewe language, and one that can best be described as a house, despite its layout around an open space. The latter is merely an adjustment to tropical conditions.

The desire to build a house dominates economic pursuits in Abutia. As with the cattle among the southern Bantu or horses among the Plains Indians, one encounters somewhat of a 'house-building complex' in Eweland. When asked the reasons why they wish to emigrate to the city, young men always mention the need to amass enough cash to build a beautiful house in the village. Houses, and not the number of wives, are the main symbols of status and economic achievement. In essays which they were asked to write in class, young boys did not mention polygyny as one of the more interesting premiums of wealth (something extremely common in other parts of Africa), but the building of a huge and magnificent house. A major form of ostentatious spending, house-building is nevertheless not an investment with a view to financial returns, since men do not build in order to rent, but simply to display their economic success and head larger residential groups. The bigger the house and the more numerous its occupants, the greater the head's prestige in the community. The few lodgers that I found in Kloe (they numbered approximately twenty-five) all lived in five enormous houses which could not be filled even with the whole minimal lineage of the late owner. Their builders died without leaving many children behind, and their heirs resolved to let the rooms (to teachers, or transient government workers) instead of leaving them vacant.

Abutia houses were formerly built out of dried mud and thatch, and apparently lasted, with occasional repairs, for the lifetime of their owner. Few of these could be seen at the time of the fieldwork, cement having replaced the traditional building material. The new concrete houses can last for many generations with only minor repairs, but were relatively expensive to build; in 1971, their cost ranged from the equivalent of US $400 to $1,000 (at the rate of exchange then prevailing), an expenditure which represented from one-and-a-half to four times the annual wages of an unskilled labourer working in Accra (the capital), or between one and three times the annual earnings of a small-scale cocoa farmer. This capital outlay, needless to say, is all the more onerous in a situation where house-builders do not have access to mortgages or to loans of any kind (except possibly from kin, though the subject was never broached).

Modern houses are personally owned by the person who pays to have them built.[1] At the time of the fieldwork, none of the new types of house had been purchased from a previous owner, and there was no evidence that such a practice would soon develop. When the original owner died, who inherited the house? To understand the transmission of houses, we have to know something about polygyny and the residence of co-wives.

Polygyny rates in Abutia are low for Africa, but there are nonetheless a few men who had been or were polygynists at the time of the fieldwork. Interestingly enough, Abutia co-wives do not coreside. As a result, a man's children will be divided in two categories: 1) those born to mothers who never lived in their husband's house, and 2) those born to a mother who lives in her husband's house (or lived there most of her life, so that her children spent most of their childhood there). After the original house-owner dies, the house he paid to have built (if built out of concrete) becomes the 'joint entitlement' of the set of full siblings who were brought up in that house, under the trusteeship of the oldest living male, who acts as 'head' (technically speaking, their half-siblings might also have entitlements but they never exercise them – since they never lived under the same roof in childhood, half-siblings never coreside in a house headed by one of them). This set of children enjoys an inalienable right to occupy one of the house's rooms, if one is available. In other words, these full siblings form a house-owning corporation represented by its oldest male member. In the absence of a son, the house will devolve to the original owner's oldest surviving daughter.

When the trustee-holder dies, the devolution is then influenced by two additional factors, namely 1) whether the next oldest brother alive has already built his own house and 2) whether the deceased trustee is survived by a grown-up son. If the trustee-owner dies before his own son has reached maturity, the house will revert to his brother next in line, whether the latter has already built a house or not. If the trustee is survived by a grown-up son, the latter will inherit the house his father headed as trustee if his father's surviving brothers have already built their own house. If not, the house will devolve to the eldest brother who is still not house-owner, and later will revert to the original trustee's own son when the brother-trustee dies (assuming that there is no other brother to inherit). At this point, this son will occupy the house as a trustee on behalf of his own set of full siblings.

If the original trustee-holder is survived by sisters only, the house will pass on to one of them if his own son is too young to head a residential group, or if he has no son. If he leaves a grown-up son behind, however, the house will automatically devolve to the latter. If the sons are still children, one of the sisters will act as trustee until the oldest son reaches maturity, at which time she will pass the house over to her nephew. When the original holder or trustee-holder has no male siblings or children as heirs, the sisters or daughters will take possession of the house and gain complete 'right of purchaser' (i.e. full individual ownership over it). Women who inherit from agnates have to pass the house on to their own sons, if they have any. If women can inherit houses, it goes without saying that they are also entitled to build their own. When a woman builds a house, however, the devolution follows different rules. First, her sons will not inherit (her sister will if she has no daughter) and a daughter (normally the oldest one) will inherit the house as personally acquired property. Houses built by women are thus bequeathed exclusively along female lines and do not become corporate property. It must be mentioned, however, that the greatest majority of houses built by women were among the smallest and could rarely accommodate more than two adult women.

Women are thus entitled to inherit their father's house and other personally acquired immovable property as residual heirs in the absence of brothers. As members of a set of full siblings, they also belong to the house-owning corporation (enjoying fewer rights than their brothers, however, in that they are the last in line to inherit) and share an inalienable right of residence (henceforth designated as 'domiciliary right') in the paternal house.

Finally, no property of any kind can be bequeathed to spouses or affines; in no case can devolution cross the affinal divide. Affines and spouses can exchange gifts, but cannot bequeath property between themselves. There is no granary, no crop even, left by the deceased husband, of which the wife could take possession. Consequently, men never build houses for their wives. Nor do they, incidentally, give houses to their brothers. I have recorded two instances of men who built a house for a sister, two others who did it for their father, and two women who did the same for their mother. In all these instances the house was to revert to the person who originally paid to have the house built when the present head died; moreover, those who paid for the house were on labour migrations and only occasionally spent time in their native village.

Returning to the topic of houses and their occupation, it is worth signalling that bedrooms are occupied in a patterned fashion. Each adult male enjoys a separate bedroom which he mostly occupies alone – a man very rarely shares a bedroom with his wife, and never with any other adult. A man's room is a very private, almost secret, place where only women enter, and exclusively at night, if invited to make love. During the day, women and children keep away from men's rooms because men keep their 'medicines' in their room ('medicines' are objects which endow them with special powers). Young men, however, do share rooms, depending on the availability of space. Women's rooms, on the other hand, enjoy very little privacy since children use them during the day, either to fetch things or to rest. Old women sometimes prefer to occupy their rooms alone, if they can, although most adult women share their bedrooms with their young children or grandchildren, and often with an adult daughter and her own children. Adult sisters, however, very seldom occupy the same bedroom. There is thus a cycle of occupation of bedrooms. Children sleep with their mother or mother's mother until their teens, by which time they share a room with peers of the same gender. Teenage girls sleep together until they bear children, whereas adolescent boys eventually move into a room which they occupy alone.

Finally, a proper (especially new type) house is not complete without a veranda, used by the men as a 'reception room'. A man expecting guests will wait for them on his veranda where they will sit to greet him. The veranda is reserved for formal public meetings, when a serious topic has to be discussed between a few men. Otherwise, men tend to spend their leisure time at the different social centres in the village – the palm-wine bar, the general store, or simply the streets, where they sit on rows of large stones set out like seats. Men thus meet each other outside the house, in one of the many public places, unlike women who tend to congregate in the open spaces around their kitchens. Men use houses mostly to eat, sleep and make love, and they spend the time not devoted to eating or sleeping on their farms or in public places. This fact underlies the very secular nature of Abutia houses, which shelter neither shrines nor commonly-owned ritual objects, and are not protected by any special spirits. There are no special ceremonies which precede the choosing of a house site, nor any to accompany building or removal. A new owner contents himself or herself with pouring libations to the 'collective ancestors' before moving into his or her new dwelling-place, but never performs any other ritual connected with it. Such secular houses compare well with European ones, but for their mode of devolution.

House transmission: changes and their repercussions

As we shall soon see, Abutia residential groups in 1972 differed vastly from anything encountered in Europe. And yet, this results from a limited set of cultural clauses, most of them recently introduced.

In 1972, many cultural practices differentiated Abutia from European cultures. First, members of any Abutia village are divided in a number of noncontractual land-owning corporations, each of which owns much more land that its members can ever cultivate. In such land-owning corporations, membership of which is dictated by the simple fact of birth (through patri-filiation if the genitor is known, otherwise through matrifiliation), every individual, man or woman, has a right to a piece of land to cultivate. Children will till the land with their father or mother but, as soon as they reach their late teens, will start working their own plot. This corporate ownership, which exists from time immemorial, implies that father and son (or mother and daughter, or husband and wife) can never be economically in superordinate/subordinate relationships because of their differential owner-ship of means of production. Sons were (and still are) economically independent as soon as they reached adulthood.[2] Let us also note that women enjoy equal rights to the main means of production (land), because they belong to the same land-owning corporations, and on an equal footing with men. They cultivate like men (although the crops differ), and have complete control over the process (they can sell their own products).

Second, inherited houses are owned corporately, giving siblings domicil-iary rights over spouses in inherited houses. Many women also own houses, the result of their success in trade and/or prostitution (both of which are female preserves; men do not engage in small-scale trade). Also, husband and wife are not culturally expected to coreside; they do if the husband owns a house and if his wife does not own one. Otherwise they will live in separate residences. This explains why I derived such an extreme individualist set of axioms from this data (Verdon 1979b, 1983). Indeed, our MRUs are reduced to three: 1) a woman with her dependent children (a matricell), 2) a man with dependent children (a patricell), and 3) a lone adult. In brief, in Abutia, the coresidence of any two adults requires explanation.

The economic autonomy of both adult men and women engendered the ideal conditions to favour residential autonomy (neolocality) although, in the four to five decades preceding the fieldwork, the cost of having a house built out of concrete made it more difficult in other ways. In other African (and non-European) societies, even where noncontractual land-owning corporations of the Abutia type are to be found, fathers can coerce sons into coresidence because they wield special supernatural powers (this happens for instance in societies with ancestral cults); elsewhere, because of dispersed habitat, people have found it safer to live in larger homesteads to protect themselves from slave raids. In the spiritual and military domains as in the economic one, the Abutia are very free of coercion. There are no ancestral cults, nor any secret society memberships that would give fathers special supernatural powers over their children; furthermore, the Abutia used to find protection in relatively large and tightly nucleated villages. In a word, the Abutia are very 'secular' compared to a host of other non-European populations.

As far as informants could recall, precolonial Abutia houses were all individually owned, and this individual ownership would have created the same situation we encountered in Europe for a coresiding daughter-in-law. But unlike European houses, precolonial Abutia ones did not have any value because they did not involve any capital outlay. As a result, they were not even transmitted. Indeed, as soon as a man had decided to get married, he then bought palm-wine and a goat to organize a work-party to help him build his house. With his peers, he would put up the main structure in one or two days at the most, from materials available to all, namely clay and thatch. From that day on, this was his house, where he lived with his wife and children (co-wives presumably lived elsewhere, but I cannot be sure in the case of precolonial days. One thing remains certain, however, namely that the rate of polygyny was remarkably low for Africa as far as I could go back in the genealogies). In those days it is said that divorces were rare, so that matricells and patricells were composed almost exclusively of widows and widowers.

When the couple died, their house was simply left to decay, or another one was built on the same site, so that houses were not even transmitted (sometimes a son would stay on if his parents died when he was not yet married, and he might then have kept the house for himself and his wife-to-be).

With men and women reaching economic autonomy upon adulthood, with houses not even worth devolution and without any supernatural sanction, we can expect precolonial Abutia residential groups not to have exceeded a nuclear limit of residential growth. And indeed, according to all the testimonies recorded from elders, precolonial (or even pre-1910) residential groups conformed to this limit (in a way not even found in contemporary Europe, it seems). In fact, house inheritance and duolocal residence were then unknown, and couples were expected to coreside, so that Abutia residential MRUs were then what they are now in Europe, but the truly corporate ownership of the main (and almost exclusive) means of production would have produced a different power configuration had people cohabited – one not unlike the Basque pattern, perhaps. In brief, conditions in Abutia differed vastly from those found in northwestern Europe, but they equally favoured neolocality. All this changed with the introduction of cement in house-building.

Dried clay and thatch were available to all, but cement could only be purchased with cash. The very task of building lost its communal character and became the new profession of a specialist – the mason. Trained in urban centres, masons demanded cash for their services, and house-building developed into a significant capital outlay. The new concrete houses could also outlast many times the life of their builders, and could be built as large as the owner was ready to afford. Their sizes thus came to reflect differentials in wealth, and these houses were inherited by the eldest son of the group of those siblings who had spent most of their lives in that dwelling, albeit as a trustee for his full siblings.

Money and masonry came from outside, and sons had to emigrate in order to procure them. Some migrated to cities in the Gold Coast in search of a trade; others had more flair and acquired cocoa farms or planted cocoa and coffee trees on their own land in Abutia. Over the years, all the sons came to depart on labour migrations. The very cost of a concrete house also lengthened the time spent on migrations, making them recurrent and extremely long-lasting, transforming the marital relationship in the process.

In precolonial society, as I was told, men built as soon as they got married because building was such an easy process. A delay in the age at building could thus have retarded the age at marriage, for men at least. This, however, did not happen. The age at marriage remained relatively the same (approximately eighteen to twenty years for women, and twenty-five to thirty for men), and in the early days wives simply followed their husbands to the city. Their presence added to the husband's financial burden, further postponing the time of his definite return to the village (when the building of his house would have been completed). The neolocal trend remained so powerful that young married couples did not attach themselves to the residential groups of other relatives in the city, but created separate households.

A migrant husband could hardly provide for two or three dependants in the city, and would send his wife back to the village after the second or third child. After a few years of physical separation (that is, of duolocal residence), the migrant husband could not resist occasional affairs with other women, and many a husband then elected to marry a second wife in the city. Having eventually to provide for two families, he would send less and less money to his 'village wife', who in turn would accept lovers to compensate for the loss of cash. Such situations could only lead to divorce.

Having hoarded up the desired money and with his house partially or completely built, the migrant husband would eventually return. If not divorced, his first wife would most likely move in with him, unless she had herself built her own house, or inherited one in the meantime. If he had divorced while living in the city and remarried a 'city wife', the latter, normally not a native of Abutia, would not accompany him to his home village, and he would move back to a large but unoccupied home.

From the point of view of conjugal pairs, these recurrent labour migrations thus prompted 1) duolocal residence, often followed by divorce, 2) marriage with individuals from different areas (outside Abutia), and 3) female emigration. Indeed, some of the brides who proved to be infertile and were divorced remained in the city and practised prostitution, trade, or both. Sometimes wives who emigrated with their husbands requested that one of their teenage female relatives live with them to assist with child-care. Through their husbands and other relatives, scores of women experienced city life for various periods of time. Some lived alone, but others found husbands from outside Abutia. These marriages outside the locality lasted only as long as cohabitation did, and ended in divorce. In the last ten to fifteen years before 1970, however, women had not even associated themselves with other female relatives in their migrations. Many of them simply imitated the men, so that the main effect of recurrent labour migrations was to level off many social differences between men and women.

This takes us back to the beginning of this section, namely the situation in 1971–3. By then, the Abutia had added a number of new practices to their former ones: namely the corporate ownership of inherited houses by a set of full siblings, duolocal residence, and greatly increased rates of divorce (as well as prostitution and greater wealth for women, many of whom spent their money on their own house). We get back to our first three atoms or, more radically, to the problematic nature of all adult coresidence. When we look at Abutia residential groups, however, we find cohabitation on a large scale, and some baffling combinations (see Figure 9.1). How are we to explain them? Before tackling this problem, however, let us introduce a classification better suited to Abutia residential groups.

Classifying Abutia residential groups

I have devised my classification on the (atomistic) assumption that children, being under the jurisdiction of adults, will normally coreside with the adults who have taken on the main responsibility for their physical maintenance and socialization. I have thus on the whole excluded children from the clas-

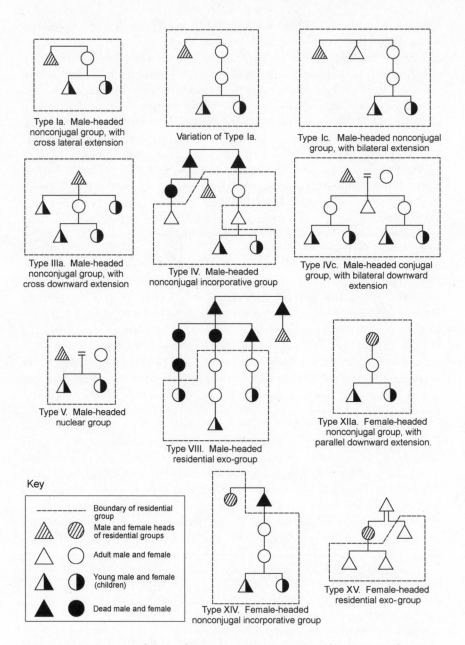

Figure 9.1 Pictograms of some of the more common residential groups in Abutia

sification of groups; if their presence and numbers are relevant, it will be mentioned in the analysis.

All Abutia residential groups designate one of their members as the 'head', and I have selected this 'head' as a point of reference, both in the description of the groups' composition and their classification. This, however, must be qualified in the light of what I asserted earlier about intermittent membership. Indeed, in Abutia the group's head sometimes leaves for very long periods of time (years), if not in some cases forever, and I resolved the problem in the following manner.

An absentee or intermittent head may be a migrant or may occupy different houses or flats at different times of the year. But, in so far as his or her existence (or that of any other intermittent member) affects the occupation of the dwelling-place (i.e. other people are prevented from occupying a given space which is reserved for that person, or because that person is a member of the household, albeit on an intermittent basis), I will nonetheless include him or her in a description of the group's composition. In instances where one person owns many houses but personally occupies only one or some of them, he or she is involved physically in the occupation of one (or a few) of his or her houses. This can give rise to one of the two following situations in the house he or she does not occupy: 1) rent is paid to the owner, in which case the person who pays the rent stands as the head, and the group's composition is defined with respect to him or her; 2) no rent is paid, and people are freely allowed to occupy the dwelling-place because of their relationship to the owner. In this latter instance, the owner stands as the head, and the group's composition is defined with respect to him or her. Individuals are entitled to occupy this dwelling-place because of their relationship to a person who is not personally involved in residence (external to the activity, and therefore to the group). I call such collections of individuals *exo-groups*, and such cases would be described as residential exo-groups.

Having identified the head, I then distinguish between the group's *core* and *incorporated members*. The core members consist of 1) the head himself or herself, together with 2) the group's *secondary members*. The secondary members comprise the head's father, mother, adult siblings, adult children, and his or her spouse (Abutia co-wives do not coreside so a polygynous head will coreside with one wife only). Spouses of secondary members I classify as secondary members themselves when their spouses are themselves members of the group.

Members of the group who are neither head nor secondary members I have grouped as 'incorporated members', with two important qualifications. The spouses and adult lineal descendants of secondary members will be classed as incorporated members when the secondary member to whom they are married or from whom they are descended is not himself or herself a member of the group. Otherwise they will be counted as secondary members, but included in the classification only if they do not compound its complexity beyond a reasonable limit.

To include incorporated members as well as lineal descendants of secondary members, and to specify the number of persons represented in each category of secondary members (number of brothers, sisters, or sons coresiding) would only add infinite variety to the classification and defeat its very purpose. I have thus preferred to exclude these elements from the classification and inserted them in the analysis when necessary.

This amounts to saying that the classification would gain in simplicity if limited to the core members of the group, a notion which further suggests distinguishing groups with secondary members (classified below) from groups without secondary members. In other words, the following households all lack either secondary members or a coresident head, that is, are without a core: solitaries, patricells, matricells, as well as what I call 'incorporative groups' (composed of a head and a medley of nonsecondary members; no more will be heard of them) and exo-groups (defined below). I shall consequently describe these residential groups without a core as 'nonnucleated groups'. As to nuclear groups, or groups extended downwards, upwards or laterally, they all possess a 'core' and will correspondingly be classified as 'nucleated groups'.

The sex of the head distinguishes male-headed from female-headed residential groups. In groups with secondary members, the coresidence of one of the head's adult siblings creates a *laterally extended* group, that of an adult child a *downward extended* one, and that of a parent, a residential group *extended upward*. The coresidence of the head's spouse also separates *conjugal* residential groups, where the head's spouse is present, from *nonconjugal* ones, where he or she is absent (because of duolocality, divorce or death). The coresidence of secondary members' spouses may yield more distinctions if necessary; for the study of Abutia, I have found it sufficient to record their presence in the analysis when and if appropriate. A couple and their dependent children alone in a dwelling-place form a *nuclear* residential group; a polygynous family coresiding independently would form a *polygynous* residential group.

In line with anthropological tradition, I have taken into account the respective sexes of the head and secondary members. In anthropology, siblings of the same sex are known as *parallel*, whereas those of different genders are termed *cross* (thus, children of parallel siblings are parallel cousins, and children of cross siblings are cross cousins). Applying this distinction to the relationship between head and secondary members, I have distinguished among the extended groups (whether extended laterally, downward or upward) those that I dub *cross* because the secondary member belongs to a sex different from that of the head (sister living with brother, daughter living with father), from those that I classified as *parallel* because both head and secondary member are of the same sex (daughters living with mothers who are household heads, brothers living under a brother 'head', or adult sons living with a father). When secondary members of both sexes are present, I shall write of 'bilateral' groups (see Tables 9.1, 9.2 and Figure 9.1).

Table 9.1 Classification of Abutia Kloe male-headed residential groups

Groups		No.
I	Nonconjugal extended laterally:	
	cross	8
	parallel	5
	bilateral	3
II	Conjugal extended laterally:	
	cross	4
	parallel	1
	bilateral	2
III	Nonconjugal extended downward:	
	cross	9
	parallel	3
	bilateral	3
IV	Conjugal extended downward:	
	cross	13
	parallel	3
	bilateral	3
V	Nuclear:	15
	Total nucleated groups	72
VI	Incorporative groups	4
VII	Patricells	4
VIII	Residential exo-groups	10
IX	Head with mother	3
X	Solitary residence	6
Total non-nucleated groups		27
Total of all male-headed groups in census		99

Table 9.2 Classification of Abutia Kloe female-headed residential groups

Groups		No.
XI	Nonconjugal extended laterally:	
	parallel	1
	cross	1
XII	Nonconjugal extended downward:	
	parallel	12
	cross	2
XIII	Nuclear	1
Total nucleated groups		17
XIV	Matricells	4
XV	Incorporative groups	7
XVI	Residential exo-groups	4
XVII	Solitaries	6
Total non-nucleated groups		21
Total of all female-headed groups in census		38

A different residential logic

Now, how do we get from precolonial neolocality to this baffling pattern, especially if we exclude marital cohabitation from the set of our atoms and reach the most individualistic formulation possible, namely that all adult coresidence is problematical? By changing the rules of the precolonial game.

In precolonial Abutia as in the Abutia that I studied in the early 1970s, all men sought to become elders. By definition, an elder is someone 'who can speak for himself', and no Abutia man can 'speak for himself' as long as his father is alive. But eldership meant more. It also meant reproductive success as well as general wisdom and a general demeanour which inspired respect. Let us equate eldership with 'jural autonomy' (Abutia women are never 'jurally autonomous', although they can be almost equal to men in all other respects). It goes without saying that a man could never be jurally autonomous if he was subordinate in any other respect.

In precolonial times, however, the jural subordination of the son meant little more than respect and deference, and letting his father speak on his behalf in any publicly important circumstances. Sons were autonomous in every other respect because they did not depend on their fathers for access to

178

land, and because they acquired a house as soon as they got married. They were themselves economically autonomous, and their wife domestically so, and their children had domiciliary rights in their parental house if they did not have one of their own.

Colonial conditions (mostly from 1920 onward) completely changed the whole logic of the system. Eager to seek a quick fortune in town, most men stopped building the traditional houses for their wives and, perforce, for their children. This meant that their children had no domiciliary rights anywhere in the village. Many relatives would welcome them, but they could always be ousted. Only in his or her father's house could a child feel that he or she was completely 'at home', and sure never to be evicted. This fostered a kind of obsession with house-building. On the one hand, the building of a house was supposed to reflect a man's economic success; on the other, it was his only way to attain 'jural autonomy'. Without his own house, his children were only guests wherever they lived, and he himself would not want to live in his father's house, a demeaning behaviour for most. In the meantime (and that meantime ran into decades), his wife and children had to live somewhere when sent back to the village. Herein lies the crux of the matter: it was the movement of women and matricells that came to determine and explain residential composition in Abutia.

Indeed, when sent back home from the city, who did a migrant's wife go to live with in her home village (always assuming village endogamy)? In precolonial days, she would have moved in with her husband immediately after marriage, in their own house. Since husbands now snubbed traditional houses for more ostentatious ones, there was no conjugal home to go back to, and no logic whatsoever in moving in with in-laws. Economically independent in the village, a woman would not easily have tolerated her mother-in-law's rule. Yet, she needed a roof and, for the first generation of migrants, her father's (or widowed mother's) house would provide it, since she retained domiciliary rights in the paternal house if her husband failed to provide a shelter.

Thus, the first generation of women sent back to the village went back to mother. Without a coresident husband, and without the weight of economic subordination to sour relationships, mother and daughter failed to create domestic subordination for a number of reasons. First, Abutia children are socialized as much by the groups of children of all ages they join to play with anywhere in the village; second, since women till the land almost as much as men, mother and daughter teaming together simultaneously reduced the weight of agricultural production for one or both of them, as it did the onus of cooking. If they cooked together, they would do so because they enjoyed doing so; otherwise one would cultivate, and the other take care of food processing. Alternatively, if there were some frictions, a second hearth could easily be built not far from the first one, and the two women could cook separately. But this made little sense and, given the extremely strong bond linking mothers to daughters in Abutia because of other practices, the two would collaborate with minimal friction in domestic activities, as they would in agricultural production. For these various reasons, duolocally married or divorced daughters initially took to going back to their mothers (and indirectly, fathers, if the mother was neither divorced nor widowed). Hence the initial transformation to male-headed conjugal cross downward extended groups (always without the daughter's husband coresiding, let us remember). And if the migrant husband had divorced all his wives by the time he came back to his house in the village, he would also welcome a married daughter to come and live with him (a daughter who also lived duolocally or was divorced); she would cook for him and do the chores that a wife normally does but, once more, without either economic or domestic subordination. There could be no subordinate cohabitation, since the daughter managed all the domestic activities, and considered the services rendered to her father as a minor trade-off for the lodgings he provided. In brief, in houses built by the male occupant, residential formation moved towards cross downward extension.

The devolution of cement houses explains the other recent residential trend, namely towards laterally extended groups. The explanation is easy. A male heir, let us recall, acts as trustee on behalf of his full siblings, who enjoy inalienable rights of residence in the paternal house (i.e. domiciliary rights), and none of the core members' spouses share this right (including the head's spouse); this fact underlies the association between nonconjugal laterally extended groups and inherited houses. A man's siblings, however, cannot claim any domiciliary right in a house which he has paid for to be built, rights which are reserved for his wife and children. If coresiding siblings are found in a house built by the head, they are merely tolerated because of extenuating circumstances.

In other words, the neolocal proclivity of Abutia men had not really changed in 1973, and understandably so. Indeed, to acquire jural autonomy, a man needed to build his own house; in other words, any adult man living in the house belonging to another adult man was somewhat subordinate to the latter, a situation men normally wished to avoid. Every self-respecting man thus aspired above all to erect his own house in order to assert his jural autonomy, especially by giving his own children domiciliary rights. Even heirs sometimes built a house, for the same reason, as an heir's own children have only secondary rights in their father's house. As a result, adult men shied away from coresidence, especially when married and living with their wife. Indeed, of the 172 residential groups of Kloe, none comprised two or more couples. *All cases of extension (lateral or vertical) excluded the cohabitation of mothers-in-law and daughters-in-law on the one hand, and of sisters-in-law on the other.* Second, patrisiblings did not live under the same roof if one of them was the head of the residential group. More generally, adult men shunned cohabitation because it contradicted their quest for jural autonomy.

What, then, are we to make of the few men who coresided with their siblings (male-headed parallel and bilateral laterally extended groups)? The evidence suggests that the coresidence of adult male siblings occurred in unusual circumstances only. In four cases, the coresiding brother had remained celibate and was completely marginal. In another case, the core-siding brother taught outside the village and rarely occupied his room. In all the six remaining instances, the siblings' mother did not come from Kloe – the lack of matrilateral ties was perhaps compensated for by coresidence. In other words, these men had much fewer residential options than those who were born of marriages endogamous to the village.

What about coresiding sons? On the whole, heads of extended groups with coresiding adult sons were older – eight of thirteen were born before 1900 (making them well over seventy at the time of the fieldwork), and the five others before 1914 (making them over sixty at the time of the field-work). In eight of the thirteen cases, their coresident son was relatively young (under thirty-five years of age), leaving a gap of approximately forty years between father and son; given the low rates of polygyny, such age gaps were relatively rare. This, alone, would somehow attenuate the reluctance of adult men to live with their father, especially as these sons had chosen to stay in the village, making it much more difficult to amass the money neces-sary to build their own house. With such elderly fathers, one cannot exclude the fact that the sons might have entertained the hope of inheriting the house as trustee. Of the five remaining instances, one was an extremely successful man who had built a house for his father, and the others were social misfits who certainly never reached the status of elder. Overall, there-fore, adult men could afford not to coreside and, on the whole, did not, except in unusual circumstances. What, now, of female-headed households?

If men disdained cohabitation with other men because living in a residential group of which one is not the head slightly prevents them from expressing their jural autonomy, it goes without saying that they would never accept coresidence under a female head. Moreover, despite their political inferiority, Abutia women preferred subordination to men (already jurally superior) than to women (their own equals; here we must except the unique mother–daughter relationship), and therefore avoided coresidence with a sister who headed her own residential group. In fact, despite their very close relationship, adult sisters only coresided when the mother also lived under the same roof. Without the mother, presumably to act as a buffer, adult sisters did not coreside (and *a fortiori* nor did half-sisters). As a result, female-headed groups were predominantly parallel extended.

This would intimate that most women heads have paid to have their own house built. There is some truth in this conjecture, as Table 9.3 suggests. Of the thirty-two female-headed groups for which I gathered information, twice as many lived in houses built by the head. Only nine women inherited houses – seven from agnates and two from their mother – and one woman had inherited two houses.

Of the seven who received their house from male agnates, only four were epiclerates, and the remaining three all had brothers who forfeited their rights to the paternal house. Or so it seems, since these brothers already owned their own house before their father died. But I am not convinced that they had completely relinquished their claim on the paternal house. A woman who inherits a house from a male agnate acts as a trustee only, and cannot bequeath it to her own children. When she dies, the house descends collaterally to her closest adult male agnate with children. This would account for the brother's charitable gesture. A man who already possesses one house can leave the paternal one to a sister without fear, knowing that it will return to his children. Fortunes may change and the female heirs may eventually treat the house as individual property, but this is left to the lineage council to decide. As to women who inherit a house from their mother, as we have seen, they do not act as trustees but as full owners, with the right to pass it on to their own children (see above on devolution of women's houses).

Despite this, the pattern noted for male-headed groups repeats itself. Women builders generated extended groups (always nonconjugal ones, since no husband would move in to live in his wife's house), whereas female heirs headed nonconjugal incorporative groups, of which their siblings' young children (and sometimes their siblings' adult daughter and her young children) were the incorporated members. Adult male siblings did not coreside with a female heir but sent their children to be fostered by her. Female-headed residential groups thus responded to approximately the same sets of factors as male-headed ones. But who were these female heirs and builders?

Table 9.3 Distribution of female-headed groups according to the manner in which the house was acquired

	Inherited	*Built*	*Unknown*	*Total*
Extended laterally	0	2	0	2
Extended downward	3	10	1	14
Incorporative	5	1	1	7
Others	2	9	4	15
Total	10	22	6	38

We have already seen that women inherited houses either as epiclerate (five of nine cases) or because their brother had already built. What, in contrast, would prompt women to build?

One could surmise that the lack of domiciliary rights would work as a strong motive. Women belonging to this category would be those whose fathers never built a house, and women not currently married to a man who had built his own house. Altogether, twenty of twenty-two female builders were deprived of domiciliary rights, though other women shared the same fate but had never built. What, then, enabled these women to do it? Their wealth. It is indeed remarkable that all wealthy women without domiciliary rights had built, although this wealth had been acquired at the cost of marital stability – seventeen of the twenty-three women builders had been or were still (in 1973) prostitutes, and sixteen had children who will never be in a position to gain domiciliary rights through their genitor. By building, these women both expressed their jural autonomy and gave their children inalienable rights of residence which would otherwise be denied to them – the very reason men built. These women were standing as pater towards their own children, whose genitor was either unknown or lived far away, and was nonexistent to all practical intents and purposes. Four sterile women had also built (from the proceeds of a similar trade), preferring an independent life, in order somewhat to redress the unenviable position attached to their infertility.

I would thus conclude that all wealthy women built, but that wealth attracted a special type of woman – those who did not care about attachment to a spouse and gave up matrimonial stability in favour of trading and/or prostitution.

Of the non-nucleated groups I shall say nothing, save for residential exo-groups (where the head does not occupy the house). These should constitute a test case of the basic cultural axiom I invoked to explain the lack of male coresidence (namely, shunning jural subordination), since the head's permanent absence from exo-groups should lift this constraint on adult coresidence. If the head does not occupy the dwelling-place he or she owns, the coresiding adults will not stand in a subordinate position to anyone else within the house. As can be expected, most instances of coresidence of collateral adult kin (coresidence of sisters, brothers, half-siblings, first cousins, and so on) did take place in such units!

A different set of axioms

Up to now, I have merely described the genesis of Abutia residential groups, although much of that description already contained explanatory elements which we can now bring together. What do we find?

First of all, for a comparative analysis, we would have to identify Abutia's limits of residential growth. In the light of the preceding analysis (and for a more detailed one, see Verdon 1979b), I would regard the *conjugal cross downward extended* type to represent the limit of growth of male-headed groups in cases where the head has built his own house, and the *nonconjugal cross laterally extended* type, in cases where he has inherited it. The limits are exceeded in unusual circumstances only.

Female heirs usually head incorporative groups; their lack of secondary members does not allow one to infer a limit of growth. Groups headed by a female builder, however, can grow to the *nonconjugal parallel downward extended* level. These three types represent the ultimate composition (or internal complexity in composition) that Abutia residential groups can reach without singular or exceptional circumstances.

How shall we explain these limits, and even internal variations? With the very elements I have already mentioned, from which one could derive Abutia's set of axioms. First, because of the corporate ownership of land and because of the fact that both men and women are engaged in agricultural production, all adults, male or female, are economically independent. Second, adult men seek their 'jural autonomy', whereas women are always jurally inferior. Because cohabitation contradicts their search for jural autonomy, men shun it, because they can afford it (nowadays through labour migrations and, formerly, through the building of their own house immediately upon marriage). Because of women's jural inferiority, moreover, spouses do not coreside in houses that have been inherited or built by a woman.

Overall, because of economic independence and the complete lack of religious sanctions, parents could not, as far as memory goes, coerce their married sons into cohabitation. All the cultural elements thus favoured neolocality. Why then should we find such an incidence of complex households (defined in terms of the cohabitation of MRUs)? Because developments from the 1920s onward prompted duolocal residence (initially, the men in town and the women back in the village) and divorce. As a result, we can conclude that all cohabitation in Abutia revolved around the movement of adult women (alone or with their children). Strangely enough, after two-and-a-half years of continuous residence in Kloe, I came across extremely few cases of difficult cohabitation (four or five). Why should that be?

First, let us emphasize that food processing was an exclusive female preserve in Abutia, so that every adult man needed a woman to cook for him. Second, women were not coerced into cohabitation by authoritarian parents, but were led into it because of hindrances (their husband did not own a house, or the women had not yet built one for themselves). Third, most women had a wide choice of residential groups to join. Since they retained domiciliary rights in their father's house, whether the latter was alive or dead, they could move back there. Also, if a divorced brother owned a house but did not have daughters to live with him, he would be delighted to have a sister to share his house. And a woman might also have decided to live with her widowed mother's mother, or father's mother, not to say mother's sister, or father's brother, and so on and so forth. In brief, there were often a number of options open to them, but women mostly chose to stay with their mother because of the positive element in this relationship, and because a woman was in fact freer with her parents than with her own husband, in the Abutia context (given women's freedom and independence). And the same applies to all cohabitation in Abutia: whenever adults cohabit, it is as a result of a mixture of hindrances (they have nowhere they can claim their own house) as well as mutual convenience. Because father/daughter, mother/daughter and brother/sister relationships are free of the tensions related to inheritance and in fact extremely close, because domestic activities are exclusively a female preserve, because new hearths can be so easily built, and because men live most of their lives on their farms or on the public place, cohabitation in Abutia is free of most of the intrinsic conflicts found in Europe.

No doubt, these considerations apply to women only. As to men, they coreside in special circumstances only, but usually for the same reason, namely because of hindrances (they have not yet built their own house). We could therefore generalize: Abutia men shun cohabitation, not because it is conflictual, for it is not, but because they seek to express their adulthood fully by attaining jural autonomy. As to women, we conclude differently: they actually prefer cohabitation with some of their relatives! No doubt, some permutations are never seen (an adult woman cohabiting with an adult sister who would stand as household head), but most are preferred, even to cohabitation with a husband – such are, for instance, cohabitation with a mother, with parents, or with a father or brother living alone. In other words, given our initial (natural social-psychological) axiom but within a different set of cultural and other elements, we find that Abutia lone mothers, matri-cells, and even married women, *seek cohabitation* with a specific set of relatives (and with someone else than the husband in the case of married women).

Like contemporary Europe, which is fundamentally neolocal and where complex households in modern cities speak of hindrances and mutual bene-fits rather than coercion, Abutia tells of a similar story, with a major difference: because of the cultural clauses incorporated in our European set of axioms, complex households remain few. Because of the new cultural clauses included in the contemporary set of axioms in Abutia, complex households are the majority (71 per cent of the sample). The reasons behind this new residential logic initially had their roots in economics and, as can be expected, new cultural codes have slowly evolved to rationalize it. But to invoke Culture to explain Abutia residential composition amounts to yet another Hegelian sleight of hand.

CONCLUSION

Many decades ago, aiming at Fortes and the followers of Radcliffe-Brown, the anthropologist Edmund Leach, perhaps one of the most celebrated in the world in his day, fired a tirade against typologies, accusing Radcliffe-Brownian anthropologists of indulging in butterfly-collecting (Leach 1961). To many, this signalled the beginning of deconstruction. In reality, Leach's accusation was misguided, for we classify the very moment we utter a sentence, and the question facing us is not whether to build typologies or not, but how to devise them, for typologies remain our only hope of proceeding with comparative analysis and, ultimately, of putting forth 'theories' which escape the grip of pure interpretation, and extract anthropology from the fold of literary criticism and the like.

In this book I have made my stance quite explicit, and will repeat it a last time. In the study of 'family history', Laslett, Wrigley and the Cambridge Group were right to hang on to typologies and to the concept of household. No doubt, as any discipline should move ahead of its founders, so should the concept of household be rid of its misleading elements, and the typology should be redefined so as to integrate power relationships through the notion of MRUs; otherwise, Laslett, Wrigley, Hammel and others laid a solid groundwork.

To redefine households and their attendant typology will of necessity imply that groups and residence be redefined, that we envision residence as an activity and as an autonomous dimension of social reality. Consequently, any attempt to reinterpret the activity of residence, such as viewing it in the wider context of kinship networks, cannot solve the problem and confuses more than it enlightens. I understand and acknowledge that students of kinship regimes must isolate that aspect of social reality (namely, kinship networks) but, from an *analytical* point of view (as distinct from a conceptual one), the particular configuration of kinship links connecting various households may at times be relevant in accounting for some features of *intra*regional variability; from the point of view of *extra*regional comparison, however, (that is, from the perspective of limits of residential growth), it seems barely relevant, if relevant at all. It certainly does not warrant reducing residential groups to an undefined, unbounded, and often misunderstood network.

Moreover, whoever writes on residence cannot avoid taking an explicit stance, either towards collectivism or atomism, and argue exclusively and coherently within that set of axioms; this is a basic desideratum of any philosophy of science. Unfortunately, as collectivism appears inevitably to yield culturalist explanations, it does not seem to take us very far and, in my opinion, only an atomistic set of axioms can bring coherence to an increasingly vast literature in family history, anthropology, ethnohistory and family demography. This, however, should not be misconstrued as a repudiation of culture. It goes without saying that residential composition always comes neatly packaged in a cultural code, but I hold that the cultural code normally comes last. First some course of events (including some cultural elements) will make it rational for individuals in a region or a socioeconomic class to adopt some collective practices (such as a residential limit of growth); then, and only then, do the same individuals invent rules which they wrap up in a cultural code to make sure that these practices perpetuate themselves and resist changes. Culture rationalizes what has already emerged as a response to a given set of circumstances, and will then act to slow change down when new conditions arise.

This new atomistic set of presuppositions and this understanding of culture should also deprive the traditional questions on 'structure or culture?' of much of their meaning. Complex households within Europe arise out of a number of factors, forces, hindrances or both, and their demise results from transformations removing these forces or hindrances. Then, and only then (and with a necessary time-lag), does a new cultural code emerge to crown the new developments.

I have also insisted in calling this set of axioms 'atomistic' rather than 'individualistic' because my 'atoms' were minimal residential units, not individuals. This wording might have been unfortunate for, were I to stick completely to the analogy from the 'hard sciences', I should conclude that if the individual is the atom, then MRUs are molecules (in chemistry, molecules are normally pluriatomic, although some are composed of one atom only; similarly, MRUs are pluriatomic, although one type is composed of individuals only); complex households, then, would appear as macromolecules. Had I called 'molecular' my set of axioms, it would have rendered clearer the fact that this new approach bypasses the antique antinomy between individual and group, between social action and social structure, and the 'chicken-and-egg' question of which of the two comes first. As 'residential atoms', MRUs are mini-groups themselves, so that, from my perspective, the constituents of complex households are not individuals, but already constituted groups. One may retort that my MRUs are nonetheless composed of individuals, to which I would reply that my definition of group leads to define the individual as the smallest group (see Verdon 1991 for full theoretical justification)!¹ Demographers have long argued along similar lines by defining a household as a collection of individuals sharing a dwelling, while calling households those residential groups composed of one individual only. With the definition of group suggested above, the individual/group antinomy simply vanishes.

Furthermore, I wish to emphasize again that I do not posit the European tendency of MRUs to residential autonomy to be natural. I insist that the only 'natural' element I invoke is the proclivity of adults (adulthood being culturally defined) to desire autonomy (or completely equal collaboration) in the run of their daily lives (while admittedly not disliking having others under their command). In brief, what I know of other societies through anthropology on the one hand, and of the contradiction inherent in any alternative social-psychological axiom bearing on this question on the other, leads me to postulate that adults do not strive to be ordered around, except in 'big' matters. Once this is posited, I then maintain that, *within the context of some specific cultural elements*, it yields a desire for residential autonomy. In brief, the proclivity to residential autonomy is a cultural corollary, given what I consider a natural axiom, inserted in a specific set of cultural elements. Within a different context, that of Abutia women, as we have seen, I would conclude that it fosters a desire for cohabitation. Stripped of its conflictual elements, Abutia women can enjoy all the positive aspects of cohabitation, so much so that many prefer duolocality to coresidence with their husband.

I was led to use an artificial construct, namely Europe (and North America of European extraction), because some themes run across most of the literature bearing on the populations of those continents, namely the intergenerational conflicts over the transmission of property and, where MRUs cohabit, over domestic activities. These conflicts seemed to be intimately associated with yet another almost pan-European feature, namely the contractual nature of the care that children give their ageing parents. I did not seek to delineate a cultural area, but the recurrence of these cultural themes through such vast expanses of the European continent before the contemporary emergence of a welfare state made it difficult to avoid referring to an already named geographical entity, namely Europe. I do not hold these themes to be unique to European populations but, in so far as I was studying the literature bearing on European societies (and North American ones of European extraction), I found it convenient to write of 'European living arrangements'. It is, and should remain, a mere presentational device, devoid of any taxonomic pretension.

Finally, I have insisted on intraresidential factors favouring parental coercion over the residence of children, but an increasing body of literature now points to equally powerful forces, namely those of extraresidential power-holders. A complete set of axioms would have to insert household dynamics within the wider context of political economy, as Kertzer (1991) has already advocated.

NOTES

1 THE UBIQUITY OF COLLECTIVISTIC ASSUMPTIONS

1 As will become clearer as the text unfolds, the Western Pyreneans have developed what I would be tempted to call a 'House complex'. Indeed, in common parlance they speak of the *maison* not as a dwelling-unit, but as the dwelling-unit together with its resident members and the patrimonial property attached to it, to the extent that all social identification is linked first and foremost to the house. This is why I chose to distinguish it from the mere dwelling unit by using the upper-case 'H'.

2 The Western Pyrenees mostly comprise the Béarn and the Basque country but, as explained in the text, the Bigorre may be understood to belong to the Béarn. The Béarn was traditionally a Gascon-speaking area immediately west of the Basque country in France. Although what will be said about the French Basque could extend to their Spanish neighbours, the following applies almost exclusively to the French ones.

3 According to Poumarède (1972), all Western Pyrenean populations transmitted their property to the first-born some centuries ago (or more precisely the eldest of the children who survived to adulthood), be it a boy or girl. The French write of *aînesse absolue* or *aînesse intégrale*. I shall similarly call it 'absolute' or 'integral' primogeniture.

4 There is an apparent consensus on this idea of overpopulation. Soulet mentions it for the whole of the Pyrenees as early as the end of the eighteenth century (Soulet 1987: 143), Augustins writes that the Baronnies have been overpopulated for centuries, but most especially in the nineteenth century (Augustins 1981: 13, 21) and, for the county of Bigorre, Berthe speaks of overpopulation as early as the fourteenth century (Berthe 1976: 41, 46). When studying the facts more closely, however, we will find this less obvious than it first seems.

5 According to Antoinette Fauve-Chamoux (1987) this matrimonial regime would have begun as early as 1650, although there is no consensus on this question (see Etchelecou 1991).

6 Indeed, it would amount to assuming that without economic incentives to living in complex households (the usual ones being economies of scale), people would prefer to live in monofamilial ones. If one wished to rely on psychological benefits, the underlying assumptions would remain the same, because this whole family of arguments presupposes a cost-benefit analysis on the part of social actors. Once residential choice results from a cost-benefit accountancy, we move right back to fundamentally individualist (and neoclassical) presuppositions.

7 A theme which Worobec also emphasizes: 'Many contemporary observers attributed the increase in premortem fission to growing individualism, influences of a developing cash economy, and a generational struggle that resulted in the weakening of patriarchalism in the post-emancipation Russian peasant village' (Worobec 1991: 79).

2 FAMILY, RESIDENCE, DOMESTICITY AND HOUSEHOLDS

1 In fact, in 1987 the periodical *Development and Change* dedicated a whole issue to publishing the results of a workshop entitled 'Conceptualizing the household: issues of theory, method and application'.
2 I will not deal with the emic/etic debate in this book but will simply mention *en passant* that I deem it a mistaken debate. Any language is arbitrary and, if we want to carry out anthropology's initial project of comparative analysis, we will not be able to utter a single sentence without having defined *our* (observers') terminology. Whether a vernacular term corresponds to it does not necessarily improve matters (from a conceptual point of view, that is).
3 Among the many meanings of the term 'function', two dominate the social sciences. On the one hand, 'function' is used to mean the role that a given phenomenon plays in the functioning of society, a role often linked to the production of solidarity or cohesion, and which often serves as an explanation of the phenomenon; this is usually associated with 'functionalist explanations'. The second peculiar usage of the term, and the one most relevant for our immediate purpose, is the denotation it carries when social scientists assert, for instance, that 'the function of the family is procreation, maintenance and the socialization of children'.

  In this and a host of similar statements, we are dealing with two separate things, namely a meaning and an implicit theory. The meaning is simple: it merely denotes 'activity' or 'type of activity'. Thus, if one declares that the function of the family is to raise children (among many other things in a multifunctional definition of group), one implies that husband and wife are involved in the *activity* of childrearing. Therefore, all the so-called 'functions' – copulation, procreation, child maintenance, socialization of children, production, transformation of products, consumption, legislation, adjudication, administration, recreation, etc. – *are only activities*. Such definitions, however, also carry an implicit functionalist theory. By claiming that 'the function of the family is social reproduction' one tacitly puts forth *an explanation* of the family's existence: the family exists in order to achieve social reproduction, a straightforward functionalist explanation. In order not to get embroiled in the theoretical and philosophical problems surrounding functionalism, I therefore advocate replacing the word 'function' with what it really means, namely 'activities', and use the term only in its adjectival form (such as multifunctional or unifunctional, always remembering that the function is only an activity).
4 From an anthropological point of view, this raises a number of problems. First, we must be able to identify a dwelling-place. It was easy for Abutia and is equally easy for most parts of Europe. Second, it also supposes that dwelling-places are there to be found, which is not always necessarily the case. The idea might be counterintuitive, but it is hard to speak of a residential group in the case of a man, his wife and child who simply hang their hammock near one another in the South American jungle.

5 As a corollary, this rules out the notion of 'coresidential groups'. Residence is an activity, and coresidence the fact that two individuals (or two units) perform this activity together. Stated differently, coresidence means 'cohabitation', and 'coresidential group' is as meaningless a concept as 'cohabitational group' would be.

6 In many parts of East Africa, when a man dies, his wife remains married to him. She goes to live with her husband's brother or closest agnate, but all the children she bears by this new genitor are socially the children of her dead husband, who thus remains their pater. Everything, corporeal or incorporeal (such as status), that they inherit will come from him. This is the precise definition of the institution of the 'levirate', classically found among the Nuer (Southern Sudan – Evans-Pritchard 1951).

7 Although cases of physical reproduction without families are numerous in many societies, this is rarely institutionalized to a whole population, and I personally do not know of any society where the family does not exist (which does not imply that the family exists everywhere; I have dealt with the notorious Nayar case in an earlier article – Verdon 1981 – as well as with marriages between women, between women and ghosts, as well as between ghosts, and found them all to be marriages).

8 These circumstances can be physical, psychological, economic or other. For instance, a physically handicapped person might get married but not form a separate residential group with her or his spouse where this is normally expected. Inseparable twins might marry two sisters and decide to form a *frérèche* where this is not the collectively approved practice, and so on. These 'out of boundary cases' will be dubbed 'exceptional' and the nonexceptional ones will be termed 'normal'. I have not carried out any study on this, but I doubt that such exceptional groups would represent more than 2 to 4 per cent of the total population, given a large enough population. I am aware that I am now summoning statistics to delineate a limit of residential growth after having rejected them to define a 'predominant household type'. This is for want of qualitative data. From a standard statistical approach, what the social actors have to say would seem to be of dubious relevance if one is bent on classifying a region by the percentages of its household types. From the perspective of a limit of residential growth, the only true way of delineating such a limit is through fieldwork but, failing this source of data, one has to fall back on statistical approximations, by default.

3 AN ATOMISTIC SET OF AXIOMS FOR WESTERN RESIDENCE

1 For the convenience of presentation later on, I shall subsume patricells, matricells, widows and widowers under the notion of 'residual families'.

2 As to consumption (more specifically eating together) it is in Europe a mere corollary of the chemical transformation of agricultural or animal products into 'edibles': the set of individuals for whom a 'cooking group' prepares meals normally eats together. Also, power relationships play themselves out through cooking, and little or not at all through eating. No doubt, women can serve the men and eat last, but this belongs to the field of gender relationships, not to that of MRU relationships. In general, MRU power games are not played out in the activity of eating.

3 As usual, some cases impose some qualifications, namely those in which partible inheritance extends to houses. To my knowledge, the best documented instance remains that of Santa Marta del Monte, where individuals retain rights over

various portions of diverse houses until they can possess a 'complete' house through a series of trade-offs (Behar 1985). At any point in time, however, they own one or more bedroom(s) in a dwelling-place, and this would be the basis upon which to delineate residential groups. In other words, in such cases (and the same seems to apply to northern Corsica), architectural structures may be continuous, but rights over them are not! I have taken this into consideration when writing of the ownership of houses, or parts of houses.

4 Incidentally, the same would apply to lone adults, matricells and patricells, with a few qualifications.

5 What I mean here is that the land will not be divided into three equal parts from the point of view of production. This would defeat the whole point of keeping it corporate property. If it was so divided, it would also be divided from the point of view of ownership and be appropriated individually. Hence, wherever we find a group of siblings or of very close agnates owning land corporately and working it together, they collectively work the land as an undivided entity.

6 That is, when two individuals, celibate, divorced or widowed, marry; when the man heading a patricell marries a single woman (celibate, divorced or widowed); when the woman heading a matricell marries a single man (celibate, divorced or widowed); or when the man heading a patricell marries the woman heading a matricell.

7 For instance, it will be more difficult for a widowed father, and still more so for a widowed mother, to maintain a forceful superordinate position in relation to the whole family (or families) of her child (or children). Conversely, it will be easier for parents to maintain their superordinate position over a child without spouse and children, and easier over a matricell than a patricell.

5 AN ATOMISTIC VIEW OF THE RUSSIAN MULTIPLE FAMILY HOUSEHOLD

1 For the sake of convenience, to avoid repeating that I am discussing multiple family residential groups of the Russian peasantry in the eighteenth and nineteenth centuries, I shall omit any further reference to the period unless otherwise necessary, and will imply multiple family residential groups when writing simply of Russian peasant residential groups or households.

2 Here, by 'complexity', I mean the fact that it is composed of more than one conjugal unit, or family, and by 'multiple family household' I designate specifically the cohabitation of the parents *with at least two of their married sons*, or of married brothers (*frérèche*) or of other more distantly related married agnates.

3   Inheritance, as defined in the Civil Code, was unknown in peasant customary law . . . which knew only the partitioning of family property among newly emerging households. In the framework of peasant customary law, the rights of descendants were not those of inheritance of the Civil Code, but those of membership of the family household unit. For these rights to become operative, it was not necessary to predicate the death of a property-owner.

(Shanin 1972: 222)

4   Unlike private property, family property limited the rights of the formal owner . . . he acted as the head administrator of the property (*bol'shak*) rather than as a property-owner in the sense current outside peasant society. An extreme expression of this feature was the legal possibility and actual practice of removing the head of a household from his position

in some cases of 'mismanagement' or 'wastefulness' and appointing another member of the household instead.

(Shanin 1972: 30–1)

5 And not the 'patriline' since a patriline includes women as daughters, and extends beyond the confines of a household. To be precise, we shall designate this male agnatic core of a residential group as a 'male household patriline'.

6 Even in the best of circumstances relations between mothers-in-law and daughters-in-law were often tense. A daughter-in-law was subordinate to her mother-in-law in the running of the domestic household. She had to take orders, complaints, and sometimes beatings from her domineering mother-in-law and at times even sexual advances from her father-in-law.

(Worobec 1991: 82)

7 Vucinigh also quotes Sir Donald Mackenzie Wallace: 'Wallace stated that discipline in the Russian peasant family was nearly perfect, but added that this could be disturbed by "the chatter of female tongues, which do not readily submit to the authority even of their owners"' (Wallace 1877: 8 quoted in Vucinigh 1968: xii). Worobec repeats the same theme: 'Russian peasant women were not unique in disrupting multiple family households in favor of smaller units over which they gained better control' (Worobec 1991: 82, who then quotes similar evidence from China).

8 In addition to drawing up contracts and dividing property among his sons in return for support, a household head had the further option of formally bequeathing his property to his sons on condition that they provide for him and his wife until their deaths.

(Worobec 1991: 54)

9 In fact, following Bohac's logic, one should conclude that, in the absence of this inheritance system, the familial units within a multiple family household would cohabit without tensions. This is a case of hidden collectivistic presuppositions: in the absence of a divisive factor, Russian peasants would have lived happily in their large and complex residential groups.

10 And it seems to be borne out by the facts: 'Daughters-in-law and sons sought to escape the domineering and oppressive authority of their seniors by setting up independent households even if that meant renouncing aid from parents' (Worobec 1991: 114).

11 Not an obvious one, as Frierson has also shown:

And, as Chernenkov astutely observed, given the natural inequality in the composition of the separate units, their interests could only rarely coincide. The haggling among the women and the conflict among the men seems not to have focused on the share of goods received so much as on the amount of work each member gave to the household. From the scattered reports to the Tenishev Bureau and in the published accounts of other observers, we find clues to when and why family fights about the distribution of labor would erupt.

The wife of the youngest son was most likely to voice her dissatisfaction with her position. She was at the bottom of the pecking order as a newcomer, as a woman, and as the bride of the most junior male member of the family. Often she had to bear the heaviest burden in child-care, because she was responsible for looking after her in-laws' children in addition to following the orders of all of the other adults in the household. The request for division often came at a moment in the extended family's cycle when one conjugal pair had more children not of working age than the other pairs did. This pattern suggests that not only the wife, but also the husband began to resent working so hard to support his brother's children.

(Frierson 1987: 47)

12 Indeed, if we remember that this equality was *per stirpes*, we can only approximate this adequation over a long interval of time. If a *bol'shak* died leaving an unmarried son of twenty and a married son of forty who had himself adult children, there is obviously no equality. But if left over a long period of time, until the younger son is himself forty and the oldest sixty, with grandchildren, it may then be argued that things ultimately even out as the larger group might have invested more labour but also consumed much more. This would justify waiting until sons are married and have children before thinking of a premortem partition.

13 [T]he threat of disinheritance was a powerful weapon in a father's hands to deter sons from reneging on their obligations or leaving the household, unless the son had sufficient means of his own to set up an independent household.

(Worobec 1991: 57)

14 Frierson writes that:

In her husband's absence, [the wife of a seasonal labourer] was often defenceless within the household. Evidence of physical abuse and general persecution of these young wives runs throughout the court cases in the report of the 1872 commission on the cantonal courts, as well as in later reports from the village.

(Frierson 1987: 49)

If so for the seasonal labourer, how much worse for the wife of a drafted man.
15 In fact, there are also extraresidential factors explaining this singularly low age at marriage for the West:

Aleksandrov cites the example of a Khar'lov landlord who established a schedule of fines to be levied annually on fathers of unmarried females – 6 rubles for women eighteen and nineteen – and threatened to transfer to another landlord or give forcibly in marriage any young women reaching the age of twenty unmarried (Aleksandrov 1976). Other landlords instituted similar fines for females as young as fifteen and introduced fines on widows up to the age of forty. Aleksandrov reports examples of similar regulations introduced as late as the 1820s, and he asserts that the landlord who did not directly set standards for the marriage of his serfs was the exception. Rules commonly required all young women to marry by the age of seventeen and young men by the age of twenty.

(Czap 1978: 115)

16 Russian agronomists and serf-owners argued passionately that the division of property led to small, economically unviable households.

(Bohac 1985: 30)

17   The Gagarins constrained partitions in part by forbidding new branches to construct dwellings and farm buildings on land designated for cultivation. One household, after twelve years of waiting, received permission to partition when the transfer of twenty-one peasant households to another estate permitted the purchase of an abandoned dwelling and the use of its land. . . . Between 1813 and 1853 the numbers of partitions roughly coincided in each of the estate's villages with the number of households that became extinct.

(Bohac 1985: 31)

18   The serf community itself supported the thrust of the Gagarins' policies because it too worried about the size and wealth of the new branches. The inability to pay rent or to survive meant increased economic burdens on the remaining households. The search for land on which to build the branches' dwellings also threatened other households. Boundaries of the plots of neighboring households might have to be altered or the village's households would have to give up an easily accessible section of communal field land for a new plot. The conditions of serfdom made postponement a strategy employed by serf and serf-owner alike.

(Bohac 1985: 33)

19 Note that it was in the *bol'shaky*'s interests to do so, but not so obviously the peasants' in general, as Czap intimates when he writes that

The large, multifocal family household was widely accepted as the only guarantee of prosperity and continuity for the estate and the peasant commune (*obshchina*) and the virtually exclusive basis of life for the individual. Therefore pressure to safeguard it, by encouraging the early formation of reproducing couples and discouraging household divisions, arose simultaneously from the landlord, the commune, *and naturally with individual exceptions, the peasants themselves* (Aleksandrov 1976: 300–3).

(Czap 1982: 6, italics added)

I do not believe that all peasants under *bol'shak* rule concurred with this idea. Those in subordinate positions were obviously aware of the economic risks of partitions, but I would submit that they would have preferred autonomy, or equal cohabitation at worst, even at the risk of lesser economic welfare.

20   The many levels of Russian peasant society also cooperated in upholding the patriarchal ordering of family and community relationships. Male cantonal judges and village elders supported the patriarch's authority against recalcitrant family members, believing that patriarchalism was the basis for a smoothly functioning peasant society.

(Worobec 1991: 13)

21 Assuming here a household composed of a *bol'shak*, his married sons and their married sons.

22 Even if brothers remained together after their father's death,

they divided the farmstead in theory but in reality agreed to keep it intact as an economic unit, thus guaranteeing the indivisibility of the patrimony. Russian peasants rationalized this practice with the saying 'Although the inheritance is not divided, everyone has to square his accounts.'

(Worobec 1991: 47)

23　The figures suggest that even in the pre-emancipation period peasants, if unencumbered by pressures from serf owners, sometimes resolved family tensions through premortem fission.

(Worobec 1991: 89)

24 Mentioning the growth of domestic industries and of out-migration even in the pre-emancipation era, Worobec explains the increasing incidence of premortem fissions by mentioning that '*Sons could afford to ignore their fathers' threats of disinheritance given the option of pursuing nonagricultural employment*' (Worobec 1991: 89, italics added).

25　The zemstvo data suggest that the stimulus to household divisions was strongest where the pressure on the land was weakest either because land was abundant or because a substantial portion of the population derived its income from nonagricultural pursuits. Accordingly, families tended to be smaller in the central industrial provinces (with the exception of Moscow) where almost every household was engaged in domestic industries. Population pressure on the land helped maintain fairly large households in Moscow province.

(Worobec 1991: 105)

6　AN ATOMISTIC VIEW OF VARIOUS STEM FAMILIES

1 This, however, does not mean that parents did not exert control. First, living as a lumberman meant being away from home five months a year. Second, moving either to the USA or to the city meant moving to an unknown situation and often (as in lumber camps) to seasonal and badly paid jobs, as well as stupefying ones when it involved (as it most often did) working in factories. As regards starting from scratch, like the original pioneers, it did not appeal very much to sons who could inherit their father's land, land already cleared, fenced and ready for production. In brief, some sons brought up on the land would always prefer to inherit an already functioning farmstead rather than start from scratch and, to many, the prospect of inheriting the parental property exerted a much bigger attraction than did an exodus which, in the context of nineteenth-century Quebec, meant moving to the cities or the US.

2 To my knowledge, only Antoinette Fauve-Chamoux assumes that nuptiality, fertility and mortality rates were all much higher before 1650, on the basis of the village she studied (Esparros, in the Baronnies).

7　THE WORLD WE HAVE LOST

1　The areas of predominantly champion, as opposed to woodland, have been reconstructed both from medieval evidence and from the later Acts of Enclosure. To sketch the distribution one should imagine a broad band running diagonally across England from the North Sea coast through the Midlands to the Channel in the south. Left of this central band are the west country counties of Cornwall and Devon; the northwestern counties of Cheshire, Lancashire, Westmorland, and Cumberland; and the southeast counties of Essex, Middlesex, and Kent. Other counties such as

Surrey, Suffolk, and Hertfordshire had a mixture of the two field types. To say that the diagonal, central band contained mostly open-field agriculture is not to exclude hamlets and farmsteads from these regions as well.

(Hanawalt 1986: 20)

2 Let us insist that, although the lord was the ultimate owner of the land, the rights of villeins over their tenure amounted to a form of ownership (Smith 1984b: 64, 1991: 45–6; Hanawalt 1986: 68; Seccombe 1992: 61, 79).

3 In other words many of the apparent sales might have been rentals in champion country (Hanawalt 1986: 74) but the fact remains that these rentals involved the temporary transfer of property in exchange for either produce or cash.

4 Through the dower, women kept usufructuary rights on a third to one-half of their husband's estate, according to the manor. Theoretically, they were expected to pass this land to their children if they remarried but, in reality, many kept the land after remarriage. In Cottenham, for instance (impartible inheritance), the widow could keep the whole tenure (Smith 1983: 125); in the first two decades of the fourteenth century, still in Cottenham, 51 per cent of widows kept their land after remarriage and, between 1260 and 1315, in the manor of Taunton belonging to the archbishop of Winchester (champion England), between a fifth and a third of the serfs married widows in order to acquire land (Titow 1962: 6–9). Also, 'On a number of manors in the West Midlands the widow could have the whole tenement or less for life, with the most common arrangement being half of it' (Hanawalt 1986: 71).

5 Incidentally, the combination of a relatively high incidence of domesticity and a relatively late age at marriage for women (it is impossible to know about definitive celibacy rates for the thirteenth century), tells of a European marriage pattern, *pace* Hajnal (Smith 1981, 1983; Hajnal 1965).

6 The possession of property allowed them to bargain for a variety of arrangements of which the medieval corrody is only one example.

(Pelling and Smith 1991: 12)

7 Data from these returns [listings of inhabitants for 1684 and 1796 in five communities] reveal that the great majority of the older generation continued to manage in their own homes. When, as widows or widowers, they were no longer able to do so, they were more likely to be found as independent lodgers than residing under their children's roof.

(Pelling and Smith 1991: 13)

Also:

In early modern England only when all else failed did an aged parent live with an offspring. All medieval evidence suggests that this was already an established pattern: People lived on their own as long as they could manage (usually as long as they had a spouse alive and were healthy), and even when they were driven to maintenance contracts only a third made them with kin.

(Hanawalt 1986: 235)

8 More well-to-do peasants, as we shall see, chose to make their arrangements by will or established their children in separate holdings before their death.

(Hanawalt 1986: 232)

9   Nor does the fact of co-residence establish who was giving and who receiving care. That the poor themselves should be paid (or simply required) to nurse and care for the sick and disabled poor, often on a co-residential basis, is a recurrent theme of poor law practice from the sixteenth century to the twentieth, and one which relates to both indoor and outdoor relief.

(Pelling and Smith 1991: 17)

10 Richard Smith, personal communication. But, as Richard Smith also remarks, retirement contracts were not the only types of maintenance contracts. There were indeed some forms of alienations which amounted to annuities:

In fact many retirements were achieved through immediate alienations of properties for sizeable sums of money from which the seller or 'retiree' could derive a livelihood in old age; some involved specified payments to the retiring generation over an extended period of time; others involved leasing arrangements that provided a regular income for the retiree(s) primarily, although not exclusively, in cash [cash for the period 1300–1400].

(Smith 1991: 48)

Since we do not know the regional distribution of this type of alienation of land, we shall therefore overlook it in our argumentation.

8 THE WORLD WE HAVE GAINED

1 Let us remember that if one applied Ermisch and Overton's definitions strictly, most of the monoparental families with a parent over fifty-five years of age would become complex households made up of two or more independent individuals.

2 Some texts resort to a false economic argument, namely that rising income levels have created a desire for privacy. Needless to say, this is just a brand of culturalist explanation. As we have already seen, explaining the rising proportion of persons living alone as evidence of an increasing desire for privacy is purely tautological.

3 Let us emphasize that the youngest U1 and U2 are those most likely to be over- or under-represented, given Statistics Canada's definitions. Indeed, loneship ratios are calculated by dividing all MRUs of a given type residing autonomously by all MRUs of this type in the population. When it comes to couples or families (U3 or U4), they remain identified as such if they choose to move back home, so that the numerator (the total number of U3 and U4 in the population) does not change. As to nonfamily individuals (U1) and lone parents (U2), especially the younger ones, they are counted as belonging to the family of their parents if they elect to go back home. In other words, a vast number thus 'disappear' from the denominator (the total number of such MRUs in the population), therefore artificially inflating their ratios. The implications are clear: they most likely explain the puzzling rise of very young lone parents from 1981 and 1986, and would also lead to underestimating the decline in U1s from 1981 to 1986.

4 Let us simply mention the weight of monoparental families in multiple family households. Whereas lone fathers and mothers account respectively for 2 per cent and 10 per cent of family units in households, they represent respectively 6 per cent and 20 per cent of family units in multiple family households. The

remaining percentages of lone parents (U2), as we shall see, share their living arrangements with nonfamily individuals.

5 A last reminder that we are here writing of complex households in the perspective of Ermisch and Overton, and that such households will not necessarily be three-generational. On the contrary, if there is an 'irreducible core', it may be overwhelmingly one-generational!

9 ABUTIA

1 In the rest of this chapter, I shall simply use 'build' to mean 'pay to have a house built' and the 'builder' to mean the person who paid to have the house built by a mason.

2 Here, admittedly, we encounter the problem mentioned in Chapter 3. Schooling has certainly changed the perception of who an adult is and, for the sake of convenience, I shall somewhat arbitrarily use the age of twenty-five as denoting the onset of adulthood among Abutia men, twenty-one among Abutia women.

CONCLUSION

1 Indeed, as I have fully demonstrated in *Contre la culture* (1991), we may multiply the criteria of group membership to the point at which only one individual would qualify. If none qualifies, admittedly there is no group because one activity must be executed in order to find a group. As I mentioned in the text, such a type of reasoning already applies in demography, and more so in mathematics. Indeed, the notion of set initially implied in its definition a collection of elements, but sets can be defined so as to contain one element only (and they remain sets). Mathematicians go further, and define sets comprising no element whatsoever (null sets), but this cannot apply for groups.

BIBLIOGRAPHY

Adams, L. (1947) 'Virilocal and uxorilocal', *American Anthropologist* 49: 678.

Alderman, H. *et al.* (1995) 'Unitary versus collective models of the household: is it time to shift the burden of proof?', *The World Bank Research Observer*10: 1–19.

Aleksandrov, V.A. (1976) *Sel'skaia obshchina v Rossii (XVII–nachalo XIXv)*, Moscow: Nauka.

—— (1979) 'Seimeno-imushchestvennye otnosheniia po obychnomy pravu v Russkoi krepostnoi derevne XVIII nachala XIX veka', *Istoria SSSR* 6: 37–54.

—— (1985) 'The evolution of customary land law in the late-feudal Russian village', *Soviet Anthropology and Archaeology* 24: 3–27.

Anderson, M. (1980) *Approaches to the History of the Western Family 1500–1914*, London: Macmillan.

Aquilino, W.S. (1990) 'The likelihood of parent-adult-child coresidence: effects of family structure and parental characteristics', *Journal of Marriage and the Family* 52: 405–19.

Ariès, P. (1973) *L'enfant et la vie familiale sous l'Ancien Régime*, Paris: Seuil.

Arrow, K. (1963) *Social Choice and Individual Values*, New Haven: Yale University Press.

Augustins, G. (1981) 'Maison et société dans les Baronnies au XIXe siècle', in I. Chiva and J. Goy (eds) *Les Baronnies des Pyrénées*, vol. I, Paris: EHESS.

—— (1986) 'Un point de vue comparatif sur les Pyrénées', in I. Chiva and J. Goy (eds) *Les Baronnies des Pyrénées*, vol. II, Paris: EHESS.

—— (1989) *Comment se perpétuer?* Paris: Université de Nanterre: Société d'ethnologie.

Avery, R., Goldscheider, F. and Speare, A. (1992) 'Feathered nest, gilded cage – parental income and leaving home in the transition to adulthood', *Demography* 29: 375–88.

Baanders, A. (1993) 'Thinking of leaving the parental home', Montreal: paper presented at the IUSSP conference.

Bachelard, G. (1969) *La formation de l'esprit scientifique*, Paris: Vrin.

Barnes, J.A. (1960) 'Marriage and residential continuity', *American Anthropologist* 62: 850–66.

Becker, G.S. (1981) *A Treatise on the Family*, Cambridge, Mass.: Harvard University Press.

Behar, R. (1985) *Santa Marta del Monte*, Princeton: Princeton University Press.

Beresford, J.C. and Rivlin, A.M. (1966) 'Privacy, poverty, and old age', *Demography* 3: 247–58.

Berkner, L. (1972) 'The stem family and the developmental cycle of the peasant household: An eighteenth-century Austrian example', *American Historical Review* 77: 398–418.

—— (1975) 'The use and misuse of census data for the historical analysis of family structure', *Journal of Interdisciplinary History* 7: 721–38.

Berthe, M. (1976) *Le comté de Bigorre: un milieu rural au bas Moyen Age*, Paris: SEVPEN.

Blanchard, I. (1984) 'Industrial employment and the rural land market, 1380–1520', in R.M. Smith (ed.) *Land, Kinship and Life Cycle*, Cambridge: Cambridge University Press.

Bohac, R. (1985) 'Peasant inheritance strategies in Russia', *Journal of Interdisciplinary History* 16: 23–42.

Bohannan, P. (1957) 'An alternate residence classification', *American Anthropologist* 59: 126–31.

—— (1963) *Social Anthropology*, New York: Holt, Rinehart and Winston.

Bonnain, R. (1981) 'Les "bonnes maisons": perception, expression et réalité de la stratification sociale d'un groupe villageois', in I. Chiva and J. Goy (eds) *Les Baronnies des Pyrénées*, vol. I, Paris: EHESS.

—— (1986a) 'Droit écrit, coutume pyrénéenne et pratiques successorales dans les Baronnies, 1769–1836', in I. Chiva and J. Goy (eds) *Les Baronnies des Pyrénées*, vol. II, Paris: EHESS.

—— (1986b) 'Le mariage dans les Pyrénées centrales, 1769–1836', in I. Chiva and J. Goy (eds) *Les Baronnies des Pyrénées*, vol. II, Paris: EHESS.

—— (1986c) 'Nuptialité, fécondité et pression démographique dans les Pyrénées, 1769–1836', in I. Chiva and J. Goy (eds) *Les Baronnies des Pyrénées*, vol. II, Paris: EHESS.

Bourdieu, P. (1962) 'Célibat et condition paysanne', *Etudes rurales* 5–6: 32–136.

—— (1980) *Le sens pratique*, Paris: Editions de Minuit.

Britton, E. (1977) *The Community of the Vill: a Study in the History of the Family and Village in Fourteenth-Century England*, Toronto: Macmillan.

Brouwer, J. (1988) 'Application of household models in housing policy', in N. Keilman, A. Kuijsten and A. Vossen (eds) *Modelling Household Formation and Dissolution*, Oxford: Clarendon Press.

Brown, S.B. (1951) 'Analysis of hypothetical stationary population by family units – a note on some experimental calculations', *Population Studies* 4: 380–94.

Buchler, I.R. and Selby, H.A. (1968) *Kinship and Social Organization*, New York: The Macmillan Company.

Buck, N. and Scott, J. (1993) 'She's leaving home, but why? – An analysis of young people leaving the parental home', *Journal of Marriage and the Family* 55: 863–74.

Burch, T.K. and Matthews, B.J. (1987) 'Household formation in developed societies', *Population and Development Review* 13: 495–512.

Burguière, A. (1986) 'Pour une typologie des formes d'organisation domestique de l'Europe moderne (XVIIe–XIXe siècles)', *Annales, E.S.C.* 41: 639–55.

Butel, F. (1894) *La Vallée d'Ossau*, Pau.

Carrasco, P. (1963) 'The locality referent in residence terms', *American Anthropologist* 65: 142–34.

Carter, A.T. and Merrill, R.S. (1979) *Household Institutions and Population Dynamics*, Washington, D.C.: USAID.

Casselberry, S.E. and Valavanes, N. (1976) '"Matrilocal" Greek peasants and a reconsideration of residence terminology', *American Ethnologist* 3: 215–25.

Castan, N. (1971) 'La criminalité familiale dans le ressort du Parlement de Toulouse (1690–1730)', in A. Abiateci (ed.) *Crimes et criminalité en France sous l'Ancien Régime*, Paris: Colin.

Castan, Y. (1979) *Honnêteté et relations sociales en Languedoc (1715–1780)*, Paris: Colin.

Chantor, M. (1980) 'Household and kinship: Ryton in the late 16th and early 17th centuries', *History Workshop Journal* 10: 25–60.

Chodorow, N. (1974) 'Family structure and feminine personality', in M.Z. Rosaldo and L. Lamphere (eds) *Woman, Culture, and Society*, Stanford: Stanford University Press.

Chudacoff, H.P. and Hareven, T.K. (1979) 'From the empty nest to family dissolution: life course transitions into old age', *Journal of Family History* 4: 69–83.

Clark, E. (1982) 'Some aspects of social security in medieval England', *Journal of Family History* 7: 307–20.

Claverie, E. and Lamaison, P. (1982) *L'impossible mariage: violence et parenté en Gévaudan, XVIIe, XVIIIe et XIXe siècles*, Paris: Hachette.

Collier, J.F. (1974) 'Women in politics', in M.Z. Rosaldo and L. Lamphere (eds) *Woman, Culture, and Society*, Stanford: Stanford University Press.

Collomp, A. (1983) *La maison du père*, Paris: PUF.

Creighton, C. (1980) 'Family, property, and the relations of production in Western Europe', *Economy and Society* 9: 128–67.

Czap, Jr, P. (1978) 'Marriage and the peasant joint family in the era of serfdom', in D.L. Randel (ed.) *The Family in Imperial Russia*, Urbana: University of Illinois Press.

—— (1982) 'The perennial multiple family household, Mishino, Russia, 1782–1858', *Journal of Family History* 7: 5–26.

—— (1983) '"A large family: the peasant's greatest wealth": serf households in Mishino, Russia, 1814–1858', in R. Wall (ed.) *Family Forms in Historic Europe*, Cambridge: Cambridge University Press.

Dechêne, L. (1972) *Habitants et marchands de Montréal au XVIIe siècle*, Paris: Plon.

Demolins, E. (1893) *A quoi tient la supériorité des Anglo-Saxons?*, Paris: Didot.

Denich, B.S. (1974) 'Sex and power in the Balkans', in M.Z. Rosaldo and L. Lamphere (eds) *Woman, Culture and Society*, Stanford: Stanford University Press.

Desrosiers, H., Juby, H. and Le Bourdais, C. (forthcoming) 'Les trajectoires familiales des hommes', in Y. Péron *et al.* (eds) *Les familles canadiennes à l'approche de l'an 2000*, Ottawa: Statistique Canada.

Dewindt, E. (1972) *Land and People in Holywell-cum-Needingworth: Structures of Tenure and Patterns of Social Organization in an East Midlands Village, 1252–1457*, Toronto: Pontifical Institute of Medieval Studies.

Dieleman, F.M. (1989) 'Divorce, mobility and housing demand', *European Journal of Population*: 235–52.

Douglass, W.A. (1975) *Echalar and Murelaga. Opportunity and Rural Exodus in Two Spanish Basque Villages*, New York: St Martin's Press.

—— (1988) 'The Basque stem family household: myth or reality?', *Journal of Family History* 13: 75–89.

Duchêne, J. (1987) 'Les familles monoparentales et recomposées. Quelles données pour une mesure de leur incidence?', in F. Prioux (ed.) *La famille dans les pays développés: permanences et changements*, Paris: INED.

Durkheim, E. (1960) [1892] *De la division du travail social*, Paris: PUF.

—— (1967) [1895] *Les règles de la méthode sociologique*, Paris: PUF.

Dussourd, H. (1979) *Au même pot et au même feu*, Paris: Maisonneuve et Larose.

Ember, M. and Ember, C. (1971) 'The conditions favoring matrilocal versus patrilocal residence', *American Anthropologist* 73: 571–94.

Ermisch, J. (1988) 'An economic perspective on household modelling', in N. Keilman, A. Kuijsten and A. Vossen (eds) *Modelling Household Formation and Dissolution*, Oxford: Clarendon Press.

Ermisch, J.F. and Overton, E. (1985) 'Minimal household units: a new approach to the analysis of household formation', *Population Studies* 39: 33–54.

Etchelecou, A. (1991) *Transition démographique et système coutumier dans les Pyrénées occidentales*, Paris: PUF–INED.

Evans, A. (1989) 'Women: rural development, gender issues in rural household economics', IDS Discussion Paper 254, Brighton: University of Sussex.

Evans-Pritchard, E.E. (1951) *Kinship and Marriage among the Nuer*, Oxford: Clarendon Press.

Fapohunda, E.R. (1988) 'The nonpooling household: a challenge to theory', in D. Dwyer and J. Bruce (eds) *A Home Divided. Women and Income in the Third World*, Stanford: Stanford University Press.

Farnsworthy, B. (1986) 'The litigious daughter-in-law: family relations in rural Russia in the second half of the nineteenth century', *Slavic Review* 45: 49–64.

Fauve-Chamoux, A. (1984) 'Les structures familiales au royaume des familles-souches: Esparros', *Annales, E.S.C.* 30: 513–28.

—— (1987) 'Le fonctionnement de la famille-souche dans les Baronnies des Pyrénées avant 1914', *Annales de démographie historique*: 241–62.

—— (1993) 'Les frontières de l'autorégulation paysanne: croissance et famille-souche', *Revue de la Bibliothèque Nationale* 50: 38–57.

Fel, E. and Hofer, T. (1969) *Proper Peasants*, Wenner-Gren Foundation: Viking Fund Publications in Anthropology.

Fengler, A.P., Danigelis, N. and Little, V.C. (1983) 'Later life satisfaction and household structure: living with others and living alone', *Ageing and Society* 3: 357–77.

Fernandez, J.W. and Fernandez, R.L. (1988) 'Under one roof: household formation and cultural ideas in an Asturian mountain village', *Journal of Family History* 13: 123–42.

Festy, P. (1988) 'After separation – variability and stability in behavior', *Population* 43: 517–35.

Fine-Souriac, A. (1977) 'La famille-souche pyrénéenne au XIXe siècle: quelques réflexions de méthode', *Annales, E.S.C.* 31: 478–87.

Fisher, J.L. (1958) 'The classification of residence rules in censuses', *American Anthropologist* 60: 508–17.

Flandrin, J.-L. (1976) *Familles: parenté, maison, sexualité dans l'ancienne société*, Paris: Hachette.

Folbre, N. (1984) 'Household production in the Philippines: a non-neoclassical approach', *Economic Development and Cultural Change* 32: 303–30.

—— (1986) 'Hearts and spades: paradigms of household economics', *World Development* 14: 245–55.

Fortes, M. (1949a) *The Web of Kinship among the Tallensi*, London: Oxford University Press.

—— (1949b) 'Time and social structure: an Ashanti case study', in M. Fortes (1970) *Time and Social Structure and Other Essays*, London: The Athlone Press.

—— (1958) 'Introduction', in J. Goody (ed.) *The Developmental Cycle in Domestic Groups*, Cambridge: Cambridge University Press.

Foucault, M. (1966) *Les mots et les choses*, Paris: Gallimard.

Fox, R. (1967) *Kinship and Marriage*, Harmondsworth: Penguin Books.

Franklin, P. (1986) 'Peasant widows' "liberation" and "remarriage"', *Economic History Review* 39: 186–204.

Frierson, C.A. (1987) '*Razdel*: the peasant family divided', *The Russian Review* 46: 35–52.

Garigue, P. (1962) *La vie familiale des Canadiens-français*, Montréal: Presses de l'Université de Montréal.

Gaunt, D. (1987) 'Rural household organization and inheritance in Northern Europe', *Journal of Family History* 12: 121–41.

Gérin, L. (1898) *L'habitant de Saint-Justin*, reprinted in J.-C. Falardeau and P. Garigue (1968) *Léon Gérin et l'habitant de Saint-Justin*, Montréal: Presses de l'Université de Montréal.

Glass, R. and Davidson, F.G. (1951) 'Household structure and housing needs', *Population Studies* 4: 395–420.

Glick, P.C. (1993) 'Living alone during middle adulthood', Montreal: Paper presented at the IUSSP conference.

Glick, P.C. and Lin, S.-L. (1986) 'More adults are living with their parents: who are they?' *Journal of Marriage and the Family* 48: 107–12.

Goldscheider, F.K., Biddlecom, A. and MacNally, J. (1993) 'Dependency, privacy, and power in intergenerational household changes in the living arrangements of the elderly in the U.S., 1940–80', Montreal: Paper presented at the IUSSP conference.

Goldscheider, F.K. and Goldscheider, C. (1992) 'Gender roles, marriage, and residential independence', *Sociological Forum* 7: 679–99.

—— (1993) 'Whose nest – A two-generational view of leaving home during the 1980s', *Journal of Marriage and the Family* 55: 851–62.

Gonzalez, N.L.S. (1969) *Black Carib Household Structure*, Seattle: University of Washington Press.

Goodenough, W.H. (1956) 'Residence rules', *Southwestern Journal of Anthropology* 12: 22–37.

—— (1970) *Description and Comparison in Cultural Anthropology*, Chicago: Aldine.

Goody, J. (1958) 'The fission of domestic groups among the LoDagaba', in J. Goody (ed.) *The Developmental Cycle of Domestic Groups,* Cambridge: Cambridge University Press.

—— (1972) 'The evolution of the family', in P. Laslett and R. Wall (eds) *Household and Family in Past Time*, Cambridge: Cambridge University Press.

—— (1973) 'Bridewealth and dowry', in J. Goody (ed.) *Bridewealth and Dowry*, Cambridge: Cambridge University Press.

—— (1976) *Production and Reproduction*, Cambridge: Cambridge University Press.

—— (1996) 'Comparing family systems in Europe and Asia: are there different sets of rules?', *Population and Development Review* 22: 1–20.

Gulbrandsen, O. and Hansen, T. (1986) *Boligetabglering i Oslo* [Housing construction in Oslo], Oslo: Norwegian Building Research Institute.

Guyer, J.I. (1981) 'Household and community in African studies', *African Studies Review* 24: 87–137.

Guyer, J. and Peters, P. (1987) 'Introduction', to 'Conceptualizing the household: issues of theory and policy in Africa', *Development and Change* 18: 197–214.

Hajnal, J. (1965) 'European marriage patterns in perspective', in D.V. Glass and D.E.C. Eversley (eds) *Population in History*, London: Edward Arnold.

—— (1983) 'Two kinds of pre-industrial household formation systems', in R. Wall, J. Robin and P. Laslett (eds) *Family Forms in Historic Europe*, Cambridge: Cambridge University Press.

Hall, R. (1986) 'Household trends within Western Europe 1970–1980', in A. Findlay and P. White (eds) *West European Population Change*, London: Croom Helm.

Hallam, H.E. (1958) 'Some thirteenth-century censuses', *Economic History Review* 10: 345–8.

Hammel, E.A. (1972) 'The zadruga as process', in P. Laslett (ed.) *Household and Family in Past Time*, Cambridge: Cambridge University Press.

—— (1984) 'On the *** of studying household form and function', in R. Mac Netting, R.R. Wilk and E.J. Arnould (eds) *Households. Comparative and Historical Studies of the Domestic Group*, Berkeley and Los Angeles: University of California Press.

Hammel, E. and Laslett, P. (1974) 'Comparing household structure over time and between cultures', *Comparative Studies in Society and History* 16: 73–109.

Hanawalt, B.A. (1986) *The Ties That Bound: Peasant Families in Medieval England*, Oxford: Oxford University Press.

Harris, O. (1981) 'Households as natural units', in K. Young, C. Wolkowitz and R. McCullagh (eds) *Of Marriage and the Market*, London: CSE Books.

—— (1984) 'Households and their boundaries', *History Workshop Journal* 20: 143–52.

Haxthausen, A. von (1972) [1837] *Studies on the Interior of Russia*, Chicago: Frederick Starr.

Heaton, T.B. and Hoppe, C. (1987) 'Widowed and married: comparative change in living arrangements, 1900 and 1980', *Social Science History* 11: 261–79.

Hilton, R.H. (1983) [1966] *A Medieval Society: The West Midlands at the End of the Thirteenth Century*, Cambridge: Cambridge University Press.

Hivon, M. (1990) *Les redéfinitions étatiques de la propriété foncière et leur impact sur la famille paysanne russe de 1861 à 1953*, unpublished MSc thesis, Université de Montréal.

Holy, L. and Stuchlik, M. (1983) *Actions, Norms and Representations*, Cambridge: Cambridge University Press.

Homans, G. (1941) *English Villagers of the Thirteenth Century*, Cambridge, Mass.: Harvard University Press.

Hoorn, W.D. van (1994) 'Living alone: choice, coincidence or fate', Luxembourg, Mondorf-les-Bains: Paper presented at the ECE/Eurostat conference.

Juby, H. (1993) *De la reconstitution à la projection des ménages: une application au Canada*, unpublished PhD thesis, Université de Montréal.

Juby, H. and Le Bourdais, C. (1995) 'Les parcours familiaux des Canadiennes', *Sociologie et Sociétés* 27: 143–61.

Keilman, N. (1987) 'Recent trends in family and household composition in Europe', *European Journal of Population* 3: 297–325.

Keirnan, K. (1986) 'Leaving home: living arrangements of young people in six West European countries', *Journal of Marriage and the Family* 48: 177–84.

Kerckhoff, A.C. and Macrae, J. (1992) 'Leaving the parental home in Great Britain – a comparative perspective', *Sociological Quarterly* 33: 281–301.

Kertzer, D.I. (1991) 'Household history and sociological theory', *Annual Review of Sociology* 17: 155–79.

King, E. (1973) *Peterborough Abbey, 1086–1310: A Study in the Land Market*, Cambridge: Cambridge University Press.

Kobrin, F.E. (1976) 'The fall in household size and the rise of the primary individual in the United States', *Demography* 13: 127–38.

Korn, S.D.R. (1975) 'Household composition in the Tonga Islands', *Journal of Anthropological Research* 31: 235–60.

Kosven, M.O. (1963) *Semeinaia obshchina i patronimiia*, Moscow: Izd. Akademii Nauk SSSR.

Kramarow, E.A. (1995) 'The elderly who live alone in the United States: historical perspectives on household change', *Demography* 32: 335–52.

Kussmaul, A. (1981) *Servants in Husbandry in Early Modern England*, Cambridge: Cambridge University Press.

Lamaison, P. (1987) 'La notion de maison. Entretien avec Claude Lévi-Strauss', *Terrain* 9: 34–9.

Lamphere, L. (1974) 'Strategies, cooperation, and conflict among women in domestic groups', in M.Z. Rosaldo and L. Lamphere (eds) *Woman, Culture, and Society*, Stanford: Stanford University Press.

Laslett, P. (1965) *The World We Have Lost*, London: Methuen.

—— (1972) 'Introduction', in P. Laslett and R. Wall (eds) *Household and Family in Past Time*, Cambridge: Cambridge University Press.

—— (1977) 'Characteristics of the Western family considered over time', in P. Laslett (ed.) *Family Life and Illicit Love*, Cambridge: Cambridge University Press.

—— (1979) 'Family and collectivity', *Sociology and Social Research* 63: 432–42.

—— (1983) 'Family and household as work group and kin group: areas of traditional Europe compared', in R. Wall (ed.) *Family Forms in Historic Europe*, Cambridge: Cambridge University Press.

—— (1984) 'The family as a knot of individual interests', in R. Mac Netting, R.R. Wilk and E.J. Arnould (eds) (1984a) *Households: Comparative and Historical Studies of the Domestic Group*, Berkeley: University of California Press.

—— (1989) *A Fresh Map of Life: The Emergence of the Third Age*, London: Weidenfeld and Nicolson.

Laslett, P. and Wall, R. (eds) (1972) *Household and Family in Past Time*, Cambridge: Cambridge University Press.

Leach, E. (1960) 'The Sinhalese of the dry zone of Northern Ceylon', in G.P. Murdock (ed.) *Social Structure in Southeast Asia*, London: Tavistock Publications.

—— (1961) *Rethinking Anthropology*, London: Athlone Press.

Lehrhaupt, K., Lapierre-Adamcyk, E. and Le Bourdais, C. (1993) 'Tendances et facteurs du départ des grands enfants de leur famille d'origine: l'exemple des jeunes canadiens nés de 1921 à 1960', Montreal: paper presented at the IUSSP conference.

Lesthaegge, R. (1980) 'On the social control of human reproduction', *Population and Development Review* 6: 527–48.

Lévi-Strauss, C. (1983) 'Histoire et ethnologie', *Annales E.S.C.* 38: 1217–31.

—— (1984) *Paroles données*, Paris: Plon.

Macfarlane, A. (1978) *The Origins of English Individualism*, Oxford: Basil Blackwell.

—— (1986) *Marriage and Love in England, 1300–1840*, Oxford: Basil Blackwell.

Martin, W. and Breittel, M. (1987) 'The hidden abode of reproduction: conceptualizing households in southern Africa', *Development and Change* 18: 215–34.

Matossian, M. (1968) 'The peasant way of life', in W.S. Vucinigh (ed.) *The Peasant in Nineteenth-Century Russia*, Stanford: Stanford University Press.

Michael, R.T., Fuchs, V.R. and Scott, S.R. (1980) 'Changes in the propensity to live alone: 1950–76', *Demography* 17: 39–53.

Miller, E. and Hatcher, J. (1978) *Medieval England: Rural Society and Economic Change, 1086–1348*, London and New York: Longman.

Miner, H. (1939) *St. Denis: A French-Canadian Village*, Chicago: The University of Chicago Press.

Miron, J.R. (1988) *Housing in Postwar Canada: Demographic Change, Household Formation and Housing Demand*, Kingston, Ontario: McGill-Queen's University Press.

Mitterauer, M. and Kagan, A. (1982) 'Russian and Central European family structures: a comparative review', *Journal of Family History* 7: 103–31.

Mitterauer, M. and Sieder, R. (1982) *The European Family: From Patriarchy to Partnership from the Middle Ages to the Present*, trans. by K. Oosterveen and M. Horzinger, Chicago: University of Chicago Press.

Moore, H. (1988) *Feminism and Anthropology*, Cambridge: Polity Press.

Mulder, C.H. and Manting, D. (1993) 'Strategies of nest-leavers: "settling down" versus flexibility', Amsterdam: University of Amsterdam, PDOD-Paper No. 15.

Murdock, G.P. (1949) *Social Structure*, New York: The Macmillan Company.

—— (1957) 'World Ethnographic Sample', *American Anthropologist* 59: 664–87.

Murray, C. (1987) 'Class, gender and the household: The development cycle in Southern Africa', *Development and Change* 18: 235–49.

Netting, R. Mac (1981) *Balancing on an Alp. Ecological Change and Continuity in a Swiss Mountain Community*, Cambridge: Cambridge University Press.

Netting, R. Mac, Wilk, R.R. and Arnould, E.J. (1984a) 'Introduction', in R. Mac Netting, R.R. Wilk and E.J. Arnould (eds) *Households. Comparative and Historical Studies of the Domestic Group*, Berkeley and Los Angeles: University of California Press.

—— (eds) (1984b) *Households. Comparative and Historical Studies of the Domestic Group*, Berkeley: University of California Press.

Norris, D.A. and Knighton, T. (1995) 'The collection of family data: limitations of traditional approaches and new initiatives', San Francisco: paper presented at the Annual Meeting of the Population Association of America.

Oppong, C. (1981) 'A note on some aspects of anthropological contributions to the study of fertility', paper on Population and Demography, National Research Council.

Ott, S. (1981) *The Circle of Mountains. A Basque Shepherding Community*, Oxford: Clarendon Press.

Pampel, F.C. (1983) 'Changes in the propensity to live alone: evidence from consecutive cross-sectional surveys, 1960–1976', *Demography* 20: 433–47.

Parsons, D.O. (1984) 'On the economics of intergenerational control', *Population and Development Review* 10: 41–54.

Pasternak, B. (1976) *Introduction to Kinship and Social Organization*, Englewood Cliffs: Prentice-Hall.

Pelling, M. and Smith, R.M. (1991) 'Introduction', in M. Pelling and R.M. Smith (eds) *Life, Death and the Elderly*, London: Routledge.

Péron, Y. (1986) 'Paysages témoin, paysage acteur d'une société pré-montagnarde sur la défensive', in I. Chiva and J. Goy (eds) *Les Baronnies des Pyrénées*, vol. II, Paris: EHESS.

Péron, Y., Lapierre-Adamcyk, E. and Morissette, D. (1986) 'Départ des enfants et contraction des familles d'après les recensements canadiens de 1971 et 1981', *European Journal of Population* 2: 155–75.

Play, F. Le (1877–9) *Les ouvriers européens*, vol. II, Tours: Mame.

—— (1907) [1874] *L'organisation de la famille* (5th edition, with epilogue and new appendices by M.M. Cheysson), Tours: Mame.

Poumarède, J. (1972) *Les successions dans le sud-ouest de la France au Moyen-Age*, Paris: PUF.

—— (n.d.) 'L'ancien droit familial dans les Pyrénées du Nord', source unknown.

Raftis, A. (1964) *Tenure and Mobility: Studies in the Social History of the Medieval English Village*, Toronto: Pontifical Institute of Medieval Studies.

—— (1965) 'Social structures in five East Midland villages', *Economic History Review* 18: 83–99.

Rapp, R. (1979) 'Examining family history: household and family', *Feminist Studies* 15: 175–81.

Razi, Z. (1980) *Life, Marriage and Death in a Medieval Parish: Economy, Society and Demography in Halesowen, 1270–1400*, Cambridge: Cambridge University Press.

—— (1993) 'The myth of the immutable English family', *Past and Present* 140: 3–44.

Rebel, H. (1983) *Peasant Classes. The Bureaucratization of Property and Family Relations under Early Habsburg Absolutism*, Princeton: Princeton University Press.

Rees, A.D. (1961) *Life in a Welsh Countryside*, Cardiff: The University of Wales Press.

Richards, A. (1950) 'Some types of family structure amongst the Central Bantu', in A.R. Radcliffe-Brown and D. Forde (eds) *African Systems of Kinship and Marriage*, London: Oxford University Press.

Riehl, W. (1856) *Familien*, Lund: Berlingska.

Rivers, W.H.R. (1924) *Social Organization*, London: Kegan Paul, Trench, Trubner & Co.

Roberts, P. (1988) 'Rural women's access to labor in West Africa', in S. Stichter and J. Parpart (eds) *Patriarchy and Class: African Women in the Home and the Workforce*, Boulder and London: Westview Press.

—— (1991) 'Anthropological perspectives on the household', *IDS Bulletin* 22: 60–4.

Rosaldo, M.Z. (1974) 'Woman, culture and society: a theoretical overview', in M.Z. Rosaldo and L. Lamphere (eds) *Woman, Culture, and Society*, Stanford: Stanford University Press.

Roussel, L. (1983) 'Les ménages d'une personne: l'évolution récente', *Population* 38: 995–1016.

Ruggles, S. (1991) 'Living arrangements of the elderly in America, 1880–1980', Newark, Delaware: Paper presented to the conference 'Aging and generational relations'.

—— (1994) 'The transformation of American family structure', *American Historical Review* 99: 103–28.

Russell, M. (1993) 'Are households universal? On misunderstanding domestic groups in Swaziland', *Development and Change* 24: 755–85.

Sabean, D.W. (1990) *Property, Production and Family in Neckarhausen, 1700–1870*, Cambridge: Cambridge University Press.

Sanjek, R. (1982) 'The organization of households in Adabraka: toward a wider comparative perspective', *Comparative Studies in Society and History* 24: 57–103.

Schmid, J. (1988) 'Principles from sociology for definitions and typologies of household structures', in N. Keilman, A. Kuijsten and A. Vossen (eds) *Modelling Household Formation and Dissolution*, Oxford: Oxford University Press.

Schneider, D. (1965) 'Some muddles in the models: or, how the system really works', in M. Banton (ed.) *The Relevance of Models for Social Anthropology*, London: Tavistock.

Schwarz, K. (1988) 'Household trends in Europe after Word War II', in N. Keilman, A. Kuijsten and A. Vossen (eds) *Modelling Household Formation and Dissolution*, Oxford: Oxford University Press.

Seccombe, W. (1992) *A Millennium of Family Change*, London and New York: Verso.

—— (1993) *Weathering the Storm: Working-class Families from the Industrial Revolution to the Fertility Decline*, London: Verso.

Segalen, M. (1977) 'The family cycle and household structure: five generations in a French village', *Journal of Family History* 2: 223–36.

—— (1986) *Historical Anthropology of the Family*, Cambridge: Cambridge University Press.

Semevskii, V. (1903) *Krestiane v Tsarstvovavnie Imperatritsy Ekateriny II*, 2 vols, Moscow.

Shanin, T. (1972) *The Awkward Class: Political Sociology of Peasantry in a Developing Society: Russia 1910–1925*, Oxford: Clarendon.

Shorter, E. (1977) *The Making of the Modern Family*, New York: Basic Books.

Smith, D.S. (1993) 'The curious history of theorizing about the history of the Western family', *Social Science History* 17: 323–53.

Smith, R.M. (1981) 'The people of Tuscany and their families in the fifteenth century: medieval or Mediterranean?', *Journal of Family History* 6: 107–28.

—— (1983) 'Hypothèses sur la nuptialité en Angleterre aux XIIIe–XIVe siècles', *Annales, E.S.C.* 38: 107–36.

—— (1984a) 'Some issues concerning families and their property in rural England, 1250–1800', in R.M. Smith (ed.) *Land, Kinship and Life Cycle*, Cambridge: Cambridge University Press.

—— (1984b) 'Families and their land in an area of partible inheritance: Redgrave, Suffolk 1260–1320', in R.M. Smith (ed.) *Land, Kinship and Life Cycle*, Cambridge: Cambridge University Press.

—— (1991) 'The manorial court and the elderly tenant in late medieval England', in M. Pelling and R.M. Smith (eds) *Life, Death and the Elderly*, London: Routledge.

Soulet, J.-F. (1987) *Les Pyrénées au XIXe siècle*, Toulouse: Eche.

Spiegel, A. (1982) 'Spinning off the developmental cycle: some comments on the utility of the concept in the light of data from Matatiele, Transkei', *Social Dynamics* 8: 30–45.

Stern, L. (1973) 'Inter-household movement in a Ladino village of southern Mexico', *Man* 8: 393–415.

Stone, L. (1975) 'The rise of the nuclear family in early modern England', in C.E. Rosenberg (ed.) *The Family in History*, New York: Harper and Row.

Sullivan, O. (1986) 'Housing movement of the divorced and separated', *Housing Studies* 1: 35–58.

Thomas, N.W. (1906) *Kinship Organization and Group Marriage in Australia*, Cambridge: Cambridge University Press.

Thomas, W.I. and Znaniecki, F. (1958) [1918] *The Polish Peasant in Europe and America*, New York: Dover Books.

Thompson, D. (1991) 'The welfare of the elderly in the past. A family or community responsibility?', in M. Pelling and R.M. Smith (eds) *Life, Death and the Elderly*, London: Routledge.

Thompson, E.P. (1978) 'The peculiarities of the English', in E.P. Thompson, *The Poverty of Theory and Other Essays*, New York: Monthly Review Press.

Titow, J.Z. (1962) 'Some differences between manors and their effects on the conditions of the peasantry in the thirteenth century', *Agricultural History Review* 10: 1–13.

Todd, E. (1985) *The Explanation of Ideology: Family Structures and Social Systems*, trans. D. Garrioch, Oxford: Blackwell.

—— (1990) *L'invention de l'Europe*, Paris: Seuil.

Tsiang, S.C. (1966) 'Walras's law, Say's law and liquidity preference in general equilibrium analysis', *International Economic Review* 7: 329–45.

Verdon, M. (1979a) 'The stem family: toward a general theory', *Journal of Interdisciplinary History*, 10: 87–105.

—— (1979b) 'Sleeping together: the dynamics of residence among the Abutia Ewe', *Journal of Anthropological Research* 35: 401–25.

—— (1980a) 'The Quebec stem family revisited', in K. Ishwaran (ed.) *Canadian Families: Ethnic Variations*, Toronto: McGraw-Hill Ryerson.

—— (1980b) 'Shaking off the domestic yoke, or the sociological significance of residence', *Comparative Studies in Society and History* 22: 109–32.

—— (1981) 'Kinship, marriage and the family: an operational approach', *American Journal of Sociology* 86: 796–818.

—— (1983) *The Abutia Ewe of West Africa. A Chiefdom That Never Was*, Berlin: de Gruyter.

—— (1987) 'Autour de la famille-souche. Essai d'anthropologie conjecturale', *Anthropologie et Sociétés* 11: 137–59.

—— (1991) *Contre la culture*, Paris: Editions des Archives Contemporaines.

—— (1996a) 'Rethinking complex households: the case of the Western Pyrenean "Houses"', *Continuity and Change* 11: 191–216.

—— (1996b) *Keynes and the 'Classics'. A Study in Language, Epistemology and Mistaken Identities*, London: Routledge.

Viazzo, P.P. (1989) *Upland Communities: Environment, Population and Social Structure in the Alps since the Sixteenth Century*, Cambridge: Cambridge University Press.

Vlasova, I.V. (1991) 'The commune and customary law among Russian peasants of the Northern Cis-Urals', *Soviet Anthropology and Archaeology* 30: 6–23.

Vucinigh, W.S. (1968) 'Introduction', in W.S. Vucinigh (ed.) *The Peasant in Nineteenth-Century Russia*, Stanford: Stanford University Press.

Wall, R. (1983) 'Introduction', in R. Wall (ed.) *Family Forms in Historic Europe*, Cambridge: Cambridge University Press.

—— (1988) 'The living arrangements of the elderly in Europe in the 1980s', in B. Bytheway, T. Keil, P. Allatt and A. Bryman (eds) *Becoming and Being Old*, London: Sage Publications.

—— (1995) 'Elderly persons and members of their households in England and Wales from preindustrial times to the present', in D.I. Kertzer and P. Laslett (eds) *Aging in the Past: Demography, Society, and Old Age*, Berkeley and Los Angeles: University of California Press.

—— (1996) 'Comparer ménages et familles au niveau européen: problèmes et perspectives', *Population* 51: 93–116.

Wallace, D.M. (1877) *Russia*, London: Cassel Petter.

Ward, R., Logan, J. and Spitze, G. (1992) 'The influence of parent and child needs on coresidence in middle and later life', *Journal of Marriage and the Family* 54: 209–21.

Weinick, R.M. (1995) 'Sharing a home: the experiences of American women and their parents over the twentieth century', *Demography* 32: 281–97.

Wheaton, R. (1975) 'Family and kinship in Western Europe: the problem of the joint family household', *Journal of Interdisciplinary History* 4: 601–28.

Wilk, R.R. and Netting, R. Mac (1984) 'Households: changing forms and functions', in R. Mac Netting, R.R. Wilk and E.J. Arnould (eds) *Households. Comparative and Historical Studies of the Domestic Group*, Berkeley and Los Angeles: University of California Press.

Williamson, J. (1984) 'Norfolk: thirteenth century', in P.D.A. Harvey (ed.) *The Peasant Land Market in Medieval England*, Oxford: Clarendon Press.

Wolf, D.S. and Soldo, B.J. (1988) 'Household composition choices of older unmarried women', *Demography* 25: 387–403.

Wolf, M. (1972) *Women and the Family in Rural Taiwan*, Stanford: Stanford University Press.

Woodford-Berger, P. (1981) 'Women in houses: the organization of residence and work in rural Ghana', *Antropologiska Studier* 30: 3–35.

Worobec, C.D. (1991) *Peasant Russia: Family and Community in the Post-emancipation Period*, Princeton: Princeton University Press.

Wrigley, E.A. (1977) 'Reflections on the history of the family', *Daedalus* 106: 71–85.

Yanagisako, S. (1979) 'Family and households: the analysis of domestic groups', *Annual Reviews in Anthropology* 8: 161–205.

Young, K., Wolkowitz, C. and McCullagh, R. (eds) (1981) *Of Marriage and the Market: Women's Subordination in International Perspective*, London: CSE Books.

Zink, A. (1993) *L'héritier de la maison. Géographie coutumière du Sud-Ouest de la France sous l'Ancien Régime*, Paris: EHESS.

INDEX

212